AGING POLITICAL ACTIVISTS

AGING POLITICAL ACTIVISTS

Personal Narratives from the Old Left

David P. Shuldiner

Westport, Connecticut
London

Library of Congress Cataloging-in-Publication Data

Shuldiner, David Philip.
    Aging political activists : personal narratives from the old left
  / David P. Shuldiner.
        p.   cm.
    Includes bibliographical references and index.
    ISBN 0–275–95045–X (alk. paper)
        1. Communists—United States—Interviews. 2. Socialists—United
States—Interviews. 3. Political activists—United States—
Interviews. 4. Jews—United States—Interviews. I. Title.
HX84.A2S58   1995
335′.0092′273—dc20   94–33258

British Library Cataloguing in Publication Data is available.

Library of Congress Catalog Card Number: 94–33258
ISBN: 0–275–95045–X

First published in 1995

Praeger Publishers, 88 Post Road West, Westport, CT 06881
An imprint of Greenwood Publishing Group, Inc.

Printed in the United States of America

The paper used in this book complies with the
Permanent Paper Standard issued by the National
Information Standards Organization (Z39.48–1984).

10 9 8 7 6 5 4 3 2 1

This work is dedicated to Joe, Lil, Jake, and Sid, who have consented so graciously to share the stories of their lives

Contents

Part Three: Summing Things Up

Acknowledgments

The original inspiration for this book comes from my parents, Sarah and Max Shuldiner, who raised me in the milieu of the Jewish Left subculture to which I returned for this study. I would like to thank Thomas O. Blank, Ph.D., Associate Professor of Human Development and Family Studies at the University of Connecticut, for providing sage counsel to me in my exploration of political activism and aging as a student of gerontology and later as a colleague. My editors at Greenwood Publishing Group, Lynn Flint and Ann Newman, have been as helpful and "author friendly" as I could have hoped for. I must also thank my British comrade and colleague, Tom Beardsley, who rescued me at the eleventh hour with his impressive formatting skills. Finally, much gratitude is due to my life partner, Anne Schick, who has made life all the more worth exploring.

Preface

Alice Kessler Harris once defined oral history as "that area where memory, myth, ideology, language, and historical cognition interact in a dialectical transformation of the word into an historical artifact" (Harris 1991). It is this wondrous complexity that has become the joy and the bane of oral history fieldwork and presentation. Our work is, however, even more complex than Harris intimated. Aside from the fact that we can never ignore the active role the historian plays in creating the historical narrative, we must also recognize that the history we are being given—the story—is not being given for the first time. It has been told again and again, and will be told again and again in the future, each time with new variations and new insights depending upon the context of the storytelling. This is especially true of political activists who have consciously articulated their views of history in a lifelong struggle to understand themselves and their world. History has intense meaning for politics. It tells us from where we came and points the directions in which we are moving both individually and collectively. It is no serendipitous coincidence that history and politics emerge together on the modern landscape.

Rarely discussed in the literature of oral history is the added complication that the interview is also the arena of intense generational conflict; not only between the interviewer and the narrator who are often of a different age, but also between the youth and the present of the narrator. The story we are being told contains within itself all of the ways in which the story teller has fused his or her present visions with the dreams of an earlier time when youth was to be served. No linear model of fieldwork can begin to encompass the multiple constructions of meaning that is the interview. It is a cultural right to manipulate history, and one of the greatest commitments of oral history is the commitment to this right. Only a dialectical model can, however, reveal the warp and the woof of the tapestry that is then presented.

Aging Political Activists is an attempt to bring to our discussions of politics, aging, and history the insights of such a method, and to illustrate the complexities of the interaction of memory, the passage of time, historical construction, and political commitment. Based upon the life history memoirs of four political activists who, as a cohort, were for many years members of the American Communist Party, and whose longer testimonies are here presented so that we can observe the process being investigated, *Aging Political Activists* traces the trajectories of a deeply committed set of activists through the memories of their passions. In doing so, David Shuldiner reveals to us the inherent tension between changing versions of the past and the unchanging commitments of his narrators. On this tension he brilliantly encompasses and illuminates the processes of fieldwork, memory, and ideology in the hope that this telling will embrace and transcend all previous tellings. When we succeed, we have a very rich document indeed; one that allows for the kinds of discussions we have here.

Considerations of narrative construction are critical to our current political understandings. Too often in our fractured world in which contingency rules we tend to view politics as a series of disparate activities for which we mobilize at one moment and relax at another. We drift from one cause to another with little or no sense of a deeper vision that would explain each, especially if that vision must be international. Is the lack of an international vision really the nature of political thought and action? Not so for the people we meet here. No matter what we may think of that international commitment to social change, to understand our history we must understand what it meant at the various times in the lives of a different generation. These stories are politics in action; they are in themselves a political summing up.

To understand the full implication of political commitment within a life span we must turn to the lives themselves and to the stories of the people themselves. The problem is then how to interpret and present the testimony. This remarkable book shows us how.

Ronald J. Grele
Director, Oral History Research Office, Columbia University.

AGING POLITICAL ACTIVISTS

Setting the Stage

Chapter One

Introduction

This book offers a demonstration of the continuing development of self-identity among aging political activists. It presents a series of interviews with four individuals in their sixties and seventies who have been longtime friends and political comrades. All are lifelong activists and continue to be politically engaged, to varying degrees, in late life. All four were members of the Communist Party for many years. Each of them severed their ties over political differences with the Party, but all continue to identify themselves as socialists. All of them are Jewish and, if queried, will specifically identify themselves as "secular" Jews.

INTERVIEW SUBJECTS

The inspiration for this book came to me when, in 1990, I conducted a series of interviews with Joseph Dimow, a resident of New Haven, Connecticut. As a "red diaper baby" (a child of parents who were members of the Party), I was intrigued by the possibility of interviewing a cohort—in every sense of that term—of my parents. It was my parents who had, in fact, given me his name and suggested that I look him up (my father had lived in Connecticut in the early 1940s and had met him "in political circles").

I then took advantage of a unique opportunity to compare Joe's personal narrative and self-identity with those of three other people who have been close to him personally and politically. One is his wife, Lillian, who was herself a member of the Communist Party, though not as active as Joe. The other two are longtime friends and comrades who, like Joe, held leadership positions in the Communist Party in Connecticut and who have continued as close personal friends over the years since their departure from the Party. Joe had mentioned each of them during our conversations.

Here, then, is a brief description of the "cast of characters" whose personal narratives are presented in this book:

A child of Jewish socialists, Joseph Dimow grew up internalizing an equation between ethnicity and activism. He found a vehicle for the expression of his political outlook in the Party and remained there until the late 1950s, when he felt that the Party no longer represented the political vision he still had. While in the Party, he did not seek a specific ethnic outlet or organizational form of expression for his political activism. However, since severing his ties with the Party he has, in fact, become more involved in ethnically identified political activities with fellow Jewish radicals. He is currently on the editorial board of *Jewish Currents*, a progressive, monthly journal of news and analysis; he is also a leading member of what was, at the time of our interview, the New Haven chapter of New Jewish Agenda, a national left-liberal organization. (The national office of Agenda has since closed, but several local chapters, including New Haven, have continued as independent groups.)

Lillian Dimow (she prefers to be called "Lil") left the Party around the same time as Joe did, in the mid-1950s. She continues to be active in various political organizations, including Women's International League for Peace and Freedom (WILPF) and New Jewish Agenda (though to a lesser extent than Joe). Much of our conversation, however, focused on her unique mid-life career as an arts and crafts teacher. She sees herself as bringing the political perspective she grew into with the Party as having an impact on the nature of her work and the students that she worked with. Like Joe, a child of Jewish radicals, Lil's ethnicity continues to be an important part of her personal and political identity in late life, perhaps more so than Joe's.

While severing his ties with the Party in the early 1960s, Jacob Goldring (his friends call him "Jake") continued to express his overall political perspective, if implicitly, in his work career as a carpenter, building contractor, and home inspector. His work also influenced more directly the character of at least some of his political involvements as well, for he has been active at different times of his life in the promotion of housing issues. While declaring that his ethnic identity has played a minimal role in his life, there are indications in

Jake's discourse that ethnicity has been a factor at different times in his life. (His father was also a Jewish socialist; much later he sent his only child to a progressive, secular Jewish after-school group in New Haven, the same one to which Joe and Lil sent their children.) Jake remarked that historical circumstances may have worked at times to mitigate opportunities for a more overt expression of his ethnicity.

Sidney Resnick is a "retired" printer who continues to work in the Law Library at Yale University. Though he shared similar experiences in the Party with Joe and Jake, he persisted much longer as a member, severing his ties in 1968. He is also a child of the Old Jewish Left. Sid, in fact, is the most ardent in his embrace of a specifically ethnic politics; his post-Party political commitments are almost exclusively to progressive Jewish activities. He has continued a "parallel" career as a journalist (he worked on Party newspapers), contributing to leftwing Jewish publications; he is also on the editorial board of the *Jewish Currents* and is active, along with Joe and Lil, in New Jewish Agenda.

ORGANIZATION

My initial approach to the dual problems of tackling the issues raised by the narratives and analyzing the narrative process itself was to address them in a relatively straightforward manner by interspersing analysis with excerpts from transcripts of the interviews. What is lost, however, in this conventional form of presentation is a sense of the "flow" of the interviews, the unfolding structure of the narratives and the nature of my interaction with my interview subjects. A major concern of mine--beyond the content of narratives of self-identity presented within the interviews--is the ways in which the narrative serves as a vehicle for the construction of a framework for self-presentation. This is a collaborative process between interviewer and subject, whose interaction "colors" the form and content of self-presentation. Only by examining the interviews in their entirety can one fully appreciate this process. For this reason, full transcripts of my interviews with Joe, Lil, Jake, and Sid are presented as the main body of this book.

With this book, I hope to stimulate discussion about the nature of self-identity, in particular political identity, from a life span perspective. I also feel that these narratives will challenge current assumptions, particularly in the fields of social psychology and gerontology, about the character of the self, ideology, and personal development. Finally, I wish to broaden the scope of the discourse about current theoretical models and research methods employed in investigating ideology as a driving force in human development.

Chapter Two

The Dialectics of Identity: Search for a Method

The dialectic approach presents a number of implications for life-span development research. These include: a model that posits the interweaving of disparate elements in life experience and self identity; an acknowledgment of the emergent/discursive rather than fixed/linear nature of human development; the recognition that development takes place within a world of conflicting forces; and the idea that a primary role of the developing self is that of mediation, of negotiating those disparate, often conflicting, elements of life experience (rather than the ultimate resolution of those conflicts).

This work is an attempt to apply the dialectic method not only to the analysis of identity, but also to the investigative process itself–specifically to the life-history interview.

The premise underlying such an approach is that the personal identity of these aging activists has been shaped through a lifelong process, set within specific individual, social, and historical contexts. It continues to be shaped by the various forms of identity and expression that have dominated their working lives. Further, it is informed by those individual, social, and historical events that have conditioned the course of their personal development.

On one level the stories of these elder statespeople of the left "movement" are seen as shaped by a dialectic relationship: among different aspects of their personal identity (in particular, occupation, ethnicity, class, gender, and age), as revealed in their self-narratives; and between their present self-identity and those forms of identity reflected in memories that reach back into previous periods of their development. Since age itself is one identity marker, the passage of time will have changed the character (and context) of that identity shared with one's age cohorts. Further, one's memory of the past is refracted through one's identity in its developmental present (that is, the time of storytelling; see "Past versus Present" later in this chapter).

On another level the stories themselves, narrative (re)constructions of identity and its development throughout a lifetime, are shaped by a dialectical process, that of the interaction between interviewer and subjects. The dialectical approach to the investigation and analysis of identity recognizes that all phenomena are aspects of an interrelated whole. Thus, the researcher/clinician, his or her subjects/clients and the social/historical environmental context in which their relationship is acted out unavoidably affect each other. One important consequence for research is that no investigative model can eliminate all of these effects.

A dialectical model acknowledges that the very structure and process of the experimental method affects research results. While controls are set up to "block out" such effects, the typical role separation of researcher and subject tends to perpetuate a false sense of detachment or objectivity. A dialectical model attempts to replace this dichotomy in the interview process with an intersubjective approach in which researcher and subject collaborate in exploring the objects of inquiry. This follows from the recognition of the importance of "praxis": the ongoing interrelationship of theory and practice in which experimental ideas and approaches are addressed in the very process of interaction with the experimental subject.

THE DIALECTIC METHOD IN LIFE-HISTORY INTERVIEWING

The recognition of interpenetrating aspects of observed phenomena extends to the experimental/research environment, where the social effects of design, context, and practice must be acknowledged as influencing outcomes. In the case of recorded life histories, the outcome of an interview may be affected by the nature of the questions asked, the character of the interaction of interviewer and subject, as well as the expectations of both, all of which are culturally encoded (though researcher and/or subject may not necessarily be conscious of such coding). Many researchers are aware of the dangers of "leading questions" in producing expected outcomes; some may not always be conscious of the social/cultural/political implications of the questions they pose. Similarly, not only questions but also the interview context itself set up expectations that may affect responses to interview questions.

IN SEARCH OF A METHOD: THE INTERACTIVE INTERVIEW

Recognizing the culturally encoded nature of the interview situation, this book is based on the attempt to employ a method that acknowledges the dialectic tensions within the self-narratives generated in the interview process. The method tested here is that of the "interactive interview," a collaborative process in which questions and responses of both interviewer and subject are examined by each in the course of tape-recorded conversations. It is, then, an attempt to implement a model for "praxis"—the integration of theory and practice—by applying the dialectic method to both investigation and analysis of self-narratives and identity.

I applied an "ideal" version of this method to the three tape-recorded conversations I conducted with Joe Dimow:

1. The first interview was fairly conventional, one in which I simply posed questions to him. I gave a copy of the tape-recorded interview to Joe to review before our next meeting.
2. In a second interview, we discussed his responses to the previous conversation. Joe offered critical comments on what he had said and, significantly, on what he considered to be important information or insights lacking in the first interview.
3. In our final conversation, I invited Joe to offer suggestions for alternative models for the interview process, as well as commentary on additional areas of inquiry that would contribute to a greater understanding of the object of research.

I must confess that the interviews I conducted subsequently did not proceed in quite as "tidy" a fashion as this tripartite scheme would tend to indicate. Initially I conceived the process, in a rather mechanical fashion, as taking place in three separate interviews. Only with Joe did I actually conduct three consecutive, tape-recorded discussions. Even in that case, the three methodological components, outlined so neatly above, insinuated themselves, overtly and covertly, throughout our conversations. I invited all four interview subjects to critique the form and content of the interview at some point, but in true dialectical fashion, these components of our interaction were themselves interwoven into the fabric of our conversations.

It would be more accurate to say that we were engaged, both consciously and unconsciously at times, in a continual process of negotiating the terms and content of our discourse. It follows that the dialectical model outlined above is designed, not as a mechanical outline for conducting an interview, but as a set of strategies in a collaborative process engaging interviewer and subject.

DIALECTICS: THEORETICAL OVERVIEW

The dialectic method, going back to Aristotle, and elaborated by Hegel and Marx in the areas of philosophy and political economy has gained legitimacy over the years as a model of inquiry in the contemporary physical and social sciences. In the late 1970s, Klaus Riegel presented strong arguments for its application to the field of psychology (Riegel 1975). Important distinctions needed to be outlined between dialectic and "traditional" linear models of conventional psychological research as conducted in Western, industrial nations.

First, like most social scientists, psychologists have tended to search for stable, universal, human traits, removed from any specific environmental, social, or historical contexts. Where these contexts *have* been considered, they have been so in isolated sets. A dialectic approach rejects all universals that tend to impute a static character to human traits and a "changelessness" to patterns of human development. Instead, a dialectical psychology focuses on the actions of human beings within constantly changing temporal, environmental, social, and political contexts.

Second, linear models promote the notion that "normal" development tends toward equilibrium, balance, or stability. Conflict is seen as "dysfunctional," resolved only by a return to some form of stasis. A dialectics of human development stresses that human beings develop and grow through problem solving, that is, by confronting and mediating personal and social contradictions.

Conflict, then, is seen as a positive mode of human experience that is acknowledged and worked with. Riegel argues that insights into human development are best derived not by searching for an elusive path to equilibrium, but by observing that problems emerge and are dealt with.

It would be a mistake, however, to "typecast" the dialectic method as a "conflict" model (Tolman [1981] notes Riegel's own tendency to do so). A dialectic universe may be more accurately defined as a "unity of opposites," one in which observed phenomena stand in contradiction to one another not as separate ontological domains, but as interdependent aspects of the same unified whole. In a commentary on the status of dialectical theory in contemporary social psychology, Georgoudi describes one important consequence of this model:

[A] common distinction is often made between the external or objective world and the psychological or subjective world. . . .[F]rom a dialectical perspective, neither of these so called 'ontological domains' possesses an independent status. Rather, they are mediated categories in the sense that neither can be defined apart from the other. . . . It is this form of mediation that is of central concern to the dialectician. (Georgoudi 1983)."

A dialectics of personality would see the emergence and development of the self as a process of mediation between individual and society, each conditioned by and conditioning the other in a continual process of social interaction. Specific biological, environmental, and historical aspects interpenetrate in the development of an ever-emergent self. A dialectics of personality also recognizes that an individual is neither completely autonomous nor a faceless cog in the social wheel; rather the self is the product of a continually unfolding dialectical relationship set within the context of social interaction.

The implications for personality research are far-reaching. Just as social interaction is culturally conditioned, the experimental situation is culturally encoded. The specific experimental context and the very character of the relationship of researcher and subject constitute a microcosm of the society of which both researchers and subjects are members. That is to say, experimental models are developed within the theoretical and methodological outlooks of the research community. Those outlooks, in turn, while far from monolithic, reflect (overtly or covertly) the dominant ideology and biases of the sociopolitical whole within which that very research community is embedded.

A major consequence for the field of psychology, of viewing phenomena as aspects of an interrelated whole, is that the researcher/clinician, his or her subject(s)/client(s), and the social, environmental, and historical contexts within which the relationship of researcher to subject is acted out become integral aspects of human understanding and knowledge as a unified field, both in theory and in practice. In fact, one of the most important contributions that a dialectical approach to psychology might make is in the area of praxis, particularly in the application of theoretical and social knowledge to the experimental context, as in the researcher/subject relationship.

Recognizing that any experimental situation is culturally (hence, theoretically/methodologically) "tainted" from the start—obviating any pretense of objectivity—a dialectical approach would be interactive, replacing the false objectivity that alienates researcher and subject with intersubjectivity, in which researcher and subject actively collaborate in the research process. This means that from the start, no "secrets" are kept from the experimental "subject," for the legitimacy of a dialectical research model would, of necessity, be based upon an open and mutual acknowledgement of its theoretical/methodological agenda. Further, since the aim of research is (or should be) the improvement of society, this collaborative approach would make researcher and subject partners in the process of social change. A genuinely dialectical approach is not "value free"; on the contrary, it places advocacy at the head of an open agenda.

Part of the problem in understanding and articulating a genuinely dialectical approach is the reluctance, at least in Western capitalist states, to acknowledge the legitimacy of a model that represents, in essence, the worldview of an ideological enemy camp (that is, Marxism). Because the model is ideologically "tainted," it has been kept from being placed on the agenda as an item of legitimate discussion among researchers in capitalist countries (or at least in the United States), preventing its heuristic value from being fully understood and appreciated in many research communities. (In a recent review of the psychological literature readily available [in English] to readers in western (capitalist) countries, I came across just one article defending a specifically identified "Marxist" theory of personality [Smith 1985], and one book [referred to by Smith] in English translation by the French Marxist Lucien Seve [1978]).

It may take a radical ideological shift among researchers (accompanying a radical shift in the social relations of intellectual production) in order for a dialectics of personality to gain legitimacy as one more application of a unified theory, not only for psychology, but for all investigative research (see Gergen & Gergen 1983). Riegel was right about the "specter haunting western psychology" (Riegel 1975); it remains to be seen whether or not a genuine dialectics of personality will be practiced, let alone have an effect on a field still dominated by hidden social and political agendas embedded in modes of investigation and analysis.

ISSUES FOR A DIALECTICAL STUDY OF PERSONAL NARRATIVE AND SELF IDENTITY

Change Versus Continuity in Self-Identity

Blank (1990) identifies an issue of central concern for the dialectical analysis of personal development: the relationship between change and continuity in the process of development. He does so within the context of a discussion of "the relationship of older persons to the political structure and, through it, to social structure and social changes." He addresses the problem on two levels: the "micro" level of personal development of political attitudes and behaviors; and the "macro" level of the relationship of older persons to the social and political system.

One of the central questions I address in my study of aging activists is the relationship between continuity and change in the character of their political self-identity. The issue is posed on a number of levels, each of them intertwined. These include the dialectic relationships among: personal and political development during their life course, individual histories and the history of the organizations in which they have been involved, individual lives and sociopolitical events, and the self and environment (temporal and spacial). An underlying concern of my research has been the relationship between change in specific political attitudes and the maintenance of a continuity in global political outlook.

Past Versus Present in Identity Formation

The past is sealed as a set of objective conditions; the present is constituted both by objective conditions and by subjective experience: people acting individually and collectively within and upon those conditions. The personal narrative represents a peculiar dialectic, for it constitutes the subjective experience of remembering imposed upon an objective set of events. That subjective experience as recounted in personal narrative becomes a "fact" itself that must be confronted. Taking it a step further, the act of remembering, while drawing upon objective events in the past, changes that past in the very selective process of reconstruction. The narrator is not simply remembering events, but is submitting the past to the present project. This is not to say that the objective past has changed, but it is to say that the narrative past (the past of the biography, autobiography, or oral history) is by its very nature revisionist: a "re-visioning" or "re-membering" of lived-in events. This "re-framing" of past experience from the perspective of the present is both conditioned and conditioning. In other words, it is both determined by the objective totality of past experiences that have left their imprint on the soul, and that subjective particularity of conscious agency exerted by a person on that objective totality.

A dialectical approach to personal narrative thus recognizes interpretation as a condition of memory. The conscious will involved in the process of recollection is never wholly without purpose, without an agenda. The remembered past is invariably fit into a framework conditioned by the specific criteria established for the project of remembering. In the present study, that project is not simply an assessment of the meaning of a past life of activity; it is a deliberate effort to construct a past that leads to and valorizes the present life course as it is unfolding for the narrator. This is precisely why a linear model is hopelessly inadequate for the task of dealing with the intricate relationship between the living present and the lived-in past of biographical memory. Memory is not a simple chronological recounting of life events; it is a story that is unfolding as it is being told and that, in fact, includes the very process of storytelling as a strategy for self-presentation.

To put it another way, we are both products and creations of our own stories. A linear approach insists upon a causal chain of events; a dialectical approach sees a shifting sea of events, consisting of both discrete, identifiable occurrences and ebbs and flows of activity. While these may be determined as "factual" occurrences, they are indeterminate in definition. The act of recounting the past, whether in personal narrative or historical writing, involves a process of identifying and assigning meaning to the contours in that sea of events.

A person makes choices in presenting his or her past through a process that is neither wholly arbitrary or fortuitous. One does not select the events of one's life story out of countless alternatives floating in a ocean of experience. Rather, a person shapes her or his personal narrative within certain bounds: on the one hand, within a specific set of objective conditions of life experiences and, on the other hand, by the subjective criteria established by a self that is both formed and forming. A story is as emergent as the self that produces it: It is both conditioned by the past (and the expectations of teller and listener about that past) and determined by the self that is engaged in the telling (including the process of exchange with the listener).

That the character of a personal narrative may change in the discourse between teller and listener was sharply delineated in a set of interviews I conducted with Joe Dimow. When I asked him to review the tape recording of our initial conversation, he wondered out loud as to whether the impression created by his own narrative was an entirely accurate reflection of his true feelings. As he elaborated on this matter he recast some of the assumptions conveyed by that first "reading."

Dominant Versus Subordinate Aspects of Self-identity

A dialectical model of human personality views self-concept as a set of interweaving relationships among multiple aspects of identity (see, for example, Shuldiner 1989). While no causal relationships are implied by this model, it does allow for dominant and subordinate relations among aspects of identity, conditioned by both objective and subjective markers. For those political activists I interviewed, their political outlook was considered to be the dominant or core aspect of their identity, providing the common thread for most of those things in their lives to which they felt the most committed, and from which they derived the most satisfaction. It was this core identity that largely remained decisive in the process of negotiating critical life transitions and choices. This is not to say that other aspects of their identity did not play crucial roles at particular points in their lives. In fact, the relationship between core identity and other aspects is not necessarily one of constant dominance or even exclusive dominion. Nor in the relationship between various aspects of identity is it possible to neatly separate and pigeonhole them. The lived-in experience of the self is far too complicated and fluid for that. Yet, directly or indirectly, the core aspect of one's identity tends to color the whole.

An obvious example of the melding of different aspects of self-identity can be observed in the relationship of ethnicity and politics in the lives of the activists I interviewed. Although all of them are Jewish, they varied considerably in the degree to which they attached significance to their Jewish identity. However, when ethnicity was self-described as an important aspect of their identity, it was invariably tied to their political outlook. In some cases that has meant active membership in organizations composed of Jewish socialists, or at least linking one's politics with one's ethnicity by engaging in political activity in the Jewish community.

Lil Dimow made a more indirect connection when she opened up our initial conversation by discussing the importance of her mid-life career as an arts-and-crafts teacher among inner city youth, young mothers, and the elderly. Later, she attributed her gift for teaching among these challenging audiences to her political outlook and experience. In this instance, she had spoken to what was uppermost in her consciousness when I asked her about her sense of self, yet underlying that was a global vision—a political vision—that has fueled the most closely felt aspects of her identity (only more indirectly, perhaps, in later years than during that time in her life when her outlook was directly reflected in her political activity).

Personal Versus Social Identity

Each of the activists I interviewed for this book was exposed to the foundation for their ideological (and ethnic) development within their immediate families. An obvious but apparently little explored area is that of the relationship between individual (personal) values and social (political) outlook when the foundation for both of these perspectives has been laid in the process of socialization by one's immediate family. Some of the people I interviewed talked of experiences outside the home and family that provided the conditions for adopting a specific political outlook or joining a specific movement or organization. Yet these later life events seemed to be conditioned to some extent by prior socialization.

Still later, personal friendships and political ties became interwoven, so that social relations analogous to earlier kin relations were formed in the "family" of political compatriots. This new political "home" became the nexus of a dialectic between the intimate relations of daily personal and political life and the global vision and goals that united comrades struggling together in a national and, ultimately, global movement.

The dialectical relation between personal friendship and political outlook has tended to reflect the shifting nature of both. Personal friction was often overlooked in the interests of political unity; it is also the case that political differences might cause irreconcilable differences between comrades as friends and between friends who were no longer political comrades. Whether personal friendship or political unity became dominant aspects of a relationship depended upon individual histories and choices; however, the choices were limited by very real political conditions. Some chose, for example, to remain in an organization whose outlook they may have personally come to doubt because they feared losing longtime friends and allies. Many who did leave became socially isolated or made friendships based on very different social or political ties. Others, like those I interviewed, severed relations with the organization but maintained friendships with those former members who not only were longtime friends, but who had also undergone parallel political changes. Thus, continuity in personal friendship and political ties has been made possible within a limited set of friends who have made similar life transitions (though not necessarily at the same rate or time).

Quantitative Versus Qualitative Change in Political Outlook

When does change in the form of political expression reflect a change in the essence or core of one's political identity? How are such changes perceived in terms of core identity? The individuals I interviewed for this book all acknowledged in one way or other in their personal narratives that they had made some changes in their political views. They saw these changes as part of an evolution of their global outlook, not a change in their core identity. Specifically, all of them described substantive changes in their views about the course of socialism and about its varied proponents. None professed, in the final analysis, however, any qualitative change in their commitment to socialism.

The question remains, though: When does a change in one's opinion about specific platforms, programs, tactics, and issues reflect a decisive change in outlook? I deliberately refrain from any attempt to make an "objective" determination of the lowest common denominator that qualifies someone to rightfully hold up the banner of socialism. What is most relevant in these discussions of ideology and self-identity is the deliberate (subjective) *choice* of socialism as a core identity marker.

All four individuals made that choice, and it is through the process involved in that deliberation that they have forged a high level of integration of the other aspects of their identity. For each of them socialism is a lived-in reality that has undergone much change, but without a fundamental loss of legitimacy.

Objective Versus Subjective Identity Markers

As the interviewer, I may intuit from the personal narratives I have heard what the "objective" boundaries of identity are, even going so far as to pronounce what the core and peripheral aspects of identity are that have been "revealed" by that narrative. Researchers, for reasons of practical necessity, set up "objective" identity markers in order to establish meaningful categories for analysis. The dialectical method recognizes that identity is actually composed of both objective and subjective elements. Paradoxically, the "objective" reality of self-identity is a dialectic between ascribed identity (a product of socialization, including the internalization of identity markers imposed by others) and self-determined identity—identity consciously formed. Both of these aspects constitute the process of identity-in-formation. Identity, then, is neither simply a given, nor is it wholly self-determined, for it is the product of a continual process of "negotiation" with others. An integral part of that process is dealing with the views and attitudes of those with whom one is negotiating, whether political comrades, co-ethnics, or those sharing any other aspect of identity.

Public Versus Private Self

Related to the issue of subjective versus objective self-identification is the issue of tactics for presentation of self based on the identities of those with whom one is interacting. For Joe Dimow, his self-conception of his Jewish identity may be the same whether interacting with fellow Jewish socialists or leaders of the mainstream Jewish community, but his self-presentation would be very different. With the latter group he may have to be more cautious in his presentation of his political self. On the other hand, the form of expression of his Jewish identity may cause problems in his negotiations with non-Jewish political activists, who may feel that he has subordinated his political beliefs in defending ethnic interests. (This becomes particularly difficult when discussing the issue of Israel and its relationship with the Arab peoples.)

Even the greatest caution in the relatively private interview situation cannot screen out the recognition of such dilemmas of the public negotiation of self-identity. Such recognition must unavoidably color the discourse. The distinction between private views and public presentation is most difficult to unravel. The most intimate view of the private self probably came from Lil, who spoke from the heart about what matters most to her, without apparently screening her views for political consistency. Yet that consistency revealed itself in her description of life events.

Joe revealed to the greatest extent the tension between public and private self when, in the second interview, I asked him to reflect upon what he had said in our first conversation. He declared that he had some second thoughts, especially about what he considered to be overconfident statements he had made initially. Was this a distinction between public and private self that my request for critical reflection momentarily breached—a rare moment of candid introspection? I will explore this issue further in a close analysis of his personal narratives.

The point is that no matter how "private" the interview, a subject may perceive it as a "public" event, presenting him/herself as for an anticipated or imagined larger audience. The form of self-narrative—and its very content—may reflect efforts at identity "management" (Compare Goffman 1959). This may be done for a variety of reasons, the common denominator being the protection of one's core identity. Thus, even though an interview may be conducted in the privacy of a subject's home, the subject may still speak (self)consciously, or habitually, in a "public" voice.

Riegel addresses the notion of a "public" voice in the narratives of authors whose activities "are not merely determined by their personal knowledge and idiosyncratic experience but also by the thoughts, intentions, and feelings of the reader in contemporary society and by those developed during the history . . . of a particular society" (Riegel 1975; Compare the notion of "dialogic principles" discussed in Bakhtin 1981). All interview subjects are "authors" of a self-narrative that, although delivered in the relative privacy of a conversation between two people, is "contextualized" by the larger sociohistorical conditions within which the "thoughts, intentions, and feelings" of the interview subject have emerged, developed, and likely have been previously articulated. Gergen and Gergen point out that narrative itself is a social process:

Narrative construction can never be an entirely private matter. In the reliance on a symbol system for relating or connecting events one is engaging in an implicitly social act . . . .In effect, narratives as linguistic devices are inherently a product not of individuals but of interacting persons. (Gergen and Gergen 1984).

Active Versus Passive Identification

In my conversation with Jacob Goldring, an intriguing concept was suggested, obvious once it is considered, yet apparently absent from the literature on identity. Jake has no reservations in asserting that his support of and commitment to socialism was as strong as ever. However, the political demographics of the town in which he eventually settled (and in which he still resides) are such that there are presently no local chapters of any of the political organizations that come closest to matching his present political perspective. While he is moderately involved in community-based political activity, his identity as a socialist is not reflected in any organizational involvements. Thus, while Jake is demonstrative in his declaration of a socialist outlook, his socialist identity is passive in relation to its concrete (or at least organized) public expression.

Jake revealed a more curious form of passive identification in our discussion of ethnicity. He asserted that he did not consider his Jewish identity as primary; moreover, he did not even consider it an essential part of his identity. Nevertheless, he observed that if there were a local chapter of an organization that consisted of politically progressive Jews, he would likely have become involved. He does, in fact, occasionally attend meetings of such an organization in another city, largely because a few of his longtime activist friends are members.

In her discussion of the "meaning of place in old age," Sandra Howell asserts that "place is necessary to identity" (Howell 1983). She discusses the concept of place, or physical environment, on a number of levels, including how one perceives his or her place, the history of one's experiences in a given place, the internalization of social attitudes about that place, and the perception of changes that have occurred in that place. One question that Howell poses in her delineation of the meaning of place is particularly germane to the present discussion: "How has a place related to the domains of the individual's life—family, work, social-educational, cultural-political experience?"

Howell places an emphasis on the importance of personal attachment to place as an aspect of self-identity. Jake, however, posed the question differently. He came to a particular place with his core identity very much intact. In fact, it was the political organization to which he belonged that assigned him as an organizer to the city in which he eventually settled, and in which he has lived out his "retirement." One could argue that his attachment to place is responsible for his remaining where he is, even though local organizational outlets for his political outlook no longer exist.

Another factor in Jake's physical environment is the home in which he lives, which he built himself on the shore of a lake. An important aspect of Jake's identity has been his trade as a carpenter and building contractor. He acknowledges that it is his attachment to his home (both the house itself and the physical setting) that is the primary, perhaps the sole, reason he has remained in place.

I will not attempt to examine the conditions under which a person's attachment to physical place may take precedence over the desire to give organizational expression to their politics. However, the questions Howell raises about one's relationship to physical place are highly relevant to the concerns of this study by way of analogy, since a central issue I confronted in the present study is that of the relationship between personal identity and environment in the broadest sense, both personal and social.

This analogy between physical and social place was revealed when, during each interview, I turned the discussion to the relation between self-identity and the sense of belonging, in particular the personal attachment people felt to the political organization to which they had made a long-term commitment. I wanted to elicit statements about the degree to which their relationship with political comrades was familial, providing a sense of belonging to a "home" and a community. It was very clear from the response to this line of inquiry that in the relationship between identity and place, "place" functions as much in a figurative as in a literal sense.

In another study of ethnic and class identity among political activists (the subjects were aged, but the focus was not necessarily on aging itself), I addressed this phenomenon as "the movable home" (Shuldiner 1984). Political activists who not only shared a common outlook but who belonged to the same organizations were often welcomed by other members as "family," regardless of where those other members resided. On an ad hoc basis, one member of a national organization might visit another member anywhere in the country, and be made to feel at home. On another level, one member might relocate to another town, and gain a new family composed of counterparts (politically, and often ethnically) of the friends and comrades she or he left behind. For one whose core identity is tied to the ideology of the organization to which one has made a major commitment, "home" is, to paraphrase the words of a popular song, wherever those who share ideological and organizational ties "hang their hats."

For those who maintain political and ideological commitments, into old age, these ties become the basis for the maintenance of close friendships or the forging of new ones. For the individuals I interviewed for this study, sense of place was still a key element in their lives, and it has been represented in part by friendships maintained among those who have shared their particular outlook all along. For it is not simply the case that they have maintained a common global vision, a common overall ideological stance. It is also the case that, whether by chance or design, they have followed similar paths in their changing perceptions of place and its transformations. It may also be a process of elimination, whereby with each twist and turn in their personal and political development, their close friends remained those who had negotiated parallel life courses. Since the four people I interviewed have longstanding ties as comrades, friends, and co-ethnics, many of these factors are at work.

Chapter Three

The Aging of Politics and the Politics of Aging

LIFE TRANSITIONS

It is the premise of this book that the formation and expression of political identity in old age is embedded in a lifelong process of ideational development. Such a view places this book comfortably within the family of "life-span" and "life-transition" studies, which portray aging not simply as a qualitatively different stage or social world, but as an ongoing movement, part of an evolving history in which it is both determined and determining. Within such a framework, personal and political development, family and social history, and historical events each have interlocking roles in the development of the whole person (see, for example, Hareven 1982; Hareven & Adams 1982).

There are virtually no studies of late life political activism conducted from a lifespan/life transition perspective. A notable exception is the ground breaking study *Lifetimes of Commitment: Aging, Politics, Psychology,* by Molly Andrews (1991). This work draws from interviews with fifteen British men and women, aged seventy to ninety, who have been political activists for most of their lives. It interweaves the personal development of their identities with the social and historical conditions in which they initiated and sustained their political involvements into late life. Many of the points that I raise in this book are anticipated in her study, to which I would refer readers seeking a thorough analysis of similar issues with reference to a different, but related, group of interview subjects.

   The literature on late life activism from any perspective is sparse. There are, however, a number of published (and even more unpublished) personal accounts written by older political activists (see, for example, Dennis 1977, Haywood 1978, Richmond 1972, Weisbord 1977), as well as biographies of activists, tracing their lives of political commitment into old age (see, for example, MacKinnon 1988, Miller 1982, Strong 1983). Still others are collaborative works between activist and biographer, based on extensive oral history interviews conducted with subjects in late life (see, for example, Healey 1990, Kann 1981, Nelson 1981, Painter 1979). Some are straightforward chronicles of activities and events, while others offer various levels of self-reflection, largely on changes in political attitudes and affiliations.

   At least one work (Gornick 1977) presents excerpts of interviews with a number of aging activists reflecting upon what their membership (former in most cases) in the Communist Party meant to them during the time they were active. Several of the interview subjects reveal something of their own personal development (mostly how they "grew out" of the Party). However, the principle aim of the author-as-interviewer was not to document personal development; rather it was to elicit subjects' recollections about what drew them to the Party. In this book, as in most of the personal accounts of aging activists, lifespan development is at best a secondary or incidental concern.

   Notable exceptions to this are to be found in feminist studies of personal narrative (see, e.g., Personal Narratives Group 1989) and biographies of women activists, guided by a central perspective (and one of the most profound contributions of the women's movement): the personal as political. As an example, a recent biography of Simone de Beauvoir by Dierdre Bair (1990), informed by feminist scholarship and enriched by extensive interviews conducted by the author with de Beauvoir (the last series completed shortly before de Beauvoir's death in 1986) reveals, in intimate detail, the complex relationship between her personal life and attitudes and her writing and political activism. (Much of this is revealed, albeit selectively, in de Beauvoir's own autobiographical writings as well, though Bair finds problems of accuracy there.) Her own writings about women (de Beauvoir 1957) and about aging (de Beauvoir 1972), both landmark contributions, are shown in this biographical account to reveal a remarkable tension between her own personal upbringing and attitudes and her perspective and sense of social responsibility as a feminist and political activist. De Beauvoir's *Coming of Age*, written in late life, may be said to be both a political manifesto on aging, and her own coming to terms (personally as well as politically) with her "condition" as an older woman.

Bair's biography of de Beauvoir reveals another insight instructive for life course studies, one that became quite apparent to me in the interviews I conducted: that of the contingent rather than fixed character of life transitions, including the "coming of age." This may be especially true for longtime activists whose political lives and agendas often set the conditions for major life changes rather than other conventional or "normative" criteria such as family, work, and retirement. Recent literature on life transitions, however, has challenged the assumptions underlying age-bound developmental models with set stages or fixed criteria. As Hareven puts it:

Historically, age in itself has not been a significant factor in the timing of life transitions and in the definitions of old age. More important than age was family status, work status, and one's relationship to the community. (Hareven 1982).

My study of aging activists deal's of necessity with the effects of the passage of time on the character and kind of personal and political commitment. It does so by observing, through life narratives, the relationship between the "individual time" of each person's life and the "historical time" through which they have lived (Compare Hareven 1982).

ACTIVITY AND (DIS)ENGAGEMENT

This study also presents an alternative approach to the issue of self-identity and aging. There is a tendency to view self-identity and its forms of expression in old age as reactive. Part of the reason is a well-intentioned critique of disengagement theory, which posits a process of gradual withdrawal from social ties and commitments in late life, usually following one's retirement. Accompanying a diminution in the number and level of intensity of one's ties is the adoption of a more reflective posture, a summing up of life experiences as one reaches its final stages. As posited in its extreme form by life -stage theorists (see, e.g. Erikson 1975) this process is writ as the culmination of aging's manifest destiny.

We should also keep in mind that much of the contemporary debate over disengagement is preconditioned by the emergence of a relatively recent historical phenomena: retirement. A product of industrial capitalism, it is a means of controlling the size of the work force based on the needs of the captains of industry. (see, e.g., Graebner, 1980, Phillipson 1983). For older workers, retirement marks their literal disengagement—often compulsory—from the work force, not only severing them from their (wage-earning) livelihood but also from what was probably their principal social activity (and frequently their primary source of self -identity).

While some writers have posited (or perhaps rationalized) retirement as a period of gradual social withdrawal and contemplation, others have focused on the possibilities for meaningful activity made possible by the free time that retirement presents. Like retirement itself, the growing field of leisure studies is also a byproduct of industrial capitalism. Leisure time for those still in the work force is a significant achievement of the trade union movement that led the struggle for the eight-hour day, along with safe working conditions and better wages, so that they might both survive the workplace and have the means to take advantage of their spare time (though this is still a dream, not a reality, for many workers).

Works like those of De Grazia (1962) and Murphy (1974) have attempted to articulate ways of conveying meaning to leisure pursuits and fathoming the implications for self-identity and value derived from leisure rather than from work. Kleemeier (1961) and others have specifically focused on leisure activity in retirement. A number of these studies offer specific prescriptions for forging a new life of meaningful pursuits in one's post-wage-earning life (see, e.g., Metropoulos 1980, Brady 1988).

Some students of activity and aging have offered a model for life in retirement that posits leisure pursuits among the aging as driven by the same "work ethic" that characterized their wage-earning careers. Proponents of the "busy ethic" (Ekerdt 1986) suggest that the moral imperative to keep occupied with productive tasks compels many retirees to engage in activities that keep them as busy (if not more so) as before they "retired." What is absent from any of these studies is a discussion of the relationship between the individual work ethic and social commitment, a central issue for political activists.

It is not surprising that political activism is either not considered a meaningful way of spending one's "leisure" time or is trivialized as "just" another form of "leisure" activity. (Actually, the term "leisure" implies activity pursued solely for self-interest, and so it is not an accurate or appropriate way of describing activity motivated by deeply held social convictions.) It is ironic that while devastating critiques have been written about the marginalization of the elderly within the industrial capitalist system (see, for example, Olson 1982, Phillipson 1982), so little ink has been "spilled" in scholarly journals about the significance of participation in movements for social change among the elderly. More than a decade ago Estes (1978) commented on the lack of studies addressing the issue of what meaning political participation might have for older people, let alone the specific types of political activity in they might be inclined to engage. The situation has changed little.

Further, in the few discussions of activism as a meaningful activity for retirees, there is a tendency to focus solely on political activity related to aging issues (see, for example, Trela 1976, Brady 1988). It is true that groups of older people organizing themselves in order to address aging issues have received much press coverage, and have been the subjects of a number of popular publications (see, e.g., Kleyman 1974, Pratt 1976). At least one publication has addressed the problems of aging in the form of a radical manifesto for fundamental social change (Bornat 1985). However, almost no scholarly work has been conducted on the development (or persistence) of political consciousness among older persons. Notable exceptions include the works of Trela (1976) and Fox (1981) that examine the conditions under which older persons might become politically conscious and politically active.

There is, however, a small but growing body of literature that addresses the lives of aging activists who carry on what has been a lifetime of involvement in social movements. The journal *Southern Exposure* devoted a special double issue in 1985 to the theme "Older, Wiser, Stronger." It featured articles on activists over age 65 living in the southern United States, many of whom continue to carry on the political struggles that have occupied them throughout their lives (and some of whom have turned their political experience to advantage in addressing issues of aging). In one such article, Anne

Braden presents, through a series of several short life portraits, the "long view of elder activists." She notes how the perspective of their years has given aging activists staying power in social movements, as well as providing inspiration for their younger counterparts. Les Lindeman, in a feature for the magazine *50 Plus*, presents first-person accounts of several older individuals who participated in a joint American and Soviet peace walk from Leningrad to Moscow in 1987. These instances are rare. This one-sided depiction of elder activists has tended to typecast them in ways analogous to that of African-American film actors like Sidney Poiter who had a hard time early in his career finding roles in which he was not primary obliged to confront "the race issue." One is hard-pressed to find studies of aging activists not devoted exclusively to "the age issue."

The life story of one of the most well-known of aging activists, Maggie Kuhn, "convener" of the Gray Panthers, is somewhat of a paradox. A lifetime activist, she gained her greatest notoriety for her incisive and creative (often theatrical) critiques of the treatment of older persons. Drawn into the "aging movement" as the result of her own compulsory retirement, she has broadened her political base once more, transforming the Gray Panthers into an intergenerational organization that integrates aging issues into those of the "global" political movement in which she has long been involved. The Gray Panthers stresses the importance of drawing older adults into the fight for peace, civil rights and basic social change.

Not only does Maggie Kuhn advocate political alliances among the young and old, but has lived in an intentional intergenerational household, and has actively promoted this form of "shared housing." Books and articles have been written by and about her (see, for example, Hessel 1977, Kuhn 1979, Lyman 1988), yet we still wait for an in-depth, lifespan analysis of her emerging personal and political self-identity.

"LEISURE," "RETIREMENT" AND ACTIVISM

From this brief introduction, it is clear that the debate about "activity" versus "disengagement" has not only created a poorly conceived dichotomy, but one that excludes important forms of expression, particularly those based on political identity and commitment. Similarly, much of the discussion about "work," "leisure," and "retirement" is made problematic by the assumptions upon which these categories of life activity are based.

The aging activists who are the focus of this book have long occupied what the literature would refer to as their "leisure" time (that is, spare time outside wage-earning careers) with activities based on their political outlook and commitments. For them, leisure time was time not spent doing either political or wage-earning work. Such time was a precious commodity when they were both activists and wage earners. "Retirement" from wage earning allowed them a little more leisure time, but their lives were still not dominated by leisure time, since their political careers persist, filling the additional time allotted to them in varying degrees. Activists like Joe considered his political "career" to be his primary occupation, even though his work as a tool maker often took up more of his time. For Joe the cessation of his full-time wage-earning career meant more time for his "principal" occupation as political activist (an issue that will be discussed further on).

In any event, both activity/leisure and disengagement theories tend to make assumptions about the kind and quality of the life and times of the aging, in particular, the nature of "retirement." Rather than reject these models offhand, I would suggest a refinement of these notions by incorporating them into a conceptually distinct dialectical relationship: one of active engagement on the one hand, and reflection upon that engagement on the other.

The four older activists I interviewed for this book have all shifted the nature and venue of their political involvement, but they vary in the degree of intensity of their political activity. All claim adherence to the core ideological belief that has fueled their lifelong activism: an abiding commitment to the overall outlook and goals of socialism. But over the years, especially (but not necessarily) in late life, and following a period of reflection, they have undergone what is arguably a process of "disengagement" from at least some aspects of the left political subculture and its worldview. These have included: a distancing from previously held dogma, doctrines, or political positions; a literal disengagement from specific organizations; and a withdrawal from some social activities and personal relationships and within the social world in which those committed to the same political outlook and organizations lived and interacted. Since the members of such a close knit community considered their political ties virtually coterminous with their primary personal ties, one cannot avoid the issue of disengagement with reference to severing political ties. The irony in this book is that such disengagement took place for all of these four activists in mid-life rather than at "retirement" age.

To summarize at this point, there are at least two fundamental problems with the application of age-bound activity/disengagement models for studying aging political activists. First, most current research is directed toward older persons active in aging issues (or other issues of immediate self-interest), but not elders involved in "global issues" such as peace, civil rights, women's movement or the environment; second, consideration is not given to political activity as a reflection of continued belief throughout the life course, rather than simply as an activity to occupy one's time in old age/retirement.

Given these observations, I would suggest that disengagement/activity be considered as relational terms, contingent upon a useful point of reference, rather than defended or rejected as developmental (let alone age-linked) imperatives. Further, allowing a greater conceptual flexibility would open up new possibilities for interpretation of late-life transitions.

An axiom of popular belief is that people become "philosophical" in their old age. To be philosophical in this sense is to distance oneself psychically from the immediate life situations in which one is engaged, in order to achieve a degree of objectivity. It is looking at a problem with a sense of detachment (disengagement, if you will), like a "disinterested" third party, without taking things personally or risking the bruising of one's ego. The expression also implies a global view, associated—interestingly enough—not just with old age, but also with a comprehensive political or religious ideology. For an aging political activist, to be philosophical is to see the world through the prism of experience, through the eyes of one who has been "through the political mill," no longer as easily misled by some beliefs, nor as easily "bruised" by being attacked for holding other views.

There is an important distinction between disengagement as a situational strategy and disengagement as a totalization (to use the Sartrean terminology), that is, as an all-embracing existential framework for experience. It is simply a discretionary position taken from time to time in order to *objectively* view life situations that are otherwise experienced *subjectively* as a totality.

AGE AWARENESS AND SELF IDENTITY

There is no denying that age-awareness is a significant aspect of self-identity. The question that arises is the character and degree of its relationship to other aspects of self-identity. My conversations with Joe, Lil, Jake and Sid offer no definitive answers to such a query. However, at least a couple of observations on the subject are useful in discussing that question. One observation concerns denial. It was certainly apparent in the interviews I conducted that, as expansive as my subjects were about political identity, they were far less forthcoming about the issue of age. It was not that they were uncomfortable with the subject; it was simply that age is a reality that has asserted itself in the course of their life activities—sometimes as an asset, sometimes as a liability—but not an issue to which they have devoted much time in reflection.

It may be argued that age becomes a primary source of identity if a person brings no other dominant aspects of self-identity into late life or has experienced the loss of a significant aspect of their identity. Rosow (1974) describes the dilemma of the "roleless" role of the aging, in which principal sources of self-identity are no longer relevant in late life, such as those associated with an occupation that ceased with retirement. But it is not a given that one's occupations (including unpaid housework) are necessarily central to a person's self-identity. Murphy (1974) argues that, for contemporary workers, leisure plays an important, perhaps even a more significant, part in the development of their sense of self-identity. If one looks beyond the narrow category of leisure, many significant forms of social involvement outside the workplace—such as ethnic, religious and political activity—may be identified as potentially central to the development of self-identity. Moreover, none of these are age-contingent, but may form the basis for lifelong ideational continuity, depending upon specific personal, social and historical conditions.

Recent gerontological studies based on life story interviews have tended to establish age awareness as a largely contingent aspect of self-identity among most older persons. As Kaufman puts it: "Old people do not perceive meaning in aging itself, so much as they perceive meaning in being themselves in old age" (Kaufman 1986). She uses the concept of the "ageless self" to describe the ways in which older persons "maintain a sense of continuity and meaning that helps them cope with change."

Applying the notion of the contingency of age, I would argue that, at least for the aging activists I interviewed, the relative disinclination to be expansive upon the subject of aging reflects, in part, a lack of age self-consciousness or, more to the point, the relegation of age as a secondary (subordinate) aspect of self-identity. This is by no means a denial of the aging process itself; rather it is a refusal to be "ghettoized" into some subculture of the elderly (Compare Rosow 1974). And rather than reflecting a pathological condition, the sublimation of age-awareness to political consciousness has invigorated their later years, perhaps even extended them (such a hypothesis awaits formal investigation).

Joe Dimow was very clear about one aspect of age which he not only acknowledged, but for which he desired recognition from others. He has been involved for many years with organizations whose memberships are intergenerational, but whose active members and leaders are predominantly younger. When he hears people discussing issues and tactics at meetings, he often steps in with advice based on his extensive experience with some of those same issues and tactics. He wishes people would take advantage—much more than they have—of his store of knowledge stemming from a lifetime of activism. In this sense, Joe places a certain importance on an aspect of age relating to both social status and self-concept: the role of the elder as mentor, and the validation of one's identity in the act of recognizing the value of one's experience and knowledge. (The term "elder" here is as much relational [indicating that Joe is more experienced than younger activists] as it is referential [signalling chronological age].)

Sid recounted his work over the years for progressive Jewish publications, and pointed to the importance of contextualizing the issue of age. He noted that his attempts to get the staff of a radical Yiddish newspaper, all in their seventies and eighties at the time, to changewith the times and involve new people in its publication were met with less than enthusiasm. Sid felt that the efforts of his younger cohorts, in their fifties and sixties, were being rebuffed, partly because of the failure of members of the "older" generation to acknowledge their own temporality. Ironically, those "elders" were too wrapped up in producing their paper and keeping up with current events to pay attention to such practical considerations of the consequences as their own biological passage of time and that of their cohorts who constituted their exclusive—and ever-diminishing—readership.

ETHNICITY, AGE AND IDEOLOGY

Much has been written in recent years about the importance of ethnic identity in the aging process (see, for example, Jackson 1985, Gelfand 1987, Markides 1987, Markides 1990). Yet there are problems that emerge in treating ethnicity as a separate issue. Jackson notes the irony in the fact that research on ethnicity and aging tends to segregate the "ethnic" elderly, objectifying them as the "other" in the process of isolating ethnic-specific variables of aging (Jackson 1985).

A more fruitful, and ultimately more equitable, approach to ethnicity is to place it within a lifespan framework, and to study it in relation to other aspects of identity, not only age, but also occupation, class, ideology, and gender (aspects of central concern here). It is this approach that informs the discussion of ethnicity among aging political activists.

Joe, Lil, Jake, and Sid are bound together as age-cohorts, political comrades, and co-ethnics. Yet while they have maintained a closeness in the intensity of their generational memory and ideological commitment, there is a greater variance in the intensity of their ethnic identity, including the degree to which they consider their ethnicity to be an essential aspect of their self-identity. However, what is essential in this observation is that their ethnicity has, throughout their lives, been linked in some way to their political identity. Three of the four have, in later life, become involved in ethnic-based political organizations.

The link between ethnicity and age among these activists is more problematic. However, there are several aspects of the relationship between ethnicity and political identity in which age may be considered factors, implicitly or explicitly.

Ethnicity and Politics and Their Persistence in Old Age

Without exception, the activists I interviewed were raised by one or more parents who were themselves not only political activists, but self-identified Jewish radicals. Liebman (1979) has described the subculture of the "Jewish Labor Movement" in the United States as composed of those who shared both class and ethnic ties, borrowing Gordon's (1964) model of the "eth-class" (also see Shuldiner 1984).

These activists, bound by ties of community and polity, were not necessarily united in the overt demonstration of their ethnicity. Nevertheless, the social ties forged and maintained within this activist subculture persisted lifelong for many members of this political "eth-class." Thus, regardless of the degree of intensity (or even overt expression) of their ethnicity, these ties have largely defined the inner circle of close friends/comrades/cohorts for many Jewish radicals in late life.

Jackson quotes Alan Harwood's distinction between "behavioral and ideological ethnicity," in which behavioral ethnicity is identified as a product of socialization: "distinctive values, beliefs, behavioral norms, and languages," and ideological ethnicity is identified as a vehicle for political expression, an ad hoc platform to advance political interests (quoted in Jackson 1985). The question arises about the extent to which the ethnic expression of politics is merely a pretext for political interests In other words, for "ethnic" activists, is politics or ethnicity the dominant aspect of their identity, their interests, their activism, their political objectives?

The weakness in Harwood's dichotomy lies in its narrow, and ultimately misleading, definition of "ideology." It fails to acknowledge an important distinction between ethnic activists who engage in social movements for *in-group* political and/or economic gains (primarily ethnic interests) and political activists who may choose ethnic forms (personal and organizational) for their political expression. "Ideological ethnicity" as Harwood employs the term, apparently refers to the former; "our" activists belong to the latter category.

The Ethnic Component in Political/Friendship Ties

Following from the close ties between ethnicity and politics in the lives of these Jewish radicals, it is not surprising that political affiliation and ethnic involvement have been intertwined for most of them. Disman (1987) speaks about the relative importance of ethnic identity and activity *during* the life course as a key to its persistence in old age. The same may be said of political identity and activity. Keith (1977), in her study of a French retirement community, noted the relevance of past political affiliation (in particular, membership in the French Communist Party) as a factor in the establishment of social networks among residents.

Myerhoff (1978), in her study of elderly Jews who congregate at a senior center in Venice, California, notes in passing the continuing importance of political history and memory, of center members, in the formation of social factions. Ironically, she treats the issue as tangential to the overarching need for communality among an ever-diminishing group of co-ethnic cohorts.

The Tension Between Ethnic and Political Affinity

The conflict between community and polity hinted at in Myerhoff's study underscores a dilemma faced by ethnic activists: a tension between the desire to maintain political integrity and the desire to be accepted by members of the ethnic community at large. Joe Dimow spoke at length on his attempts to interact successfully with members of the mainstream Jewish community as part of his political organizing efforts. It was more than just a demonstration of his willingness to work on a tactical basis with people with whom he had little in common politically. He also wanted to be respected as a person—more, as a co-ethnic—in spite of mutually recognized, irreconcilable, political differences. Acceptance, if any, must of necessity be conditional or limited to specific domains of ethnic expression. (I would argue that ethnic unity is at best conditional for those committed to fundamentally divergent political goals or outlooks.) What is important is that the desire for acceptance from those united primarily on the basis of ethnicity reflects not just the need for ethnic identification but also the need for some sense of communality among co-ethnics regardless of political affiliation. Does the need for ethnic communality intensify in late life (as has been argued for religion)? The results are mixed for those I interviewed.

PERSONAL NARRATIVE AND LIFE SATISFACTION

These interviews challenge yet another set of assumptions about self-concept and aging, those that arise from studies of "life-satisfaction" and morale. A central problem in the critique of such studies lies to a great extent in the fact that "there appear to have been few attempts to specify the conceptual and theoretical domains for either life satisfaction or morale" (Sauer& Warland 1982). Neugarten, Havighurst, and Tobin (quoted in Sauer& Warland 1982) define five components of life satisfaction: "zest (versus apathy), resolution and fortitude, congruence between desired and achieved goals, positive self-concept, and mood tone."

Lillian Dimow opened our initial conversation with the remark that she was very dissatisfied with her life. Yet, during the interview, she demonstrated zest for much of her life activities and commitments, resolution and strength in her political outlook, and positive self-concept in terms of her sense of certainty and acceptance of her core identity. What she has lacked is satisfaction with specific accomplishments that, in her estimation, have perpetually left room for improvement.

Part of the problem may lie in the failure to apply life-satisfaction measures to specific contexts or domains, as do studies of "locus of control," in which subjects are queried about their sense of competence within a specific domain of life and activity. For example, to meaningfully assess the level of one's "life satisfaction," it would be important to make a distinction between the sense of control one has over internal affairs versus control of external affairs in one's life. To make such an evaluation would require eliciting from an individual his or her assessment of the relative importance of control over personal life and/or emotional state (internal) versus their sense of control over global outlook and political activity (external).

While they were constantly frustrated about local and world affairs, the aging activists I interviewed were consistent in their certainty of the overall perspective that guides them. In this respect it would be fruitful to further qualify the term "external control." One may employ this term to describe a "global" sense of control over external affairs (an illusory goal!). A more fruitful definition of external control would address the sense of control a person perceives in terms of her or his stance, place, or position, in relation to the external world. Following this latter definition sense of the term, one could pose a model of external control which allows for a richer, multilayered understanding. On the one hand, the remarks of our activists, who express great certainty in the ideological foundation of their outlook and activity, reflect a positive sense of external control because of their confidence in the viability of an external ideological framework and a continued positive sense of its relevance to their ongoing political work. On the other hand, these same individuals express periodic dissatisfaction with those same external relations because, as committed activists (like creative artists), they are never completely satisfied, always making an effort to "fine tune" both theory and practice. External control may may viewed "globally," but is contingent upon "local" conditions.

PERSONAL NARRATIVE AND SELF-CONCEPT

The significance of a conditional, or domain-specific, context in the valuation of life-satisfaction is related directly to the significance of context in the valuation of self-concept. In discussing the dimensions of self-concept and self-esteem, Breytspraak and George (1982) note that:

The most popular theoretical classification is the distinction between actual self-concept ("what I am really like"), ideal self-concept ("what I would like to be like"), and perceived self-concept ("how others see me"). In this system of definitions, self-esteem is sometimes operationalized as the discrepancy between actual and ideal self-concepts, with a large discrepancy assumed to reflect negative affect and self-evaluation (Breytspraak/George 1982).

What is most telling in this description is the negative valuation of the discrepancy between actual and ideal self-concepts. While the apparent lesson is that those who fall shortest of their ideals are the least satisfied with themselves, it may also be said that those with great confidence in their outlook set high goals or standards of which they may invariably fall short, but which at the same time may not sway their self-confidence. Again, what needs to be done is to look at the specific contexts of aspects or domains of self-concept, in addition to the above dichotomies.

In this way it is possible to speak of a person being "satisfied" with (certain of) his "global" or ideal self-concept, yet dissatisfied with his self-concept as a "work in progress," that is, with the relative failure of specific activities or projects (as self-evaluated) to adequately reflect his ideal self-concept. In a discussion of personal theories of life-span development as revealed in autobiographical writings, Handel (1987) provides a perspective on self-concept that is particularly applicable (though not necessarily exclusive) to creative artists, political activists, and others committed to life projects on a grand scale.

Handel compares the accounts of middle-aged and older autobiographers on self-concept with the findings of studies in which self-appraisals have been solicited. He concludes that there are contrasts in approaches to the issue of selfhood that lead autobiographers and researchers in different directions.

Handel suggests, for example, that "traditional" studies have tended to focus on whether subjects felt that they had changed or remained the same as in the past, evaluating the subjects on the basis of their responses to this issue. Autobiographers tend to compare their present self not only with "retrospective" selves, but also with a "desired self." He later points to the sense of indeterminacy of autobiographical accounts of the self, descriptions that present the self as in a perpetual state of emergence, insinuating that there is always a gap between the present self and the full realization of the "true" self. This notion precludes the sense of closure that is the putative goal of self-reflection in life review among the elderly, as argued by Butler (1963) and others. While Handel does not identify it as such, what he is describing is a dialectical process of self that is open-ended rather than a linear pattern of development that "demands" an end point or "closure."

Many self-narratives speak of a sense of estrangement with former selves, emphasizing "the radical nature of the transformation of self" (Handel 1987). Yet while feeling that her former self is a "stranger," the autobiographer may still argue that her "essential" self is still the same, that, for example, her faults are the same but her perspective on them has shifted. Here again, self-narrative reveals a dialectical relationship between form and essence—the changing forms of the self in time set within the context of a core identity ("true self") that is ontologically constant.

Personal theories of the self revealed in autobiographical narratives present a challenge to prevailing notions of a developmental imperative in selfhood that has implications for prevailing gerontological models. This is particularly true in the case of those approaches to reminiscence outlined above that posit life review as a means of providing closure in life's final stage. Handel points to the perpetual distance between that desired closure and the sense of incompleteness of the "true self" as expressed by autobiographers.

This observation bears comparison with comments made by Kaufman on "adaptation" in her analysis of the life history of "Millie," an 80-year-old woman living in a nursing home who has had to change the "themes" of her self-concept in adjusting to surroundings that continually compromise her needs and desires (Kaufman 1986). In her concluding remarks, Kaufman observes that "the meaning attributed to adaptation which has . . . shaped nearly forty years of research is contentment." Successful adaptation is equated with happiness and, like closure, any other outcome would tend to be viewed as pathological. Like the autobiographers that Handel has "read," Millie, in Kaufman's view, has not found "happiness" but *has* found ways, through the telling of her life story, of constructing the "themes" that comprise her sense of self and provide meaning to her life. Like the autobiographers (and the activists I interviewed), it is the search for meaning, rather than "contentment" or "closure" that propels her existence (and, one might add, that fuels her personal narrative).

Handel briefly compares oral life histories to (written) autobiographical accounts and sees the latter as "an essentially reflective reconstruction of one's life history," while he views the oral history elicited in an interview as more spontaneous. (In describing the latter as "an expression of a sudden impulse to vent some fierce, hitherto suppressed affects . . . , " he may be referring more to life review interviews conducted in a clinical setting than to conventional [nonclinical] oral history interviews). Reading Kaufman's account of Millie's oral biography, there may be more of a comparative construction of one's self through personal narrative in the two approaches than Handel is willing to grant. The works autobiographers actually share with the oral histories under consideration here (as well as Millie's personal account) underscore the fact that past experiences are, in the process of retelling, cast in an ideological mold that "fits" the reconstructed self of the present. And in both cases, there is, at least implicitly, an acknowledgment of the incompleteness of life's project and, by extension, of the self. (Recent works on personal narrative that contain references to self-concept and/or life satisfaction include Bertaux 1981, Burgos 1989, Cohler 1982, Denzin 1989, Plummer 1983, Polkinghorne 1988, Titon 1980, and Watson 1985.)

AGE OF WISDOM, AGE OF COMMITMENT

This book tackles a number of issues related to the development of self-identity in late life from a life-span perspective. It is not my intention to derive from this analysis a definitive theory on late-life ideational development. My aim is rather to chart the ways in which Joe, Lil, Jake, and Sid have each dealt with these issues while negotiating a sometimes tortuous route through their personal and political life courses. I will look at and compare their evolving views on a range of subjects, critically examining the ways in which they have shaped and defended their core identity as political activists. I may challenge the degree to which each of them has maintained "fidelity" to the political ideal of socialism that they continue to adhere to, without exception. However, I will ultimately yield to the surety of their own demonstrated sense of self, reflecting a remarkable capacity to adapt to changing conditions. They have held on to a core identity that has not only enabled them in late life to maintain a sense of commitment, but that has also given them a privileged position from which they may look back, with more than mere nostalgia, on accomplishments made possible by the constancy of that identity and commitment.

The Stories

Chapter Four

With the Feelings That I Have About the Capitalist System

[First interview with Joseph Dimow, conducted at his home in New Haven, Connecticut, on April 12, 1990.]

[The conversation we had about the terms of the interview in general and occupational identity in particular, just before I turned on the cassette recorder, prompted Joe to make the first recorded remarks.]

JOSEPH DIMOW: Occupation and work involves, to my mind, two different things. One is the work you do in order to earn a living, which to me has always been separate from "occupation," or things to do because I want to do them. One took time away from the other. One was something that I had to do in order to enable myself to do the other. So if someone were to ask me, what were you doing at such and such a time in the past, in say the 1960s?, I would probably respond by talking about the things I did *off* work that interested me. That's not to say that there weren't some interesting moments at work, too. And I did have some throughout my working career, as a toolmaker. I had times when there were interesting things happening as a toolmaker, interesting things happening in the shop [where] I worked and [with] the people I worked with. But there were also things that had nothing directly to do with toolmaking. I might have been interested in Jewish community affairs or in civil-rights movements, or in community projects, political campaigns, and so on, which were also occurring at the same time that I was involved in [work, but] off the job.

So I just wanted to make clear that I'm confused when you talk about occupational identification. Sometimes if somebody asked me what is my occupation, I would say I'm retired. From what? As a toolmaker? Yes, I'm retired as a toolmaker, but I don't think of myself in those terms. I think of myself in terms of the organizations I belong to and the activities I was involved in.

DAVID SHULDINER: I think that's a very good point of departure, Joe, because the aim of our discussion is really, at root, to get at the important sources of identity in your life. We begin with the occupational, because that is something that dominates so much of one's working and waking life, and in most societies is the central [activity]. There may other forms of social organization-ethnic, social, religious, etcetera, but work is the driving force. But you make a good point. It's not necessarily work that may provide a dominant identity. There are many, many sources of identity.

JD: Well, let me start this way. When I finished high school, I was thinking in terms of what to do with myself, and I felt [that] my parents wanted me to learn a trade. They felt that it would be impossible for me to go to college and that I should learn some sort of skill so that I could earn a living. I had notions of possibly being a political activist of some [sort], but there was no way to earn a living at that, and I thought their advice was good. And I didn't think I could swing it through college, 'cause there was no way they could help me, and I didn't see any scholarships or anything of that sort available.

I got interested in toolmaking because at that time it was the "aristocracy of labor." It was also the area [where] there was a lot more math and some sort of planning and thinking involved. There was also [the fact that] they weren't outdoors clamoring around on things; it wasn't hard physical work. I did take some courses in it, and worked in a shop before the United States got into World War II. During my term in the army, I also went to a machine shop course, worked in machine shops in an ordinance battalion of an armored division, and picked up some experience with it there. While I was in the army, I was encouraged by several officers that I had met to apply for Officer's Candidate School. And they all told me that I had a high score on whatever the army IQ test was at the time. And I did, but that resulted in an interview with Army Intelligence on my political background. And nothing came of that, though that's not the same experience that many other people had, with a similar background.

At any rate, when I got out of the army, I went to work in an automotive machine shop, but I also became politically active at that time. In the shop, a union organizer was trying to organize the shop just at that very moment, and I immediately got involved in it. As a matter of fact, the owners of that shop concluded that I was the one that started it, even though it had already started before I got there. But we did organize a union in that shop, and I did work in the field. But at the same time, I was politically active. I had notions about going to school on the G.I. bill, about going into some profession. But I was already married. The pressures—there was a child on the way—I was a little scared about going to school, [wondering] how we would earn a living, how we would get by. At the same time, I was offered a job full-time as a political activist. I took that job for a while. That was at the time of the Smith Act trials of the Communist Party here, and I was arrested then. [Originally enacted in the 1940s to curtail union activity during wartime, the Smith Act was used after World War II to prosecute Communists and others viewed as "threatening to national security."] And after the trial—by the time the trial was over, the notion of going to school seemed a little impractical to me. I had two children, I had a trade that I could work at, and trying to go to school then and put[ting] the kids and my wife through that kind of pressure seemed an impractical thing to do.

So I went to work in machine shops and continued at that until I was in my sixties and able to retire. As a matter of fact, I still go into a shop once in a while, but not so much to work as toolmaker, but for consultation, [to] do some purchasing, estimating, laying out procedures on jobs, and so on. But I don't regret it. There are times when I wish I had gone to school and done something like law or teaching, something of that sort. So many people have told me that I would have been efficient at that or capable of it. But I don't regret it that I don't know if I would have made a much greater contribution to myself or to society that way, or that I would be any happier, or anything.

But working wasn't bad for me, working in machine shops. I worked in several different types of shops. I tried to organize unions in some and got fired a couple of times because of that. Some places

I lasted a week or a month, or so, getting fired because they found out that I had been involved in unions in the past. Otherwise, I had some good experiences in helping teach other people. I ran into several occasions of helping black co-workers learn more on the job. I also went to work for some new businesses on some inventions, where I had total control of my time, and with engineers and so on. I was able a couple of times to get involved in new, innovative projects for architects or for other experimental ideas, and found some of that interesting.

Then, I eventually went to work for a man, a black man, who was starting a business, who had worked with me in the past, and [who] knew me, and regarded me as one of the few white toolmakers around that he could trust to run a shop. So I wound up working for him for many years, running the shop. And that put me in the position of having pretty much complete control of my time. I could decide if I wanted to take time off or not. I could arrange my day, what I would do. I made decisions of how jobs would be done, how it should be organized. [There were] conflicts, with a lot of debate and discussion, but I was basically the one in charge of running things there. [It never] gave me a feeling that the job was something that I couldn't stand, that I had to get away from. I was able to go to work and [garbled].

But in all this time, all the decades that I worked in shops, my other activities in the evenings and weekends (not separated in that sense, though most of the time we put into it was evenings and weekends), they always were as important or more important to me. I worked in electoral campaigns, I worked in community groups ranging from neighborhood improvement organizations to tenants' groups to ethnic groups. At one time we lived in a neighborhood that was mostly black (we were one of the very few white families), and we built some community organizations that got funding into the neighborhood, some city projects, and so on. I was a member of an advisory committee to the community school, the city-wide president of that for several years. And we organized a number of activities to be done in the schools after the school hours to use the facilities and the buildings there. I was involved in several minor party efforts to get on the ballot—the Progressive Party, the Citizens Party, the Peace and Freedom Party—every third party organization that came along. I was helping them to try to get on the ballot and change the political system some. I was also a member of an advisory committee to the police department, to the police chief, on community relations. We worked on getting more minorities on the police department, changing some of the rules and regulations, attitudes of police toward women, toward community members, and so on, civilian complaints, and all that sort of thing.

At the same time, I was very much involved with *Jewish Currents* magazine, a couple of Jewish organizations, so that I found [that] there usually wasn't enough time in the evenings or weekends to do all the things that I wanted to do. So when the opportunity finally came for retirement, at sixty-two, I took that. I continued to work part time, just in order to earn more money, to have something that would enable me to take a vacation or to take some of the trips or attend some of the functions that I want to, like a convention or whatever it might be. I was fortunate enough that I didn't have to work to such an extent that or such a manner that it dominated my life, and that I identified myself by my work only.

Retirement meant for me a reorganizing of my time, to do more of the things that I had always wanted to do, and less time, or practically no time, working. Like now, I have an appointment to go to the shop tomorrow morning, but it's the only time this week that I'll have to [be] there, and I'll go in there for two or three hours. I was in there for two or three hours last week, one day. I help out there and earn a few dollars that way. But my time this week, I spent mostly putting out a newsletter for New Jewish Agenda—typing it up and writing the articles in it—and reviewing an article for the *Jewish Currents* magazine, and catching up on some reading that I'm doing. I'm preparing next week—I have a current events discussion—making some notes in preparation for that discussion.

DS: A current events discussion at...

JD: The West River Senior Center [in New Haven].

DS: And how long has that been going on now?

JD: That's about four years now. I've been doing that once a week. [It's a] well-attended group, ranging from—I think the lowest we've ever had was seven people, up to about twenty people, depending on the weather [and] the time of year, because sometimes in the winter some people go to Florida. Then also it depends on the menu of the lunch program [at the Center] for the day—whether people want to have the particular meal that they're offering. But we have discussion right after lunch, and usually there's about ten to fifteen people present. We discuss current events in the sense of how people feel about it, what significance they've put [on] it; sometimes clarifying the confusion or misunderstandings about what's going on; discussing possible alternatives. For example, for the last several weeks we've frequently discussed the [New Haven] city budget and the financial crisis that the city is in, and what alternative would be possible. And we get into such things as following a line of thought and see where it comes out. For example, I might suggest the idea: Supposing the city were to save money by cutting out the fire department and going to a volunteer fire department. It wouldn't have to pay all the firemen, then. What would happen? And after a while, people said, well, it would be a poorer fire service, and therefore the insurance rates would go up. And also the businesses would not want to go into the city because of that factor. So the city would lose money, or the people would pay more in other ways for the lack of fire service. And that's too big a price to pay to give up the fire service. So then we dropped that idea and we go to the question: Supposing we were to cut out some of the schools, could we do that? And [we would] follow that, again with the same kind of reasoning, and see how some of these things come out: what the problems are that the city is dealing with in how to balance its budget, how to get a proper amount of revenue in, and so on, and compare it with what happens to other cities, and what would be a fair and just way of raising the money for a city to pay its bills.

DS: So in a way, this current events program is a microcosm of all that has been a part of your political life from an early stage.

JD: My political life had a great deal to do with [it.] In the beginning [I took] some fundamental classes in economics and how the economic system works, from a Marxist point of view. With all the criticisms of Marxism, I think the critique of capitalism is still valid. Nothing that has happened has made it invalid in any way that I can see. In the beginning we did a lot of that, and then we were involved to a great extent with foreign policy, though I think the current events group, [while] we discussed foreign policy, were also more interested in domestic issues, too.

DS: Now, [about] your own interests, in the sense of your own developing political identity. We began talking about occupational identity and have quickly moved into political [identity]. I think it's important to go back now and look into the formation of your political identity and then come once again to that point where you entered into the work force. What are the roots, Joe, of your political identity?

JD: My parents were socialists, communists, and secular Jews who were very much Jewish. That is, they spoke Yiddish as their major language, read the Yiddish press, and were very much interested in anything Jewish. But they were also socialists, or—my father was a member of the Communist Party. And so at the same time that he was involved in that he was also involved in organizing Yiddish schools for children. And my siblings and I attended the schools. And I got interested in socialism in that aspect. And then, I was the youngest of four children, and from my siblings I also acquired some interest in this. Some people say that people such as myself only got involved because we inherited it from our parents, much as most people sort of inherit their religious beliefs from their parents. That may be true, but I consider it fortunate for me to have had that opportunity. Instead of having to come around the long way, I was able early on to catch on to some of the critiques by the socialist world of the capitalist system, which as I said, I think is still a very valid critique. What I'm trying to separate there is that it may be that the socialist world has made some dreadful mistakes, and even committed some dreadful crimes, but that doesn't mean that capitalism is a better system.

[While] I thought it was fortunate on my part, I did go through periods of rebellion. You know: "Don't make me into something that I don't necessarily want to be." But as I looked around and grew older, religion or any other philosophy of life seemed to have either no meaning or no rational basis. And being a political activist and trying to change the world for the betterment of mankind seemed to be a proper and worthy way in which to live. And while philosophically I don't know what is going to happen (I can't define any ultimate purpose in life), I do have the feeling that helping other people, helping people less fortunate, or helping people to understand the society in which they live and to reorganize it in a better way is a worthy thing to do.

Part of that I think may be [my] Jewish training, in the sense that I think that Jewish life has always taught people, (whether religious or secular [Jews]) that you should be doing something, that life is serious, and you should be doing something with your time, making some contribution to society. Some people may make it in the form of charity, and some people make it in the form of political activism. But I think that's a worthy thing for people to be taught. I like that part of Jewish tradition—teaching children that you should be doing something with your life, not just diversion, and pleasure, and so on. As a matter of fact, I think that doing something with your life can be pleasurable; [it] is a higher form of pleasure than just having fun, so to speak. I acquired that from my parents and my siblings and got more and more involved in it. I don't question why I do the things that I do, I accept it because it gives me a sense of purpose and gives me a sense of accomplishment, and it gives me a sense of self-pride that I'm involved in something worthwhile. I also get from my associates and the other people with whom I deal a constant reinforcement and commendation for doing these things and being involved in this way. So for these reasons I continue to be politically active. I don't know if I can succeed in changing the world. But like the old philosopher said, the important thing is that you try and make your contribution. Whether it's going to happen today we don't know. So I do try to make that contribution.

DS: It seems that your very strong sense of identity comes from the fact that you were raised in a family, political, [and] cultural atmosphere where the political and the cultural (in this case, Jewish values) were seen as fused, that each fed the other. I was wondering, did your parents, or people that you grew up with, ever also stress the aspect of working class identity?

JD: Yes, very much. As a matter of fact, to them it was immoral to exploit anyone else, and I have a strong feeling of that sort, that there's something highly immoral, unethical about cheating someone or exploiting someone. The notion of hiring people, of making profit off their labor, makes me feel uneasy. I never wanted to do that. I have never considered going into business. At anytime in the past when I thought about what I was doing with my life, if it was not working in a shop, then it would have been something like—as I said before—going into academics, into teaching or some sort of a self-employed profession, but not in a business of hiring other people and exploiting them.

My parents were—my father was a carpenter, and he was a worker all his life, that way but, again, with some intellectual leanings. He tried to read a lot, he tried to get into discussion groups and so on, but he had very little formal education, just enough to enable him to read and write. But he felt that way, it was very clear, and I feel that way. My mother felt the same way. She never encouraged me to go into business—neither of them. She encouraged me to learn a trade, like my father did, to get a skilled trade, where the boss could not exploit you too much and where you could talk back to a boss. That's one of the things, why I say that the toolmakers were the "aristocracy of labor," as I said before, not only because they earned more money at that time.

Toolmakers were also then (and still are today, to a great extent) the aristocracy of labor, in the sense that the owners of industry conferred with them on a more equal basis. I've seen executives and owners of companies seeking and accepting advice and the opinions of skilled toolmakers, while they totally reject and ignore (completely ignore as though they didn't exist) the workers on an assembly line, machine operators. So that if a toolmaker came up with a proposal [that] we ought to do something a certain way, the factory owners would listen, and discuss it, while they wouldn't take that from other people. So in that sense also, toolmakers were the aristocracy of labor, and I think that is one of the senses in which my parents suggested it to me. To be a skilled carpenter or a toolmaker [was] something where people recognized your skill as giving you an equal intellectual status, in addition to the fact that it paid more than an unskilled worker.

DS: How was it that you made your way into the tool making profession?

JD: In 1940, I went to Hartford—my sister was there. There was a shortage of work at first. I got a job at first at a fur store. And then, when the war broke out in Europe, and some of the factories in the United States started to get some big contracts (particularly I'm thinking of Colt Industries in Hartford [that] got some big contracts from Britain), they instituted a statewide program for training machine workers. I took one of the courses and got a job in Colt's.

And then, when the United States got into the war, I volunteered into the army. But in the army I was assigned to an ordinance battalion of an armored division. There, too, I did machine work, keeping tanks and armored vehicles moving. We used to work at night, in a blackout tent or in a blackout truck, to repair anything that could be repaired overnight. If it couldn't be repaired overnight, it had to be either left on the field or shipped back in some way for more lengthy repairs. But anything we could do overnight, to keep an armored column moving, we did overnight in the dark in the blackout truck. And then for a while I worked at a base camp, in the same way. There again, some of the experiences that I remember are refusing to work with German prisoners (prisoners of war) in a machine shop there, and making a political issue out of it.

DS: Some of them were conscripted to work?

JD: Yes, some of them were conscripted to work, and we had all kinds of prisoners there, and some of them were skilled workers, but I didn't want to spend my day working with a German prisoner of war in a two-man shop.

Anyway, after the war, I went to work, first in an automotive machine shop, which [was] what I had been doing in the army, and then went into other shops later and gradually acquired the experience that I needed. I also took a correspondence course in blueprint drawing and reading, just to get a little bit more proficient at that, and learned the trade that way.

DS: Did you learn also from your co-workers?

JD: Yes, I learned a good deal from co-workers who taught different methods. I saw from observation and discussion and learned different methods of doing things, different ways of doing things. The field is constantly changing, too, so that by now, there is so much computer controlled machinery in there, and people have to know how to program the computer to run the machines, which is a whole new field by itself. But, as I said, when I got into one aspect, I began to get into a lot of experimental work. I worked directly with some engineers from some of the companies around Connecticut, like Olin Industries, or Upjohn Chemical Company, and a few of the others. Two engineers I know who were into some inventions asked me to work with them for a while. They set up a company and I was running a shop there, on some experimental devices.

DS: So you did a lot of collaboration with engineers and others, not just with other machinists.

JD: That's right, though for some things I had to get advice from other people, and went to people that I had met and knew and discussed some problems with them about how to do certain jobs, and gradually got more and more skills and knowledge of my own. And then, once you have a basic knowledge of what a machine can do, sometimes you can come up with your own innovations on designs, on how to do something that hasn't been done before, how to make new parts.

DS: There's a lot of creativity involved.

JD: In model-making, pattern-making, for jigs and fixtures and new parts, there can be a lot of creativity, and you get a—for many people there can be a strong sense of accomplishment. In taking something that's abstractly described and converting it into something you're holding in your hand, making the tools with which to make it; or to get a rough sketch—an engineer's rough sketch—and design something that will be shaped approximately like this, to do such and such. And then you have to make that part. You may have to experiment with making it out of soap at first.

DS: Did you use models, then?

JD: Yeah, sometimes I've done that. You take wax or soap and carve it, make it, [to] see how it's going to look at some point. And then you have to make [the] fixtures [to] make it with, to hold it, and so on. So there can be a strong sense of accomplishment in making something, not like somebody who's working on an assembly line, who just does one or two operations all day long on the same part, and most of the time without even knowing what the part is. I've had people that I supervised who were in that position, and I could empathize with them very strongly.

I remember one young woman who was a member of the Jehovah's Witnesses—either that or Seventh Day Adventist, one or the other.

And she found out that some part she was working on was called a trigger, and she refused to work on it, said it was against her principles to work on guns. The fact of the matter is it was a trigger for a door-closing mechanism for a fire door that is made out of a piece of metal [that] burned through or broke under heat, and would activate the door-closing mechanism. So the trigger held the door back, held the mechanism back, until the heat snapped the holding part. But I couldn't persuade her [laughs] until I was able to get an entire assembly and show her how it looked, because [for her] a trigger was a trigger. There's only one thing a trigger is for, and that's to shoot a gun. But she was typical of many people who worked on something without knowing what the part is, or without knowing what it's going into, what the ultimate part is, and so on. That happens very often.

So I got into the trade, in the beginning, because I took some courses and I had a job. But during the time [when] it might have been opportune for me to go into some profession or go to school, the pressures on me were—first, political pressures, that I didn't want to give up the activity I was in, and that for part of that time I worked full time—I gave up working in shops and worked full time as a political activist, as an organizer. So I didn't have an opportunity to go to school. Then, when it seemed there was an opportunity to go to school, the other pressures were that a family had already started, that I had obligations that I just couldn't give up, or couldn't abandon. So I stayed with it, 'cause I was able to earn a living at it. And that's the way it developed.

DS: Did you ever work a job where you had a large number of co-workers? What was the size of the shops you worked in?

JD: Well, I worked at Colt Firearms, which probably had several thousand people at that time. But that was in 1939, 1940. Other than that, I think the largest shop I worked in was U.S. Motors, which made electric motors, in Milford. I also worked at Schick Razor Company. In both of those places, after a few months I was called by personnel people. They had found out that I had been involved in unions in other places, or else they got some information about my political background, and I was let go. Other than that, I decided to forget about big shops after that. I worked in an automotive shop with maybe eight or ten people, and most of the shops I've been in have been about that size, about eight, ten, twenty people. I worked in one [plant] in Milford for a little while, [that had] about seventy-five people, but even there, the tool room was separated, and so the tool room probably had about seven, eight people working there then.

And there was another place typical of what I meant before. The owner was—it was a family, several brothers who were the sons of a former toolmaker. They had been to school, and they ran the place. And they treated the toolmakers in a totally different manner than the other workers. They would come in, almost like a co-worker, discussing jobs, how they're going to do things, and so on. They would even get to the point of discussing why they had taken some jobs. They took a bunch of contracts from some larger company at one time, which would include a few of what used to be called "dogs," meaning that they were difficult jobs with probably very little money in them., But they took them in order to satisfy the buyers and get the large quantity jobs that they would make money on. They would sit down and discuss these dog jobs with you: "How can we get this out as fast as possible, and get it off our backs?" Very often they would wind up [saying]: "Do whatever you think you have to do, and just get it out of here." But [as] I say, that's what they do with the skilled workers.

I never had a feeling of "who am I?" in the sense of, "am I a toolmaker or am I a political activist?" I always felt, without any problem, that I was both. Even in political activism, I had certain satisfactions out of working in a shop, in the sense that the vast majority of people I met who were activists were either self-employed, professional, or academic people. Some of them never met a worker. I've known some left-wing political activists who not only never worked in a shop or worked for wages, but [who] didn't know workers [and] had no acquaintance with people who worked for a living. To them, I was an object of—I was unique. They would hang on my every word, as though I had some source of wisdom, working with my hands, that they didn't.

I never really regretted working in a shop. I don't know if I would have enjoyed any other [kind of] work any better. And I was raised at a time when I had to go to work, I had to do something. I had an older brother who tried to go to college. He did for a couple of years until he was unable to keep up with it; he had to get job. And his sisters never went to college either. Most of the friends I have now did, and certainly all the young people I associate with, did. The vast majority of them are Jewish, and the statistics on that scare me—[I] read how many Ph.D.s and Master's there are among Jews, something like eighty percent. Someone did a survey in Detroit, if I remember, [where] something like eighty percent of the Jews over twenty-five completed college, and a large percentage of those have higher degrees, Master's or Ph.D.s. One time I was at a meeting where I asked people who had degrees to raise their hands; the bulk of the audience had degrees. There were three of us—my wife Lil, Sid Resnick, and myself—[who] once were on a panel on the history of the secular Left in the Jewish community, and particularly the history in New Haven. During that discussion, I asked if people in the audience [would] raise their hand if they had a masters degree or higher, and I think three quarters of them did. And [here] we were, three people who never went to college, explaining things to this group of people. I don't know [how it] would have been if I had [gone to college]. I looked at people who have gone to college, and they look just as unhappy about some things, just as confused [laughs] about other things, as I am. Or just as confident on some things.

DS: Now, this brings us to another area, in fact, the area into which this has all been leading, and that's the whole area of retirement. Clearly, from the discussion, our talk about retirement will be a little different, because the transition for you has certainly not [been] an abrupt one—and also not a clear-cut one—since you gradually phased out of toolmaking. And your own sense of that part of your life, your work, is not one where it was ever something that dominated you[r life]. Often questions [about] retirement are (and I will pose them to you anyway): How does it feel different for you now, not having a work routine? How significant has that been for you in retirement?

JD: Not really. The major difference is that I can sleep a little later in the morning [laughs]. I plan my day, because I've always had this—I've lived with a kind of structured time frame. So I do plan my day: what I'm gonna do, and so on, where I'm supposed to be. And I have time for reading. Reading has always been important to me, and I've also found that it is difficult for me to read in the evening. I fall asleep. I gave up trying to do that. So I spend the evening sometimes talking to people on the phone. I make whatever calls I have to make (and that's when people are available anyway) or watch some television, or just go to bed. During the day, I try very often to get some exercise, for an hour or so—a walk [or] a quick hike. Otherwise, I spend my time either reading or writing or doing some of the things at the senior center.

Since I retired, I took a course in music, something that always intrigued me in the past. What is it about music that interests people so, and moves people so? I enjoy music, but very often I would also get bored. I find a full evening concert boring. I wondered what is it that I'm missing in that? Also, what are people talking about when they use some of the descriptive terms in music? I had a cynical attitude, that they don't know what they're talking about, [that] they're just using some fancy words, though I also realize that it's very difficult to describe sound in the same way that it is difficult to describe color. We have to use words like "warm" and "sweet," and so on, to describe music, and when you examine them, they sound— you look at it and say, what do you mean, "warm"; "sweet"? It's hard to find better words. Anyway, I was interested in that, and I took a course in music. I even tried to learn to play a recorder, but I realized very quickly that it was going to take a lot more practice than I was willing to give, in order to become proficient enough to enjoy it. So there was no sense in wasting a lot of time, so forget it.

I took a course in the history of Western Civilization, which I had never really done before. Though I had read a lot, there were some things with which I wasn't familiar. And I took a course in psychology, in cultural anthropology, some comparative philosophies. And right now, I'm taking one in comparative world governments. I also took a course in the history of art, modern art, and just before modern art. In much of them, the material is familiar to me, I know much of these things. Certainly the one in comparative governments, I know more than the instructor in some cases. In the history of Western Civilization, there was a lot that I knew. But there [were] also such things as: What did Machiavelli really say, or who was, what's his name, [Girolamo] Savonarola [(1452-1498), Italian religious reformer executed as false prophet]? How did people change from this big emphasis on religion to this big emphasis on science, which occurred during this whole period? In my readings, very often I would find [a] reference to something that I just didn't know about. I took the course hoping [to] freshen up on that. Then in addition, I got involved in doing this course on current events [at the senior center].

But ([and] it's a major part of my time) I write a monthly column for *Jewish Currents* magazine. It involves doing a considerable amount of reading, and culling from some of the Jewish press, though they also do some at the office of the magazine. Then I also edit the monthly newsletter for New Jewish Agenda. I go to Steering Committee meetings of New Jewish Agenda and attend the meetings that we organize. I sometimes contact a speaker or discuss the problems of the organization. I attend some national meetings. With the *Jewish Currents* I attend the national meetings of the editorial board that they have every few months. And I'm also involved with an organization, World Fellowship, that runs a summer camp [with] educational programs. I'm on the board of trustees, and that involves occasional meetings, over-the-telephone discussions, lining up speakers and programs for the summer, and then business meetings during the rest of the year, on such things as maintenance, salaries, and so on. I have to organize my time around these things. Sometimes there's a weekend meeting out of town.

There are other organizations that I meet with, too, [like] Veterans for Peace. I helped organize a chapter of that, and we occasionally have a meeting or telephone discussion. And then there are other activities in town that I try to keep up with, [such as] organizations doing things on Central America. I'm not directly involved (I just can't find enough time to get in that), but I do go to some of their events, like to hear a report on people involved in the elections in Nicaragua in February, people who went down there to observe. Or there are meetings of the Women's International League for Peace and Freedom [Lil is an active member], and they have a speaker that I go to hear occasionally. So I organize my time around these activities. Lil doesn't drive, so I find [and] organize time for her, too. Then we have to do things like shopping [and] problems of maintenance around the house. I still do a little work around the house. I built a closet, do some minor repairs—plumbing and electrical repairs, and so on. But, as you noticed, [there's] some painting I don't want to do [someone he and Lil had hired was painting the house as our conversation was in progress].

DS: It seems that retirement is different from the rest of your life largely because of the reorganization of time. I get the sense that your outlook pretty much has continuously been one that acknowledges your occupational identity [Joe might well have interjected that I really meant "work" identity (apropos his definition)], but really is more informed by [your] political outlook. I was wondering, though, if you ever felt (and you certainly did allude to it) that there was something special or unique that informed your political outlook, because you, in fact, had been a worker?

JD: Well, I don't know exactly how to deal with that. My attitude is that, with the feelings I have about the capitalist system, that the changes that come about in this society are going to come about mainly because of changing working conditions and changing working relationships. Many people on the left share that view, but some carry it over it over into what I consider to be a romantic view of the working class.

Chapter Five

When I Left the Party, I Left for a Number of Reasons

[Second interview with Joseph Dimow, conducted at his home in New Haven, Connecticut, on April 19, 1990.]

DAVID SHULDINER: I had mailed you a copy of the tape of our last conversation in which I had asked you general questions about your life activities as a worker and [more importantly] as a political activist. This discussion will be more [about] looking [at] what you said [in terms of] the character of that discussion, [and] what it revealed about your identity. Perhaps the best way to begin, since you've had a chance to listen to [the tape] is [to get] some of your feedback. You [said] just before we [turned] the tape on that you began by looking at it objectively, as though it was another individual. Why don't we look at that and then let the subjective part [enter] in as you examine your reasons, or your explanations, for why certain things were said in the way [that] they were said, or why things are noticeable by their absence. So, why don't you start with some of the comments you had.

JOSEPH DIMOW: The first comment of any significance here is [that] looking it as objectively as I could, it seemed to me that the person speaking said that—myself—I don't regret it being a shop worker. And I wondered if somebody might feel "but the tone of saying that means that you do." That has been tossed around in my mind. Is it something I regret or not? And I said in that interview that I didn't regret it from the point of view that I don't know if I would have been happier doing something else. And yet, thinking about it, I recall other times when I thought about it and felt that I would have. So I think I would modify that and say, Yes, I do have some regrets, but they're not very [deep]." I don't belabor myself. I'm not going around saying, "Jesus Christ, I fucked up my life, I should have become a professor of history," or something like that. I don't do that. But I think there is more [to it]. There is a greater element of regret than I expressed in that first interview. At the same time, it also seemed to me that there was a certain amount of enthusiasm about describing shop work. That seemed to me to come through in the interview also.

DS: Is that an accurate reading?

JD: I sort of surprised myself a little bit, that there was more enthusiasm about describing shop work and creativity than I would have thought I had. I'm not sure if that's accurate. But again, trying to be objective, it occurred to me, if I were listening to this, would I say that this guy enjoyed work in a shop? And I think the interview did carry some of that in there. The truth of the matter is, of course, that there were times when, yes, I felt creative or a sense of accomplishment. At the same time, there were often times when I thought, I got to give up this stuff—it's nonsense, wasting my time away, working with a piece of metal. But that [was] a kind of ambiguity about regret, and about how I felt about enjoying shop work [and] it seemed to me as part of the interview. The only clarification I would want to make was that there were all kinds of reactions that occurred during that period.

At one point I felt that there was more in the interview about shop details and less on political activity. Then shortly afterward, I told an anecdote about graduate degrees. That anecdote also gave that feeling: Was there a sense of regret that other people have graduate degrees? I did, listening to it, [think]: "Is this guy also expressing, underneath, that feeling?" But it also made the interview cover both aspects of "occupation," of working in a shop as well as political activities. It began to balance. I thought the interview was more heavily on working in the shops for a while, but then it came around. That's it. Basically, there was nothing I would want to change, except how candid you want [me] to be about political activity and organizations? That's what we're going in[to] today, right?

DS: Yes, that's one of the issues I'd like to take up, particularly because, again, just before we turned the recorder on, we were talking about this notion that, as you're being interviewed, you weren't just thinking about us talking privately in your kitchen, but [also about] what [the] possible hypothetical audience for this tape would be. Particularly, having been a lifelong political activist, you were always aware that even in your private-most conversations or thoughts, there was always the "public voice" for the public audience. Part of it had to do with the nature of political activism, translating your thoughts your strategies so that they could be used, but it also had to do with protecting your identity—your political identity—which is, for you, clearly, your core identity. And so there's a certain self-protection involved there. I was wondering if you felt in [this] second interview perhaps [you might be] a little more comfortable about being candid about what that was, and maybe articulate more your reasons for feeling protective about it, all the various reasons, subjective, as well as objective.

JD: Firstly, I'm not sure—I hesitate about the question of candid[ness], because there's a lot of ideas that come into my mind. Firstly, being in a particular organization is not the only way in which I, or anybody else, identified their political activity. Now, I was an organizer for the Communist Party for a couple of years, but I left the Party. But I did not leave political activity. I tried to find other ways of doing [politics]. So the one problem that occurs to me is that if I start talking about being an organizer for the Communist Party, a full-time, paid, professional organizer, that was only two years out of a—I'm seventy years old now, and that was in 1948.

DS: How long were you a member, though?

JD: Well, I actually was—I joined the Young Pioneers, which was a children's organization under the sponsorship and supervision of the Young Communist League, which in turn was a youth organization under the sponsorship and supervision of the Communist Party. The Party had adult advisors to the Young Communist League, and the Young Communist League had advisors to the Young Pioneers. Young Pioneers was kids ranging in age from about seven, eight, to about twelve or so. And we had uniforms— uniforms consisted of a blue shirt with a red bandanna. But we had classes, discussions, and turned out to march at demonstrations, and so on. We also had a dramatic group, and we put on plays. We put on *Waiting for Lefty*. . . .

DS: [By] Clifford Odets?

JD: [The] Clifford Odets play, yes. As a group we participated in demonstrations or rallies or whatnot, and we also had discussion classes. Then I was in the Young Communist League for a while, though there my membership was a little spasmodic at first, because I was also going through a period of rebelliousness in the family. I felt I was being pushed, and I wanted to sit back and examine it. I never really said I don't agree with what you're saying. Everything I read made me more convinced, and everything I heard made me more convinced. At the same time, I had that feeling [that] I'm not coming at this from myself, I'm coming at it because somebody is guiding and giving me things. And I said, "I don't want to do this, this way, let me think about it a while." Then I went into the CCC.

DS: Civilian Conservation Corp., under [the] W.P.A.?

JD: Yeah. But after I left that in 1939, I joined both the Young Communist League and the Communist Party. And I was a member of both organizations and very quickly got into positions of leadership in both. I was in Hartford, then. Then the war interrupted that. After I got out of the army in 1945 (and I remained in touch with people all the time I was in the army, too) I got back into the Party, and immediately got caught up in reorganizing the Party in New Haven. By that time Lil and I had married, and we lived in New Haven when I got out of the army. I very quickly became Party chairman in New Haven and reorganized it, that is, drew up lists of people who had been members, what had happened to them, and so on, and went to visit people, and got them together, and organized clubs and groups of people, either by industry or community and so on.

Then, when I went to work for the Party, I was asked to go to Hartford. I was the chairman there, and I was in Hartford for about a year as chairman of the Party, and then moved back to New Haven. I was in charge of educational programs for the Party and also for circulation of the paper, the *Daily Worker*. Which was all, again, interrupted by the Smith Act arrests and trials in the early fifties. So, though in 1949—late 19[49], I think—due to the attacks on the Party, and the Smith Act arrests of the top leadership, and the fact that the Party had lost some members and some money, [I] went off the payroll and took a job in some shops then, though my major activity was still trying to keep the Party together, and [deciding] how to deal with the possibilities of arrest, and so on—making plans to keep the Party going, if it was declared illegal, which it was, in a way, though in another sense, not. So I spent a lot of time on that. But then, in 1956 I left the Party, after the Khrushchev revelations about Stalinism and the discussion we were having. [Following Nikita Khrushchev's denunciation of Stalin at a Party congress in the USSR in 1954, many communists in the U.S. became disillusioned and left the Party.]

To me, the Smith Act trials played a peculiar role, in that they brought some questions up for discussion which otherwise would not have been discussed. The charge that the government made, for example, that we planned to achieve socialism by force and violence, [that] we planned to advocate force and violence: did we? The question came up, What did we really plan to do, how did we conceive of doing this? And [it] became a practical question: How do we answer that charge, and what is our actual feeling? 'Cause many of us had sort of drifted for a while on that. We got into many theoretical discussions about that, and how we felt about some of the things in the Soviet Union and Eastern Europe, and so on. By then [mid-1950s] there had been a revolt in Hungary and [a] revolt in East Germany, and how did we feel about the way these things were handled? Was it counterrevolutionary action or was it a legitimate demonstration on the part of working people in those countries against the communist governments? So it wasn't just these revelations about Stalinism, but it was those other factors, too.

So when I left the Party, I left for a number of reasons. But I also maintained connections with a number of people with whom I had serious disagreements. Part of that was due to the fact that we had amassed a sizable sum of money before the Smith Act trials that we used for bail. We had borrowed this money and given people certificates, very often without any name on it—sort of an I.O.U. because people didn't want to use their names. By the time the trials were over and the bail money was to be returned, we didn't know who some of the people were. Some of them had died, some didn't step forward to claim their money. We advertised in the left-wing press; we advertised in the foreign-language, left-wing press. We tried to track down people, and then many people said that they didn't want the money—it was a hundred dollars or two hundred dollars that they had loaned us, and they didn't want it back. Others we could never find. We wound up with thousands of dollars left over. I was the treasurer of that fund, and we had to then decide what to do with that money—who did it belong to? Years before, it would have been easy. We were all leaders of the Communist Party and we would have reached an easy decision on how to deal with the money. But at this point we had disagreements [laughs] among us. Some of us wanted to give it to one newspaper—a donation, say, to one newspaper. We argued that this is what the people who loaned us the money would have wanted to do if they were still alive or around. Others said no, not that paper, because that paper has become critical of the Soviet Union, and they want to give it to this paper, which was still supportive of Soviet policy or to different organizations. This necessitated meeting a lot, trying to find ways to compromise different views between people who had disagreements. I did that and maintained my connections.

I never gave up the notion and still, to this day maintain that all of these people on both sides were good, sincere, idealistic, well-meaning people, committed, trying to do whatever they could to improve conditions in the world for working people, poor people—trying to achieve socialism, not a utopia, but as a better way of organizing society, to do away with some of the evils in society like war, oppression, and so on. I still—all the members of the Communist Party that I know, and knew, and to this day know—still meet that description. I don't think that's necessarily true in a country where the Communist Party is in power, by the way. There, the party can easily be perceived as a vehicle to power, and there, of necessity, a Communist Party is going to have in it a lot of people in it who are simply bureaucrats, or careerists, who see that as the avenue to power.

DS: All of this raises a very interesting question—

JD: Yeah, alright, go ahead—

DS: Well, you keep going—

JD: Well, at any rate, I left the Party, then, in 1956. And that means that now I've been out of the Party for almost thirty-five years. It's obvious that it's very important to me—that history is a very significant part of my life. At the same time, if I describe myself as a political activist, the bulk of my political activity has been *since* then. The bulk has been that thirty-five year period since then—outside of the Communist Party. So I feel a kind of ambiguity in saying I was a political activist, without making it clear that I was a professional organizer for the Communist Party; at the same time I don't want people to get the impression that [that] was it [in defining my political activism], and the other things weren't [important]. The other things weren't as highly organized, as specific—well, in some ways more specific, like a particular election campaign, to get somebody on the ballot or something, where it could be very specific. But they changed and varied, whatever I thought was an appropriate thing to do at some particular time—some kind of left-wing political activity. So, I do have that sense of, what do we mean by candor? I don't want to create a wrong impression, in saying that I was an organizer for the Communist Party—[because] that becomes the definition, [and] it's not. At the same time, it's an important part.

DS: I'm glad I backed off interrupting you earlier, because this statement you've just made is, to me, indicative of the fact that, for you, the issue of your political identity is clearly related—analogous—to the issue that we [started] this series of discussions with, the issue of occupation. As you said before in the earlier tape, you wanted to distinguish between "occupation" and "work," work being something you do for a living, [and] occupation meaning something that occupies—

JD: —Right—

DS: —your time, and in that sense dominates, or "occupies," your identity. What you've said—correct me if I'm going off [on] the wrong track, but it seems clear that all of your experiences as a political activist, in whatever context, reflected a continuity in terms of your political identity, even given the drastic changes in the political makeup, the historical experience, the divergences of opinion in terms of tactics, and even the breakup of an organization that was critical in the formation and growth, early on, of your political identity—in the Communist Party. Do you feel that there was a point, or were points, in your life where your core identity (I'm assuming that would be your political identity) came into question, not just [views on] an issue of tactics, but in it's essence?

JD: Yeah, in a sense—well, there are several ways that that happens—that it came into question with me. First, it was that after I left Party—though I still maintained some connections with individual Party members, it gradually got less and less, though I still see some people personally, and I bump into people. New Haven is not that big of a town, and so, if there are some activities of any kind of a left-wing nature, I bump into people who I knew as members of the Party. From our conversations, sometimes it's clear to me that they still are [members]. With most of them I have fairly good relations. [With] some people, it's kind of cool and distant, but with many people it's very warm and friendly.

The problem that I had was getting into other groups. So, for example, I got involved in a community betterment—neighborhood improvement—group. And I had a sense of satisfaction in being involved, dealing with people, working on some problems that we had mutually. We had a hell of a fight with the water company, which we won. I had a lot of personal input into that. And I also got to know a lot of black community people who accepted me. Very often I was the only white person involved in a black community group. One of the leaders of the tenants groups, and so on. But, I also felt that I was missing some of the things that I had in the Party. I missed the more intellectual conversations. I missed the theoretical discussions that took place—[the] linking up of things around the country, with whatever we were doing; the sense of an ultimate goal beyond what we were working on, and I wanted some of that. That was one way in which I felt a peculiar identity, that I was there and satisfied, but it wasn't quite enough of what I wanted from it.

I also joined, or was involved with, other left-wing organizations in which many of the people there were former members of the Party, or what used to be called "fellow travelers," sympathizers. And many of these people would look to me for leadership. They would look to me for leadership in the way that they used to look for leadership in the Party, which was by deferring to the Party secretary or the Party chairman—chairperson. If there was a discussion or disagreement about something, the Party secretary had the last word, and that was the line. And many people looked to me for that, and I felt very awkward about that kind of thing; I didn't want to be in that position. I thought that was one of [the] things for which I left the Party, that we should not operate in that fashion.

DS: So, regardless of how you identified yourself, people were attributing an identity to you.

JD: That's right. People [were] looking to me with "what is the line?" on such-and-such a question, even though they were all out of the Party and knew I was out of the Party, but "what was the line?" Some of them looked to me to carry the banner against the Party people that they knew. If somebody said something, there were people in an audience who might look to me, expecting me to rise up and pick up the gauntlet, you know, and lead the charge of whatever it was [that was] in dispute. I sometimes found myself saying to people, "Look, if you feel that way, speak up, say what you want. Don't ask me to carry the ball for you." And they would look at me a little in surprise, because their attitude toward me was that I was the spokesman, I was the leader of that, a spokesperson for the group. So I felt a peculiar sense of identity very often, in that regard.

Then I began to move over to *Jewish Currents* magazine, because there, I found a group of people, some of who were my age, some a little bit older, who were the people who I had admired and looked to for leadership myself when I was in the Party, or in my youth— even in the Young Pioneers and in the YCL [Young Communist League]. And they were trying in an organized way to carry on some sort of socialist movement, at least in the Jewish community, with a magazine, a periodical [that] came out regularly, and it had an audience, a base. They also spoke the shorthand that I understood, and they understood my shorthand, so to speak. You know, in every technology [laughs] you have your own shorthand. Just like in a shop, you talk about parts of a lathe, and people working there understand each other. When we say an "arbor" or a "center," or something like that, we know what we mean. And the same thing in political activity; when you talk about "dictatorship of the proletariat" [laughs] or "democratic centralism" or some other term from Marxist vocabulary, people understand what you mean without going into long explanations.

DS: It's an occupational language—

JD: An occupational language, right. So in the community groups I belonged to, I didn't find that. I had to avoid such language, that people would be bewildered by. "What are you talking about?" So, again, there was a sense of identity, sometimes. Around *Jewish Currents* I had an identity, but for a while I went through a period of wondering, am I really that interested in being Jewish? I was, as a child, steered by my parents into Jewish left-wing schools, and so on.

I had never been involved in Jewish community work, in the Party, working with the organized Jewish community. But in *Jewish Currents* magazine we discussed that, got into it. And I had a feeling, here I am, a secular—nonreligious—Jew, never very much interested in it, and now getting interested in it. What's gonna happen; am I gonna become a religious Jew; am I gonna (as I saw some people doing) join a synagogue and all this stuff? I thought, no, I just don't believe that's gonna happen to me, and I don't believe that's what I want. I felt I had enough sense that my convictions were correct, 'cause I wasn't going to follow that kind of path, and I haven't. I never became a religious person, though I have changed my attitude toward religious people, I would say that. Some religious people I've met I not only accept, but have admired their attitudes. And some of the things that I used to mark down as dogmatic, I've found they're much more flexible than I had previously thought.

But, anyway, I never did in any way become a religious person, but I did have a sense of "what am I doing here; is this where I want to be?" But I got used to it, accepted the idea. Yeah, there are problems about it. I'm not totally accepted in the Jewish community. I'm accepted in the New Haven Jewish community by most people I meet because they know me, they know me as active, they know my family to some extent. I come around, so they accepted me. "Yes, you have a place here, you have a right to speak." But I don't get into the big banquet things or the "big ticket" events that they have. So I'm on the fringe, on the acceptable fringe of the Jewish community. But there was (and occasionally still is) an identity question there, too. So, those are some of the ways in which identity has come up to me, working in community organizations in which I was not [at the same political level] much differently than we used to work in the Communist Party years ago. Also, what people expected of me, people who were left-wing people: whether they were or were not members of the Party, some of them expected something of me that I was not sure I wanted to do, or should do. And then getting involved in the Jewish community in a way that raised identity questions to me.

DS: "Retirement" is sort of an odd term to use here since, as you say, your core identity or "occupation" is political and you've never "retired" from that. And retirement in the sense of work is applicable only to the fact that you left the world of the toolmaker. However, I was wondering if these questions [of identity] or others like them came up as you made the transition from wage earning as a toolmaker to the more full-time occupation of political activism or organizational involvement.

JD: Well, it came up [in] the last thing that I mentioned, of relationships in the Jewish community in New Haven. That came up more because, prior to retiring from working in a shop, I had very little contact, except with some people in the Jewish community who were directly related to civil rights activities, for example. So I bumped into the director of the ADL, I knew him—I used to know him.

DS: The Anti-Defamation League—

JD: Yeah, the Anti-Defamation League. I've bumped into him and some people who are in the Jewish community and also involved in other things. There used to be a very progressive rabbi around. [I'd] meet him at different things. After I retired from working in a shop, and I had a lot more time, I began to attend meetings of the Community Relations Committee of the Jewish Federation [the organizational "center" of the mainstream Jewish community]. Other activities—I've called or met with some rabbis or heads of different organizations and got to know people that way. I got to know many of them on a personal basis, and I found that one thing is that most of these people respect age. And also, when I meet many of these people, they begin to ask, "Who's your wife's family?" and, "Oh, I know you, your brother-in-law was in the painting business," and "His brother was such-and-such," and "Yeah, I know that family," and so on. I find a lot of that when I go around.

Just several months ago, I had occasion to meet with a group from an orthodox synagogue, about—actually it was about buying a cemetery—and got into that sort of exchange. And one of them said, "oh, I know your family, you were from the Bolshevik Jews." [laughs] But he said it, not in a derogatory or antagonistic manner. He knew— that's how he identified them—the left-wing Jews, the Bolshevik Jews, but [nevertheless] part of the Jewish community. As I say, when I go there, nobody challenges my right to speak, though I've heard young people that I know come into Jewish community meetings and right away a whisper goes up, "Who's that kid?; Where [does] he or she come from?; Is this a Yale student or something?; they come and go," and so on. So I have that kind of fringe acceptance. And I call and speak to many of these people on a first-name basis and [we] get along. Since retirement that has happened, mostly because I just have more time to spend there.

Other than that, some of the things that I do is go to meetings of other organizations in which I'm not active but just interested in some issue. And I meet people, some of whom I've know for years and have been active around town. Some people get involved in South America or Central American issues. So I know some of the people there. I know people who are involved in labor issues, and so on. Occasionally we do something together. Just recently I spoke to some people in some of the unions about a campaign to get Yale to pay taxes to the city. There are people in the Green Party in New Haven who I bump into every once in a while, and we talk and sometimes do something where we're all involved together. Next week there's gonna be a May Day rally on the [New Haven] Green, and I'll be there with a table from New Jewish Agenda. But there's also a lot of other groups, and I know that many of the people who are there from different organizations cooperate on some of these things. Some of them I know, as I said before, some of them who were members of the Party or some who I'm sure still are.

DS: Do you feel that since you've retired, your sense of identity is more inclusive, [that] you're willing to accept a sense of your Jewish identity that was a little more expansive? Or your political identity? JD: There's a contradictory feeling that I have, in that I feel [that], yes, it's expanded in one way. At the same time, I'm not happy over the fact that many young people in New Haven have known me as a left-wing Jew. They identify me as a guy who is a left-winger in

the Jewish community. "That's the guy from New Jewish Agenda."
"That's the spokesman for New Jewish Agenda. He's a left-wing
[Jew]." Thirty years ago it was different. Then I was a spokesman
for the Left, and for the Party, thirty-five years ago, or forty years
ago, say, 1950, 1948. But these people don't know me. Many young
people know me as a Jewish guy. They think my primary interest
[is] in Jewish community activities—from a left-wing point of view.
They credit me with that. Because they're leftists, they credit me
with being a leftist also. But I know people in the Sister Cities projects
with Nicaragua or the Committee in Solidarity with the People of El
Salvador, and so on, and they consider me a supporter, a sympathizer
with their view. But they think of me, I know, as the guy from New
Jewish Agenda, which I'm not entirely happy with. I would rather
be thought of in a broader way than that. On the other hand, I
recognize the reality, that that's the primary place I'm active in, and
that's what they see. So you get that.

DS: When you describe desiring that your identity be referred to by
others in a broader sense, are you suggesting that although you
identify both as a Jew and as a Marxist, that you would rather that
the general political category be considered the dominant one, of
which being Jewish is an important aspect, but an *aspect*?

JD: Yeah, I would rather see—I also feel I have a lot to give to these
people, even if it's just history. But as long as they don't see me in
that light, [if] they only see me as a one-dimension person, then
they're not going to get it. They're not going to ask for, or make any
effort to get, what I can give them. It's difficult for me to break
through with them because they see me in that way, and I just don't
see enough of them. If I saw more of them, got more into their
activities, then that could change. Then they would see it differently.
But I don't. So that's just one shortcoming, a minor problem that I
see. There are people like myself who have advice to give or
connections to give, and many of these people don't know. Just an
illustration of that is, again, this "Tax Yale" campaign. I went to a
meeting at the Central Labor Council headquarters, and there were
people there from different ethnic and religious groups—some
ministers, some priests, a couple of rabbis, as well as some
community organization people. They got into discussions about
taxing Yale, and I found I had a lot of information to give 'em on

past campaigns to tax Yale and what some of the problems were
that they knew nothing about. To them I suddenly became a source
of—a resource. There was also a discussion there about the difficulty
in Connecticut of getting the suburban towns to take their share of
responsibility for the poverty problems that occur in the larger cities.
And some of them kept saying that this was a problem, and expressed
this as though the idea had never been expressed before, and that
something should be done about. I started to tell them some of the
things that were done, to my knowledge, back in 1935 and 1940, in
some of the campaigns we conducted, to try to get over that hurdle,
and what the difficulties were, and how people could go about it.
And, again, [I] was a resource to them. So that can happen
occasionally, but most of the time they think of me as the guy from
New Jewish Agenda.

DS: So, ironically, your acceptance in the wider Jewish community
is contingent upon your identification being Jewish *primarily*—

JD: Right—

DS: —but ironically that acts as a disadvantage in the larger political
community, because then—

JD: —[the] larger left-wing political community, yeah, right. They
see me as the guy from the Jewish community. So [laughs]—

DS: It's a dilemma [laughs]—

JD: Well, it's a reality that comes out of the facts of people's lives. If
you see somebody under certain circumstances all the time, or in
certain circumstances, then that's how you identify them.

DS: So, then, let's look at what we have so far. [Initially] we chronicled
the ways in which your activity as a worker and as a political activist
have reflected your growth and development, [the] continuation of
your identity, and [noted] that your political identity was dominant.
[This] did not mean that it overshadowed [other] identities. You have
a very strong ethnic identity as a Jew, in addition to your identity as
a worker. Then I asked you if you felt there was any shift in your
sense of identification. Now, you indicated that you still felt [that]

your political identity was dominant, but that your interaction, since you retired, has shifted because your time has been reorganized. And the nature of your activities has been such that you have come to be identified perhaps even in different ways than you might think of yourself, in terms of your core identity.

But coming back to that question: Do you feel, in regard, let's say, to your Jewish identity, that there have been shifts in your own sense of who you are, given the fact that you have made a Jewish organization—a Jewish political organization, which is important to emphasize—your primary activity? What do you feel, deep down, were the personal reasons for choosing a specifically Jewish vehicle?

JD: For one thing, as I've said before, I found around *Jewish Currents* magazine some of the people who I [had] missed having discussions with [in the Party]. And they exist around the magazine. And even in the form of—what I was primarily thinking of is the editorial board discussions. But we also organized—another fellow and myself—a reader's discussion group in New Haven. We would have meetings, bring in a speaker once in a while. This was prior to the formation of New Jewish Agenda. We organized a *Jewish Currents* readers group in New Haven. And so we would have discussions occasionally, that kind of thing which I used to have in the Communist Party, a discussion of the theoretical implications of something, how something related to the socialist movement, how a domestic issue related to foreign affairs. All this sort of thing, and what we felt was happening in the socialist countries or in the Soviet Union, and what was happening, all the issues that we wanted to discuss from a Marxist point of view, we were able to do that around *Jewish Currents* magazine. So I got more and more involved in that way and more and more accepting of the idea that that was a way for me to be active in the Jewish community and in the left-wing area.

DS: Right, now both of those were desirable, though, not just—

JD: Both were desirable—

DS: —political activity but—

JD: Yeah.

DS: —Jewish. Now, given the fact that you had not been active in any Jewish organizations—political organizations, certainly, and I don't know about cultural—in your adult life, was there a particular reason why, in retirement, you chose those things?

JD: The Jewish issue—in the exposure of the failings and the shortcomings of the socialist experiment, the Soviet experiment, and the exposure of Stalinism, the Jewish aspect had a great deal to do with it. It's not just of interest to Jews, but the Jewish role in the Communist Party and the building of socialism throughout the world, the prominence of Jews in the socialist movement, Jewish theoreticians, and so on, and the question of anti-Semitism in the Soviet Union—all were significant parts of both Jewish life and the socialist movement. And there was a big tie-up in there, also. There seemed to be a very clear role for Jewish socialists.

DS: And you still felt clearly—and continue to feel clearly—identified as a specifically *Jewish* socialist.

JD: As a Jewish—and a democratic [socialist]. I still felt the notion of a democratic socialism was a very worthy objective. I still feel that today. It's a very worthy objective, and I wanted to be involved in that. And here is a group of Jews [around *Jewish Currents*]. That's what they want to do, to retain the good features of that democratic socialist movement and to throw out the bad features of the undemocratic socialist movement. So that had a strong grip on me. Also, the people there—many of them were people I knew already who were friends. They were people I was associated with in New Haven anyway and who I saw socially, close personal friends [who] were also involved in this. So it had that aspect to me. On the other hand, there were other organizations with which I could have gotten involved—other movements. Some of them seemed a little too artificial for me, a little too awkward for me. I don't know if that's the right word, but—for example, Central America: I can see myself getting involved in the issue of Central America, and yet there's no personal connection the way there is with the Jewish thing. I don't have any family there, I don't have friends there. It's not a personal issue to me.

DS: So, in terms of the Jewishness, there's—

JD: It's a more—

DS: —always been for you a communal sense.

JD: Yeah, there's more a communal sense in there, also. [In] the other area, though, like some of the peace organizations that existed, I did not want to get into organizations where I would be in disputes or in competition or in arguments with people I knew in the Party. I did not want to be involved in something where my main function would be to begin to take issue with so-and-so because they were the leader of this [organization]. Most of the left-wing peace groups were of that nature. I didn't want to go into, say, a peace committee in a synagogue. I wasn't a member of the synagogue, I had no intention of being a member of the synagogue, I wasn't going to join a peace group (though I was involved with some of the individual people in there) in such a committee.

DS: And the political center [of that committee] would have been further to the right—than would be comfortable?

JD: Yeah, but something like the [Joe names a peace organization in New Haven], for example, where there's a lot of Communist Party influence and some people who I know as Party members. I felt that I could be supportive of some of the things that they do, [but], first off, I disagree with some of their positions [and] if I went in there to work, I would have to express those disagreements. By them, I would be seen as a disruptive force, and I didn't want to spend my time battling with them. I preferred something else where, in a sense, you have your area of work and I have my area of work, and when we meet in some cooperative endeavor, fine, we'll cooperate. So that aspect has always been important to me, that I don't want to take that role of fighting some other group on the Left.

DS: Would you say, then, that after being raised in a left, socialist, [a] Jewish socialist, family, and yet having spent your adult life as both a political activist and as a worker, but not necessarily in Jewish organizations, that perhaps joining *Jewish Currents* in your retirement, in a way was a "homecoming"—

JD: Yeah, yes—

DS: —politically and culturally?

JD: —it was, sometimes, I thought, in a sense, as some people do in going back to their roots, when they feel lost. I never felt that lost that I wanted to go back to my roots, but I wonder if a more introspective view might be applicable to what I experienced. Yeah, *Jewish Currents* is sort of a home, like the Communist Party was a home. Not quite so, because people don't want to let it become that much [laughs] of a home. But in a sense, yeah. New Jewish Agenda is not. New Jewish Agenda—there's a lot of younger people in there. Some of them are religious people. Some of them are far less political, in a sense [than] for building socialism, or something like that.

DS: Different class background, too?

JD: Different class background. Most of them come from parents who are fairly well-to-do. Most of them, their parents are academics. We have professors who are sons and daughters of professors. So there's that difference in class background. Some of it—they were raised in synagogues, and so on, so they may be to one extent or another [either] nonobservant or very observant. It's different than *Jewish Currents*, which is all like me. So *Jewish Currents* is very much of a home. I enjoy going to an editorial board meeting of *Jewish Currents*. You sit down and enjoy arguing with people there. We can argue with people and still be best of friends afterward.

I see contradictions about working in different kinds of organizations. There are some that I have [participated in]. I helped to form a chapter of Veterans for Peace. I was talking to a fellow I know who has never been a member of the Party, or anything like that, a left progressive guy, and we were discussing it one day, and we decided to form a chapter of this, and we did. We went about it carefully, not to let it become an area of dispute with other people on the left.

There are two organizations in New Haven that are involved with South African anti-apartheid work. One of them considers the other to be dominated by the Communist Party and doesn't necessarily object to that, but they don't want to be—they are sometimes critical of the Soviet Union [and] they want to be free to be that way. The other one is [a] more standard CP-type organization. And they sometimes compete. I go to either one. If they have something I'm interested in, I go to either one, and I know people in either one. I would be reluctant to be very involved in either one because they get into disputes with each other sometimes.

There's other issues. For example, in the [peace organization with many CP members], their position now on Israel and the Middle East is pretty acceptable to me, but four or five years ago it was not. They've changed their position, in the same way that the Soviet Union has changed its position. And though I sometimes like to point out to them that they don't acknowledge that they've changed their position, that they merely state that this has always been their position, and it's not. And then there are other groups that they want to associate with. Like this May Day thing—the Communist Party is prominent by its absence in this May Day Committee. They're having their own May Day celebration. But I will go to either one if I want to. But I don't want to get into those disputes. I would also like to give them the example that their disputes are really not that important in a larger sense.

One of my philosophical observations of life is that there are values greater than ideology, which I wasn't always sure about; but the older I get, the more sure I am that there are values in life more important than ideology.

DS: You just raised an issue that relates to something else you mentioned before. You talked about [how] as you grow older, you tend to think more globally, in terms of values that transcend particular political differences.

JD: Not necessarily more global; sometimes more personal.

DS: But personal values become more—

JD: The values I'm talking about can be of different natures. One of them, for example, can be not to hurt people. And just because I disagree with someone who basically is a good, well-meaning person—just because I disagree with them, I don't want to get into denunciation [or] hurt their feelings, necessarily. I want to try to be tactful and understanding. I try to look at people in their whole life, not just because somebody's a schmuck about this particular issue. I don't want to denounce them, or separate from them. I think a value like that can be greater, more important, than ideologies. I've seen people driven to tears because of ideological differences. I just don't think it helps. I don't want to hurt people that way.

DS: Adding that thought to the earlier thought: when you retired and joined the *Jewish Currents*, you felt it reflected a turn in your life toward becoming more introspective. I'd like [it] if you could talk a little more about any feelings you might have that changes in [your] worldview have taken place since you retired, changes in your way of looking at things in the political spectrum.

JD: Well, one thing that is [a] much stronger and stronger conviction [is] that simply because somebody is articulate and well read does not make them correct, necessarily. I've seen too many people who make some flat out statement about something, and it turned out to be wrong—sometimes seemingly the most knowledgeable people. I've also felt that my own judgment or doubt should be listened to; that I shouldn't, as I used to (especially in my youth), tend to be persuaded more easily by somebody who would appear to be in a position of leadership, [someone] respected, knowledgeable, and so on.

My general world outlook is that—well, something I'm totally convinced of [is that] the Marxist critique of capitalism is valid but that not everything in Marxism is valid. As a matter of fact, very often I think that the Marxist movement might do well to drop the phrase Marxism [and] find something else. Describe it as a theory of dialectical materialism or something like that. Because, attributing some sort of all-knowing wisdom to an individual is bad news— you shouldn't do it. Marx was not always right. And there are many aspects of Marxist doctrine that I question. I question his theories of relative and absolute impoverishment. I certainly question much of Leninist doctrine. Just examine Marx's writings and some of the anti-Semitic, anti-black, anti-Hispanic, anti-Slavic statements that he made at various times—which today would be denounced by the Left here [if they] knew. [If] some people that call themselves Marxists knew what Marx himself said at different times about blacks, Jews, and so on, they would denounce him all over the place as the worst racist [laughs] around. So much of his theories, I think, are right, but some of them are questionable.

Though the critique of capitalism is valid, Lenin's theories of what kind of a party is needed for a move to socialism, I think, should be totally discarded and totally examined, every aspect of it. There is, in his notion of the state, I think, a lot of validity. His book *The State and Revolution*, I think, has a lot of validity, but his writings on the Party, I think, are a hundred years out of date. They were written at a time when nobody knew anything about nuclear war, environmental pollution problems, overpopulation, or all of the things that we try to deal with now. And they were written [with]in a type of government that now longer exists. It should just be discarded. So, I would discard the notion of Marxism-Leninism. Marxism—the word carries a certain meaning that still has some value, though, as I say, sometimes I think we would do better to drop even the word, just to get away from naming something after an individual person and get away from this notion of creating a god or creating someone who you turn to and look, and whatever they wrote, and accept it as gospel.

DS: Of course, there are people like yourself who have rejected the political theory because of all the individual exceptions or instances you mention—historical and otherwise—just as there are those in the political movement who rejected Judaism [for] pressuring one to make decisions on the basis of ethnicity rather than politics, those who consider themselves internationalists. I get the sense from you that, at least politically, you consider yourself an internationalist, although you still strongly identify as a Jew. Do you feel that there [were] any times in your life where there was tension around that?

JD: Oh, yes, yes—always, always. [I] always felt contradictions between identifying as a Jew and identifying as an internationalist. You can easily say that when the time comes we give up our Judaism. I'm even ready and willing to say that when the time comes, we should be the first to give it up and go into the international brotherhood and sisterhood of peoples. But the time hasn't come, and considering the experiences and anti-Semitism in the world, it's, to me, perfectly valid for people to still feel a strong ethnic identity because we're Jews, to still feel that. In the same way, I cannot—for example, the state of Israel—it's a contradiction to form a state for Jews and then claim it's democratic. But the same thing exists in many other states. France worries about keeping its character as French Catholic, with the influx of so many Algerians, Arabs, and so on. Other countries take measures to maintain their identification, and so on, and we don't consider it undemocratic. I think there *is* an element of "undemocraticness" about that sort of thing and we should be more international, but that's obviously for a more future time.

In the same way that we have affirmative-action programs for blacks. One could easily [say the] same, that it's undemocratic. Why don't we simply say no more discrimination, period. But no, we also talk about more compensatory programs, because we know we're not going to resolve the problem of two separate races unless we take some specific action to help to bring blacks into positions of—better jobs, and so on [phone rings] Excuse me. [answers phone] . . .So, where was I?

DS: Well, we [were discussing] the whole issue of the tension between nationalism, or ethnicity, and internationalism.

JD: I feel that for myself, very often. As I said, the world is in contradiction a lot. There's a lot a contradictions going on, and right now, it seems to me that there is no real contradiction [in] saying that I am an internationalist. I advocate and encourage international brotherhood and sisterhood. But I also know that people have feelings, that they feel ill at ease or like outsiders in one group, [but] at home with another. You have to deal with that and relax to live. You have only one life to live; you want to live it as happily as you can. So, you compromise these things. I try to get along with other people, try to demonstrate that in various ways. We were the only white family in a black neighborhood for twenty-seven years. We belong to all kinds of different organizations: human rights, human relations groups, mayor's committees, police committees on inter-ethnic relations, the *Jewish Currents* magazine writes about it— especially black-Jewish relations.

DS: And those involvements were important as a reflection of your identity.

JD: Yes, a reflection of my identity as an internationalist. At the same time, when you say you want Black-Jewish relations—which is the black and which is the Jew? You're one or the other. You can't go in there and say, I'm an internationalist. You're somebody. I hope that the time will come when ethnic identification will disappear, fade. Some people say that they have found it. I haven't, and most people haven't.

DS: Is it safe to say then, Joe, that as you've grown older your basic philosophy or outlook has not changed, but [what has changed is] the way in which you've articulated it through activities and organizations.

JD: Yes, that's very safe to say. The tone of denouncing capitalism and asserting that socialism will resolve all of these problems—I've dropped that. Obviously, it doesn't happen that easily. The notion that a revolution was necessary in order to do that, and that some sort of class struggle is going to culminate in a victory of the working class, and a dictatorship—I've dropped that entirely. The notion that a party, guided by some principle called "democratic centralism," which conceives of itself as the general staff of the working class— that I've dropped, certainly for the United States.

So I still believe in socialism, but not with all that stuff. I'm willing to give a lot of time [and] effort to campaign to elect a mayor on a Democratic Party ticket, for example, which is a long, long, long way from socialism. But it may help improve conditions a little bit today, too. It may help get people into motion. I think it's important to get people active, [to] get people into motion about the problems in their life, [to] help them acquire a feeling that they can have some control, that they can have some effect on the conditions of their life. And I think that's more important than the actual result, very often. If people have that feeling that, if [they] organize and get together, they can do something to effect conditions of their life. Not to wind up in despair and desolate.

So, [as] I conceive of myself, I still hold many of those same principles, but I also find other things are important. Helping a friend or relative who's in some difficult circumstance is important, meaningful in life. Having a relationship with one's children, or something, is an important thing. The concept of a professional revolutionary, in the Leninist jargon, was someone to whom the revolution was totally important, and a wife or children or something like that is less. Now, I just can't accept that that's a viable way to build socialism or to build an organization to move toward socialism or that's the way I would want to live or to advocate it for anybody else.

DS: So, you've "retired" from aspirations to an occupation of full-time revolutionary [laughs]—

JD: Well, a full-time revolutionary, yeah. But I've also found that people with whom I disagree have good features, too, and can be worked with. Now that doesn't mean that I say that capitalists are just as good as workers. Capitalism is no good. Capitalism makes people do things that I consider to be bad to other people. And restraints can be put on that. But there may be [the case that] with some capitalists you may be able to work one way, with some, another way, with some you can't work at all.

DS: So, maybe one thing you've found as you've retired and moved back into the political community, that you're better able to work with individuals, regardless of their particular background, and maybe are a little more willing to accept differences than you were—

JD: —right, yeah—

DS: —when you were juggling work and political activity.

JD: I think so. I think I'm more willing. One thing I'm much more willing to [do is that] I don't understand religious people, but I'm much more willing to accept them. I used to be so disturbed by the notion that "how can somebody believe in something that's such obvious nonsense, and what can I do with a person who believes in such obvious nonsense?" And now I find that there are things that we can do, even though they say they believe that obvious nonsense. You don't have to get into a fight over those things. There are still things that you can do. Yeah, some people say [you] just get more tolerant.

This guy who just called might relate to this in a way. He's a professor of, I think, English [or] philosophy, I'm not sure, at Quinnipiac College, and he wants to organize a movement that would help to answer, to define, the questions that are going to arise in the next century. It's part of an international movement. The founding organization behind it is a British group [that] he says is the Temple of Understanding, which sounded to me like a Moonie organization. But I checked around with several people and the ones who have heard of it say, no, it's not. It's been in existence since before World War II, and it's an effort to bring people together to understand each other. What he wants to do is bring together a group of people from various ethnic and occupational backgrounds who would sit down and kick around some ideas, and eventually draw up a list of, say, twelve or fifteen major problems that they think the world is going to be faced with. Then, these [topics] would go to other groups to be discussed and eventually [be] brought together so that out of the international discussion there would come some kind of consensus on what the problems are, what people should work on. And he's been after me to get involved in that. And, again, he knows me through World Fellowship. I went to one meeting we had, just to meet some of the other people there. I didn't think it was going to go very far; [if it] gets organized a little better, I might go back.

I also had another man, also at Quinnipiac, a professor of sociology who wanted to organize a series on peace: How to achieve peace, how to maintain peace, and so on, into the next century. And he knew me through New Jewish Agenda. He wants to apply for grants, I think from the MacArthur Foundation. His idea was [that] he would organize a series of seminars and discussions with some prominent speakers. To get the grants, he wanted to get input from nonacademic people not involved at Quinnipiac College. So he called a meeting together, and at that meeting, in addition to a couple of colleagues, he had Pat Dillon, a state representative, and he had Bishop Rosazza, the archbishop for the New Haven Area, a minister whose name I don't recall offhand, and myself—eight people there, kicking around ideas for such a series of seminars and what the topics would be, who some of the speakers might be.

So, I do get into some of these things which are not strictly Jewish, for me to get involved in that. We did draw things up, and now he's trying to write a grant [proposal]. It's another way of being active and involved with people and having some input. It's not strictly Jewish. It is left-wing, to my mind, but it also relates with other people who are not [of] that same philosophical outlook.

Chapter Six

I Would Probe Into Their Feelings About How They Missed the CP Life

[Third interview with Joseph Dimow, conducted at his home in New Haven, Connecticut, on April 25, 1990.]

DAVID SHULDINER: Today is April 25, 1990, and we're continuing our discussion [about] the identity of Joe Dimow [laughs]. And what were you just about to say before we turned the [cassette recorder on]?

JOSEPH DIMOW: The thing I did think about is, if I were to interview other people in a similar situation to mine, what would I ask them about? I didn't think that I would ask them anything different than we had been talking about, but I think I would probe more deeply into some areas. And the areas I would be concerned with was the question of what I called regret, though, again, I'm not sure that's the right word. I'm using that word to remind you of it [That is, previous remarks Joe made about regret], an area of thinking that [poses the question]: Should I have made certain decisions, or should I have done different things at different times?

In speaking to other people—I'm particularly keeping in mind two people with similar backgrounds in the sense that they were [manual] work[ers], one a printer and one a carpenter. [Joe is referring to his two friends Sid Resnick and Jake Goldberg.] Do they feel that they should have made other decisions when they were young; that it was wrong or mistaken to have put so much time and energy into trying to build the Communist Party, in that movement?

Then I would also try to probe more into their feelings of how they missed—another form of regret—how they missed the CP life. And I don't think we went quite enough into that. What I mean is that being in the Party with a group of people is—the only thing I can possibly compare it to is being in a family [with] people who you know [and] share experiences with. The experiences are often emotional and important to you—deep. It's like going through triumphs and disasters together, and you build up sort of an *esprit de corp*, a feeling of comradeship, of brotherhood and sisterhood. And it's people who you know you can always turn to, and [who] will turn to you if they need help. I could think of dozens of anecdotes to illustrate that; of people—total strangers—coming from another town, and you welcome them into your home, share your food, your bed, your home with them, and everything else, because they're part of the same movement. And that sense of belonging and acceptance is—leaving the CP puts you—there's nothing else I've ever seen like that, to replace that, except a personal family. I think that would be an important area to probe in a psychological investigation of identity. Because it's very much a question of being one of a group, and being—it's like that old [saying]: A home is the place, when you go there they have to let you in [laughs]. And the Party is the place where, no matter what happens to you, they take you in. No matter how bedraggled you become, or what you have gone through, as long as you're still a part of that belief system. It's only when you leave that belief system that you begin to separate from people and separate from the group. That, I think, is an important area for discussion.

DS: Absolutely. It becomes so critical to this whole question of the relationship between your identity—in this case we're talking about your core political identity—and that principal group of people that you associated with on a social basis, and, from what it sounds like, on an intimate basis—like a family relationship. The question [that is] raised when you are separating from that group, and unavoidably [you] have to raise for yourself, [is that of] personal questions of identity, since it *was* so much a part of your life.

JD: Yeah. When I think of these people—the two I mentioned before and others—I know that I don't think of them in terms of their work identity. I don't think of this carpenter as a carpenter. It's strange for me to think of him that way. I know that that's what he did for a living, but when I think about him, or talk to him, or mention him, I don't think of him as the guy who was a carpenter. I think of him as the role he played in the Party, or what political activities he's in, or what campaigns, or things he has said about some ideas or theoretical notions or philosophical notions, and so on. And the same is true of the printer. I don't think of him as a printer, but I think of him as his interests. He's very much interested in Jewish history, in Jewish affairs, speaks Yiddish, reads and writes, translates, and so on. And I think of him in those terms—the topics in which he's interested, his enthusiasm about it. Very rarely have we talked about his work experiences, job experiences. [He] sometimes mentions something, as I did, but that's not what we think about, and that's not the way I identify him in my mind—as a printer. I identify *with* him as a colleague or as a guy who was a Party organizer, a youth organizer for the Party, and then was very active in Jewish [activities]—not community activities, but in Jewish *left-wing* activities.

[With] other people that I knew in those days, I very rarely thought of anybody in terms of their money-making identity—their jobs— but rather their identities as political activists. Sometimes, the fact that somebody had some expertise in a technical area might come in handy. But even then, if I needed advice on insurance and I said, "What am I gonna do?" suddenly I think, "So-and-so's been an insurance agent all his life, he knows all about that—why didn't I think of that sooner?" The reason I didn't think of it sooner was I didn't think of him in those terms, as an insurance agent, but rather as a political colleague. But racking my brain, it occurred to me that he was.

The same thing is true of many people that I could think of. So that's another area—I'm sure they thought about me the same way. So I would, as I say, want to probe more into whether people have any feeling that they should have done some other thing; whether they feel that life in the Party was a waste; whether their political activity was a waste or not; whether they're doing these things out of habit; if they can identify why they want to be politically active now, in terms other than rhetoric. I confess that, for myself, I find it difficult, other than rhetoric, to explain why I want to be active. Sometimes I can think in terms of anything, ranging from a fear of boredom all the way out to some altruistic, abstract notion of building a better world. And I think all of these things [are] part of it [laughs].

They're both true, but it's not complete that way. We used to have a slogan many, many years ago: "For life with a purpose, join the YCL"—Young Communist League. And I thought that was one of the greatest slogans I've ever heard or seen, because it seemed to me very real and applicable. The purpose got hit [laughs], you know: "What are you doing now?"

So I think, what's missing out of the interview is more depth on that sort of thing. And I'm not sure it's the kind of thing you can cover in a brief interview. It takes a lot more than that. Or else, it would take brief interviews with a dozen or more people. You might get a feeling of it. Did you ever read that book, *The Romance of American Communism,* of Vivian Gornick's?

DS: Oh yeah, I've heard of it.

JD: She interviewed about twelve or fifteen people and got some kind of smattering of different views. There have been other books by people in similar circumstances to mine who talked about their history, and somehow it always seems to me that they fell a little bit short. They did not really explain why they were doing these things. I don't know that I would have the words to articulate it either.

DS: [About] why you were politically active.

JD: Yeah, why people are politically active. Some people I know [who] are politically active—you look at some of the candidates for office, and it's obvious that they just want that feeling of power, of influence, and importance. I think everybody wants a feeling of importance, a feeling of acceptance, or something, and the only way you can really get that is if other people say you're important. If you're the President of the United States, you know that you're important, because a lot of people are waiting in line to see you [laughs], talk to you, and ask you something, and so on. So you can have some sense that you're somebody.

That's one of the things I wonder about—how to explain why we are active, why we do that. I don't know that I can explain it, and I don't know that anybody else has really explained that either. That's the kind of thing [that] is missing from this sort of interview and this sort of process.

DS: Actually you've raised several issues. One of them has to do with a critical view of the whole notion of occupation that began this series of discussions. I began with "occupation" as work, and you were saying that "occupation" is what you choose to fill your time; work is what you may have to do instead of the—or sometimes in lieu of what your primary life choices might be. And that for you, your occupation was political; that there was a brief opportunity to engage in it full time during your work career, but that in a sense you really felt your life career was political; that your sense of commitment—all the kinds of things that [are] talked about in the literature on work—the sense of commitment to your work, wanting to be accepted for what you produce, for the skills you may offer— all of these things [apply] for you, I'm certain. You talked about the sense of accomplishment at work, but it seems that those same things apply, perhaps even more intensely, in terms of your personal identity, to your involvement in the Party, to your political activism. Maybe a fuller picture of quote-unquote occupational identity might expand that notion of "work" to "life career"—what your *central* commitment is, what [it] is that really gives you satisfaction, a sense of commitment or purpose, one in which the acceptance of your fellow worker or, in this case, political compatriots becomes important. It sounds like from what you were saying that your desire for acceptance, let's say, from political comrades, would be much stronger than your desire or need for acceptance of a kind at the workplace. I don't know if that's a correct reading.

JD: That is, that's a correct reading. I'd go even a little further. The organizations to which I belong now, I find that some of them are closer to my personal feelings in that I can share—I have a sense of belonging more with some than with others. And it's not on the basis of which one is politically important but on the basis of people there having common experiences. So then I say, well, aren't I here more for the social life, for what is social life for me, than for what I identify as political goals? And I think, yeah, it's part of it, it's mixed in there. I don't know if you can or should separate them. People have mixed motives and there's nothing wrong with that. If somebody wants to accomplish a certain political goal and at the same time is also seeking approval, a pat on the back, recognition, and so on, there's nothing wrong with that, unless they elevate that search to the point where they sell out or compromise their principles, ideals, and so on. So, again, that's another aspect of identity. I'm there as a political activist, but I'm also there because the people I know are there, and I want to be with them, and I want to be among them, and I want to be accepted and approved by them. That's a big part of identity also.

So, again, I think these are areas of identification that come into it. It's a lot more than occupation. The occupational part of it recedes in importance, to me, as I think about these things. Some people can be identified as, let's say for a man—as a father, as a brother, as a son, in addition to their occupation. [They] can be identified as a member of a group, of some association, even if it's just a social club or a senior center or whatever it might be—[they] can be identified in that way. Though I'm pretty sure that nobody is fully satisfied with their identification. People go around with a smile on their face, but that doesn't mean that they're satisfied, that they are properly identified to themselves or to others. I don't go around asking myself who am I or what am I. Well, in a certain context I ask myself that. I put it that that's the primary thing in my life. Every once in a while I ask myself, "What am I doing here, in these circumstances?" I'm sure everybody else does, too. That's the whole point of doing research on the topic we're in now.

So, I don't know where to go about—where I'm supposed to pick up the interview. As I said, in the area of how I would conduct an interview, I think those are the areas I would want to probe into. I don't know if you can do it right away with people immediately. [It] would take a little time, I imagine, but that is the area that I would want to go in[to], and which I think is a little bit missing in what we've done so far.

DS: I think it's a point well taken, Joe, that the deeper you probe, the more complex the question becomes. If we had settled on the first interview as the summation of your thoughts on identity, we'd be missing a tremendous amount. The second interview revealed yet another level, and the third interview seems to indicate that, although of necessity you had to have a more narrow focus in the first interview we had here, identifying specific areas of identity—occupation, then later politics, ethnicity, et cetera—that [in] each one of those identity is expressed sometimes not only in a variety of ways, but, as you say, is conveyed in certain mixed messages. [As for] political identity, trying to isolate it makes it problematic, because it's never a question strictly of political identity, as you aptly put it, it's a question of social identity. You joined the Party because of the politics, but clearly, throughout the years, the desire for social acceptance [from] a group of cohorts with whom you could share a sense of belonging and purpose and commitment is important. [Joe gets up to answer the phone.]

Then, again, what you just said raises once again the whole problem of dealing with such a problematic concept as "retirement." It's easy when you talk about a work career that has ended. You cease being a wage earner and you collect your pension or Social Security, or what have you. It's much different when you talk about leaving a political occupation—in particular a party that you [have] been involved with for so many years—and find yourself facing those same sorts of issues [as] you would in retirement, to the extent that since the Party dominated your social, personal, [and] political identity for so long—in a way, it would be analogous to leaving a shop that had dominated your working life. And it's very telling that when you separated yourself from that, you eventually came to join a group, [the people involved with the publication] *Jewish Currents*, because they were cohorts of those who shared not only the same ideology, but the same experiences—I assume within the Party—

JD: Mmhmm. Right.

DS: —and then became active [later on] with them. It's very different than talking about retirement as a break from work, because this represented a transition to a different kind of work. And yet, nevertheless, [when] you speak of your "divorce" or let us say "retirement" from the Party, even with your other involvements, your other work that comes to fill in that gap, you still speak of it with intense feelings, like regret, almost the way in which a retired worker speaks of not having the satisfaction of really being on the job with people who are fellow workers, fellow sufferers, who have the shared experience of the intensity of the work environment.

JD: There's a couple of other factors or ways of looking at it. One is: as we get older, we retire, not only from work, but also from certain types of activities, in the things we want to do—just physically less active. I don't run around as much as I used to. I don't go to as many meetings or visit people or try to recruit people or this sort of thing. So there's a sense of—the same kind of sense I think older people have, no matter what their occupation has been—a sense of loss of power or loss of influence. I go to the senior center, and [I] am active there, know people, and so on. At the same time, I think I have the same kind of feeling there that I think other people have: that your society has, in a blind, unconscious, unfeeling, unthinking way, pushed you into a corner. Go entertain yourself there until you're gone. It's hard to separate those feelings from other feelings about retirement.

It's difficult to put the time in the Party in proper perspective. I left the Party in 1956. That's thirty-four years ago. The bulk of my adult life has been outside the Party, though never really away from its influence or its aura or something like that. The other people who were members had their say, or some of the things I read that are much influenced by their views, or reading their view directly, or talking to some of the members, and so on. At the same time, I think it would seem unusual or striking to say, here's an organization you left in [19]56, and you're still talking about it. What the hell is this? It's very hard for me to explain what it is. It's not just the Party, it's being raised in a family that was associated with [it]; it was siblings that were associated with it, even though I have one sibling who left very early [and] became a critic of the Party. I often think we get a distorted view—or I am giving a distorted view—of what it was all about when I talk about something that ended in a way thirty-four years ago, though it was a big, important part of my life. I don't like the notion that I stopped living thirty-four years ago [and am] living in nostalgia and retrospect since then. It's not true. That's another area that I think needs probing.

And also, as I said before, this question of diminishing health, [of] increasing concern with health and sickness, and apportioning your physical energy, and so on—which I think is a problem for all older people—how does that relate to this type of discussion? It seems to me that when I meet with people at the senior center who retired from their occupations, and now spend most of their—[end of tape]— that a big part of our time is taken up talking about health problems. A major concern is obviously health problems—fear of catastrophic illness, and so on. There's very much an atmosphere like in that old movie "Marty" where somebody says, "Did you hear about so-and-so, he died, and so-and-so, he's in the hospital, and so-and-so, he died, too." You have that. Every time you go to a monthly meeting at the senior center, they give you a list of so-and-so who died, so-and-so's in the hospital, will die [laughs] soon. When I meet with my colleagues in political activities who are my age and background, same thing happens. You hear stories about "so-and-so died," and so on. I still subscribe to the *Daily World*, the weekly edition of the paper of the Communist Party. And sometimes people ask me, "Why do you read that?" I say [laughs] one of the main reasons is I look at the death notices [laughs]. I see who's died, who's now eighty-five or ninety years old, and something like that. You read about these things, too.

So it strikes me, though, that we don't yet know then, the way in which we get older, other than the question of retirement. Just getting older and less able is a big part of our discussion. I go to *Jewish Currents,* and they talk about having a picnic, and they say, "Well, if we have [it] over there, so and so can't come because he can't walk anymore, or so and so can't do this—they need a ride"—this sort of thing. So that's [a] factor in the question of how you identify yourself and how you see yourself. It's just a common problem for older people. That, I think, has to be a part of the picture, also. These two guys that I mentioned before both have health problems. One is sixty-nine, and he has problems that he's seeing medical people about. Another is seventy-five and has slowed down a lot. [They have] problems which are on the top of their minds, as mine are very often. This phone call that just interrupted our conversation was somebody inquiring about my brother-in-law who's in the hospital. Again, you get the same kind of thing.

DS: That's interesting, though, Joe, because very often retirement from work comes, obviously as one is growing older and one is phased out. Sometimes it's mandatory on the part of the employer, but very often it is correlated with, not necessarily declining health, but maybe just diminishing capacity, or just a feeling that you just don't really have the energy or desire to keep up as much, even though there still may be income needs. But certainly aging is very much a factor. Whereas your leaving the Party [given that it happened when Joe was in his thirties] was almost in a sense more like what someone would call a "career decision." [But] after a gap of more than twenty years or so, you deliberately chose to become involved in a group of political-slash-ethnic cohorts [*Jewish Currents*].

Would you say, perhaps that age was a factor in your choosing that particular group, in addition to the political and the ethnic factors? [NOTE: This last question was prompted by the mistaken assumption that Joe hadn't become involved with *Jewish Currents* until his "retirement" from shop work. It was actually not much more than two or three years after he left the Communist Party, a point that is clarified below. Nevertheless, the question leads to additional revealing insights from Joe.]

JD: No, I don't think it was a factor when I first made that choice. I didn't think about age then. But that was thirty years ago.

DS: So you joined the *Jewish Currents* group thirty years ago?

JD: Yeah, twenty-five, thirty years ago. I don't think I thought about age then. But it has become a factor later. That, plus all of the developments—politically and ethnically. And the problem in left-wing circles of Jewish identification has become sharper and of more emotional significance than it was forty years ago. At that time, to be Jewish and to be a left-winger was not uncommon, but most left-wing people paid no attention to being Jewish. It wasn't a major factor in their life.

DS: To be Jewish [and] left—you mean to be Jewish-identified?

JD: Yeah, to be identified as Jewish, to have an important concern about being Jewish. Many of them paid no attention [to ethnicity]. In no way was their life influenced by the fact that they were Jewish. They didn't observe any customs or traditions; they didn't observe any holidays; they didn't read the Jewish press; they didn't belong to any Jewish organizations. They just happened to be of Jewish origin. There were many people who lived their entire lives that way. That's perfectly alright with me. I have no objection. If somebody is of Jewish origin and that's all they feel about it, or that's all they know about it, and they're satisfied, I don't object. But, it seems to me there were more people [like that] in those days, forty years ago. As some of the anti-Semitism that existed in the Soviet [Union] and socialist bloc in the world became better known, and became more exposed, undeniable, then some people began to feel twinges or discomfort or unease [and] got very much interested and involved, and so on. Especially after not only the establishment of the state of Israel, but [also] when the Israeli government in the late sixties began to become more and more right-wing [and] intransigent in its hostility to the Palestinians, to the Arab world, and more supportive of those aspect of American imperialism which we opposed, then, too, the problem of Jewish identification became sharper. As the criticisms of Israel from the socialist world sharpened and some of them became tinged with anti-Semitism, to a greater and greater extent sometimes, then the ability to be both a left-winger and Jewish also became a problem for many people.

And then age entered into that. The people who had lived through World War II and the Holocaust—leftists who felt that they could, by creating new political conditions, by helping support a socialist movement in the world, could eliminate anti-Semitism or lessen anti-Semitism—they became disappointed that they hadn't. Many of them became very disappointed that they began to see or feel anti-Semitism among the left-wing groups [that] they supported. So that feeling began to sharpen, and there were divisions and tensions in the Left, which still exist now in some left organizations. But again, the older people got much sharper about it, and as they began to look back on their lives and what they were doing, and what they were contributing to, and so on, a kind of resentment, or an emotional reaction from (to them) unexpected quarters—and disappointing for us—became much more meaningful to them. Age—you could see the division in age.

Another area in which I see a division in age is on the growing movements in the Left [that] have to do with topics that the older generation never dealt with or [are] totally unaccustomed to, for example, the gay [and] lesbian rights movement. A whole slew of what you might call lifestyle issues—families, how to raise children, how to choose careers, and so on—began to divide many of these older and younger people. The sharpest way in which I see it is on the gay and lesbian issues, where almost all the older people I know feel that this is an issue that has no place in what they call the left progressive movement. They say, "Alright, gays and lesbians shouldn't be discriminated against, but why are they raising it here for? What's that got to do with us, and what's that got to do with the situation in Poland or Eastern Europe, preventing war, improving the economy, or getting the United States out of Central America. All these extraneous issues [are] dividing us and distracting people."

The younger people are all for it. This is a hot issue, and it's important to them, and it leaves the older generation somewhat bewildered about that. So I see age coming up in that issue, particularly on that. I see age coming up on ethnic identification. But it was not a factor when I made a decision to get more involved with *Jewish Currents*.

DS: I was wondering—and this may seem a little discursive—you retired at age sixty-two, a conventional time for retirement. Even though [your] work as a toolmaker was not necessarily your primary identity [it] nevertheless involved a good part of your waking life, [your] active time, during the day for so many years. That would mean also that the amount of time that you would be devoting to, let us say, agonizing over issues of politics and ethnicity, would simply be limited. Do you feel that there has been a change in the ways in which you have grappled with this issue [of political self-reflection] following your retirement from work? [Is it] growing in intensity or taking [on] a different character, if for no other reason than the fact that you've more time to devote to those issues, and in particular those activities and organizational involvements that raise those issues?

JD: There has been a change, but I'm not sure that I attribute it to the fact that I reorganized my time. Perhaps it is; I'd really have to think about that. I attributed the growing interest in change more to the fact that I've become just more involved with it—more concerned—and [to] the different experiences that I have had. Particularly I'm thinking [that] in New Jewish Agenda, I've met a lot of people who were politically either liberal or vaguely liberal, or [who] may have had some vague connection with a radical movement, in the sense of a relative or something like that, but who were never really involved in it. I met a lot of people who are religious. Their entire life is wrapped up in Jewish community affairs, and so on. You would never see them at anything to do with Central America, or with the economy or [even] with civil rights. Some of them you might see at some civil rights things, a few limited ones. But meeting a lot of these people, naturally [you] become influenced by the pressures of what they're interested in. So I attributed my changing outlook [to that].

I think I've become much more conservative—well, I don't want to use that word, let me change that—I've become much more interested in working with people on the level they're at, on the interests they're at, rather than pushing a radical program that will only attract a tiny handful of people. Let me illustrate that: A big argument in New Jewish Agenda for several years has been whether we should call for a cut for U.S. aid to Israel. The argument is stated in various forms, anything from just simply calling for an outright cut in aid to Israel, to ideas about [cuts] commensurate with the amount that Israel spends in the West Bank, what they spend for military purposes, and so on. The argument has been around the tactic (and nobody in Agenda really disagrees with the principles that are involved in that) that somehow we should try to get the [U.S.] government to put pressure on the Israeli government to change its policies. The argument is whether by openly calling for such a move, we would be cutting ourselves off from the Jewish community. There are some people who say I don't care if I do, it's morally right, and we should do it. It's morally right, and if we cut ourselves off, we'll just go along with whatever we can do. But somebody's got to say this direct thing. And other people say there's lots of things that are correct to say, but you don't say them in the wrong place in the wrong time, and the wrong way, 'cause you just hurt your own cause instead of helping it. I have come down more on the side of a more conservative view on this: not to isolate ourselves from the Jewish community. I would prefer to put it [by] saying that we should not say anything [that would] appear to be negative and punitive toward Israel. We should be critical, but not negative and punitive, and that we can be sharply critical and not isolate ourselves from the Jewish community, so we maintain some voice there.

I don't know to what extent my position is a result of [the] influence of many people I meet in the Jewish community, that I [have] a contact that I don't want to be disrupted, or whether it's something that I've really thought out, you know, come to. I don't really think that anybody really thinks out a position and comes to it strictly on a theoretical basis. I don't believe anybody sitting in a library or laboratory really comes to a conclusion or something based solely on objective evidence. We all choose what evidence we want to hear and see, and we choose what evidence we want to overlook. We come with our biases, and so on. At the same time, we're influenced by the things around us. So I don't know how to separate those things. I'd say yes, no matter how [I arrived] that's where I am now. But part of it I'm sure is the fact that I meet with a lot of people outside the Left, and their influences [are] a big part of what makes me come down on the side I come down on, on this issue.

Now, that happens to a great extent, since I retired. I don't think it has anything to do with retirement except that I have more time that I spend in the Jewish community and more time to meet with these people and to be influenced, one way or another by it. But it's that because of retirement, I thought more about it and [have] come to some conclusion.

DS: Well, since you mention the idea of choosing evidence, choosing aspects of your conviction—

JD: That might be a little too crude, putting it that way—

DS: —that there is a selective process.

JD: People try to be objective. Most people try to be objective and look at the facts, and so on. I don't think we can help but be influenced.

DS: But what you see—you're exposed to different points of view, and then you make choices, is what I was getting at. To put it another way: When you were working in the shop, there were not only work pressures, but time pressures as well, and outside of work, the amount of time was limited, and it seemed to me that there would be some pressure in terms of choices of associations, activities, et cetera, that you would have to make. I was wondering if, for no other reason than the amount of time that was available in retirement, that perhaps your choices were greater [in number]. Do you feel, perhaps, that there was less pressure to confine yourself to certain activities? Did you feel, perhaps, that there was an opening up to a wider range—in particular a wider range politically, in terms of your contacts—that might have given rise to the influence of a wider range of ideas?

JD: I'm not sure I understand what you're asking.

DS: Well, were your contacts with this wider political spectrum greater [in number] following your retirement as a tool maker?

JD: Yes, yeah. Because of time. There is an implication in there that maybe I could have taken the time, while working, to do that, instead of the things I did. I made that choice while working.

DS: There were pressures, and part of the pressure was time.

JD: Well, that's still pressure—that's still part of the pressure now—time and money. There was an ADL [Anti-Defamation League] banquet the other day—their annual banquet—and I didn't go. Mostly it's expensive, and I choose not to associate with the people at that type of function. Before retiring, I didn't go to anything in the Jewish community, very rarely anything in the Jewish community. Afterward, I do. So now, as a consequence, I've met people, but I've also become interested in some other things. So if some other group, somebody, is doing something of interest to me, I might go there. I wouldn't have even known about such things before retiring, because I didn't even meet the people who would have told me about it.

DS: Now, the choice *not* to attend those functions—and I assume you're talking about [in] the mainstream Jewish community —while you were still working, did that have to do exclusively with the limited time available to you, or—

JD: No, it had to do with time and money and that I wasn't known to these people, that I would have to break into it, that I would have to overcome some hurdles in the beginning. And I wasn't that interested. I wasn't that much interested in that sort of thing.

DS: So, was it more important for you to, say, move in and become more accepted by the mainstream Jewish community following retirement?

JD: Well, partly because I was interested in New Jewish Agenda, and—

DS: When did you join them, before retiring or after?

JD: I joined just before retiring in 1980. I retired in 1982. But just before retiring I joined Agenda. There had been another organization preceding Agenda called *Breira*—I don't know if you've ever heard of that?

DS: I think I have.

JD: *Breira* is a Hebrew word meaning choice [laughs].

DS: That was, I assume, specifically in response to policies in Israel?

JD: It was a response to policies in Israel, and it was destroyed by the mainstream Jewish community. And I mean destroyed in the sense that they put out booklets and pamphlets talking about what it was that this organization wanted—they called it anti-Israel and anti-Semitic. People working for Jewish establishment organizations were threatened if they—with loss of their job if they went to a meeting or had anything to do with this organization. That organization died. It was formed in the seventies and died after a few years. Then [in] 1980 Agenda was formed. In 1982, the war in Lebanon gave Agenda a big boost, because a lot of people were critical of the Israeli government. The Peace Now movement started up in Israel, and a much more sizable section of the Jewish population accepted the notion—perhaps, begrudgingly, but anyway they accepted it—that criticism of Israel could be legitimate. We still went through a lot of attacks, a lot of people saying that they didn't want to hear us say the things that we said. They didn't want to hear all this kind of stuff—that we were anti-Israel. But we also had some defenders, enough so that we managed to exist. By now there's a broader consensus in the Jewish community. I think Agenda's gonna have to find some way to change some of its program a little bit and grow some, or else it, too, is gonna die or be replaced by other things. [Agenda did, in fact, dissolve as a national organization in 1993; the New Haven chapter, however, voted to continue as an independent group.] There's this Jewish Peace Lobby now, which is raising more money and pushing many of the same ideas as Agenda. The national director of the ADL, [was] openly criticizing the Israeli government at this banquet, which is extremely unusual. The stupidity of the Israeli government policies is also [laughs] contributing. It's always true: Your opponent's mistakes are often your strongest weapon.

DS: It sounds like—maybe you[r] joining New Jewish Agenda coincided with the period just before your retirement.

JD: That's when it—yeah, it did—

DS: That's when it emerged—

JD: I was involved with *Jewish Currents* before, so when a group of people got together in New Haven to try to form a chapter, I was one of them, in Agenda.

DS: Now, was *Jewish Currents* supportive of this emergence of New Jewish Agenda?

JD: Yes. I think I told you, *Jewish Currents* used to have regular—well, irregular—discussion groups, invite speakers, and so on. Actually what happened [was] there was a *Jewish Currents* meeting with a historian, [to] which we invited a number of graduate students in history. Out of that, a chapter of Agenda was formed. We had—it was amusing—we had Paul Buhle. You know him? He's a historian, labor history.

DS: Labor historian, yeah.

JD: And Paul Buhle is a guy—he's not Jewish, but he became very much interested in the cultural aspects of labor history, the labor groups that formed glee clubs and bands and drama groups and all this sort of thing. And he also was interested in the left theoretical discussions in the labor movement in the United States, and the Jewish component of that was very important. And they had the strongest type of cultural group in the unions, and in the left-wing organizations in the Jewish community. So he went and studied Yiddish, so that he could read it directly, you know, understand it. To anybody [laughs] who spoke or understood Yiddish, his speaking was funny, you know, the way he pronounced words and so on. But he could read Yiddish and understand what they were saying. So we invited him to speak on some aspect of this. And a whole group of people came from the history department at Yale. A number of them were graduate students who were interested either in Jewish history or women's history or something like that, and from them we formed a chapter and recruited more people from these two groups, from *Jewish Currents* and from these Yale students. We formed a chapter and then got some community people into it as well.

But I think it was just coincidence that it happened at the same time that I was retiring. Before that I was involved with *Jewish Currents,* and then after that—still involved with *Jewish Currents*— Agenda was a local organization that we could do something [in]. By now we have sort of given up *Jewish Currents* running anything. We haven't done anything for years, as a reader's group, mostly because it would be a kind of duplication of effort [of] the people who would come to this as part of an organization now. But anyway, I don't think that it was because of retirement. It was coincidental. At the same time, having more time after that enabled me to start going to meetings in the Jewish community, some of which take place at noontime. They're accustomed to businessmen's type meetings. They meet for an hour, hour and a half, at noon. Or they'll have a speaker—the lawyer's division, or something like that, of the Community Relations Council [of the Jewish Federation], or whatever it might be. But then they have an urban task force in the Community Relations Council that would run some things [such as] discussion groups, or they'd have someone like the Superintendent of Schools, somebody from the Hispanic community, come and speak to them. I'd go to those meetings and meet a lot of people who were involved in the Jewish community. Then we ran meetings of our own at the Jewish Center. We would invite some rabbi or some[one] to moderate; invite other people to participate in one way or another.

And in that way we became acquainted with a lot of these people. And [I] began to meet them, then speak up at some of the meetings, get to know people that way; introduce resolutions or proposals for some action, and so on. We introduced a resolution on a nuclear freeze to the Jewish Community Relations Council. They had a series of meetings they were going to have on brotherhood, so they decided to invite somebody from the black community, from the Hispanic community, and from the Italian community. So I proposed somebody from the Arab community [laughs] and got a very militantly hostile reaction from some, but also a more intrigued and accepting reaction from others. So we could begin to see who's who in the community. Then we sent out letters proposing that we meet. We offered to play a tape of some discussion we'd sponsored.

It was a tape that appeared on public TV, nationally, of a tour that we had sponsored with an Israeli Jew and a Palestinian, and this was in 1983 or 1984.

DS: This was a New Jewish Agenda-sponsored tour—

JD: New Jewish Agenda sponsored the tour, and they made a tape, [which] appeared on TV. And we had a copy, and we offered to play it at anybody's home [where we] could have a discussion on it. And we had a response from a woman who is now the president of the Jewish Federation in New Haven, asking us to come to her home, not with the tape, but to come and talk—have a discussion of what Agenda is all about. And we did. She had invited four or five people active in the Jewish community. So we went there, had a very good discussion. They were asking us why we were picketing General Sharon [commander of Israel's invasion forces in Lebanon in 1982] when he came to Connecticut. And they were asking us why we participate in things about South Africa, but not about the Soviet Union, and so on. And we responded, how could you let General Sharon come to Connecticut and *not* picket him? How could you let him pass himself off as Jewish hero after what happened in Lebanon? We discussed the question of the Soviet Union, what our position was, South Africa, and so on. But, again, we got to know some of the people better, so we were able to make some contacts that way. We managed to make some good connections. We ran a film to make some money. We rented a movie theater [and] showed an Israeli film, an antiwar, pro-cooperation film. And we made up a list of sponsors to put on a film, and people made a special contribution as a sponsor. And we got a few [of] these people from the community to sponsor the film. So, again, it increased our credibility and acceptance in the community, and contacts with people. By now I know a half a dozen rabbis, the leaders of the [Jewish] Federation, and so on, many of whom consider me a leftist Soviet apologist, or something like that, but many of whom are accepting that this is a legitimate view in the community. I have a problem with most of them just on an income basis. Most of these people are higher-income people. And their homes, and their lifestyles [are] beyond my means. But nevertheless we can talk—

DS: —in spite of the class differences.

JD: —and some of them are—there are people who tell me they don't want to say the things that I say but they're glad that we're saying it. I don't know if you've seen some of the latest surveys of American Jewish opinion, which show that well over half of the American Jews would accept negotiations with the PLO if there was a commitment on the part of the PLO to certain conditions. Or some of them are ready to accept it without any conditions. I think actually [that] private opinion in the Jewish community is a lot more favorable to our view than many people think. [The reaction of American Jews to the "peace accord" signed by Israeli Prime Minister Rabin and PLO leader Arafat in 1993 was mixed, but many expressed cautious support.] Anyway, we built up with that, and my involvement in it started before I retired. After that, retirement just gave me an opportunity to be more involved.

DS: More involved in the wider Jewish community.

JD: Yeah.

DS: It's interesting, though, Joe, that we began this interview with your critique of what you felt was missing, and a crucial aspect of that missing element was the need to delve deeper into the sense of loss, or regret, among those who were separated from a group that was really like a family. And for you, the wider Jewish community was never that family—

JD: —and it isn't now.

DS: For you it was [a] specific group of Jews—not New Jewish Agenda, but actually the *Jewish Currents*—that was that specific cohort of both co-ethnics and political comrades—

JD: —right—

DS: —whose experiences you shared over many, many years. And that insight was something that was really brought home in your remarks. Perhaps you might give us a few parting shots. It would be really important to look at the whole issue of what a person in their work career, their life career, has seen as their personal, their social, their political, or their spiritual "home"; the people that they associate with that are most like a family—of course, including their immediate family. But is that family sense—I mean outside of the home—found in the workplace? Is it found, as it was for you, in a particular political movement? And as you move into retirement, where does that sense of "home" or sense of place come from?

JD: Well, for me it was never in the workplace. I know there are some people who do find a family in their workplace. Sometimes it seems to me it happened in kind of institutional workplaces, or places where people—their work is different in a way. I think some cops have it, where their friends are fellow cops, things of that sort. Sometimes, it seems to me that certain levels of people working in places like Yale University, have both a personal [and] social life with the people that they work with. But for me, it was never the workplace. There [were] only two occasions [in] which I invited people that I knew from work to come to my home—well, there were more than two which I invited, but two where it was accepted. And I've only been invited twice by other people that I worked with. One was a Puerto Rican family, a Puerto Rican couple working in a shop, that invited us to a picnic. There was another picnic that I was invited to. So for me, [it] has never been the workplace where I found a social life or a family or home. It was among people with similar backgrounds that I found it, as friends, as social friends. Like most of our friends are people we've known for forty or fifty years, that we see occasionally, have dinner together, or go out to a movie together. But the social life, the family life, the sense of acceptance, this is from people that we have known through political activity of one sort or another, then became friendly, and still see each other in that way. Some may simply belong to an organization [but] are not active in it. We have that sort of relationship that developed over years, but [it] had nothing to do with the workplace relationship. I just never had the experience at work of finding people there that I felt warm and close to socially. That's one of the things that I never really puzzled about, or thought about. Unless you're working for some organization, newspaper, or something like that. I don't know how I would deal with that. I can conceive of ways in which a workplace might also be a social place, but for most people it isn't, and for me it wasn't.

DS: So, any concluding thoughts you might have on the issue of—

JD: —identity?

DS: —identity, retirement.

JD: Everybody ought to retire as soon as possible, and find some—well, I suppose the main thing I would say is, I think that we need a purpose in life, some kind of purpose. I don't think you can examine it too deeply, 'cause I think if you go too deeply there is no purpose anyway, there is no ultimate purpose in anything. Life is to be lived, that's all. But we have to have a kind of purpose that satisfies us in the sense that this is worth doing. And I think that there are plenty of things worth doing. So I think that it's important to me—and should be important to anybody—to find things that you think are worth doing and try to do them, even if it's not totally successful. That makes life worthwhile.

DS: So, for you, the things that have given life purpose are those that gave purpose before and after you retired—

JD: Before and after retirement. They changed some—like forty years ago I had nothing to do with the Jewish community. And I was one of those people who was [simply] "of Jewish origin." That phrase I got from a guy who was a Zionist philosopher, and he says that we live now in a post-Zionist world. Zionism accomplished—partially accomplished—its goal. They got a state, though it's not the state that they envisioned. The [state the] original Zionists envisioned never will be. People aren't all flocking there from—all the Jews in the world are not gathering in there. He says [that] in Israel you can be a Jew without being religious. Outside of Israel, he says, it's gonna die out—being a nonreligious Jew. I don't know if it's accurate or not, but that's the way he feels. So then he says outside of Israel [Jews] are identified either because they're religious or they're simply people "of Jewish origin." So you can say a lot of people—Einstein was a man of Jewish origin, to him. But I'd say there are ways for people to be Jewish without being religious, at least for the present period of time, like I am.

I think there are other people who are not leftist, who don't consider themselves to be political activists but who are Jewish. And many of them, more so as they retire, because otherwise they're—their life, too, that's the way they find some meaning. I know people now [like that]. I met a guy recently who just returned from a convention in Phoenix, of Jewish community relations councils. He had been to Israel twice, and he would probably go twice more this year, on various commissions, and so on. He's not a religious person at all, doesn't attend any synagogue regularly, doesn't observe [Jewish customs] regularly, considers himself not religious. But he puts meaning and purpose in his life. Otherwise, what's he going to do, play golf? So that's what he does; there are people like that. Maybe that won't last very long, but for now that gives him meaning, and it gives me meaning and purpose. It's also, for me, a way of tying together this question of ethnic identification and political identification.

I can very easily see losing the ethnic identification. I can easily see that something might happen [that] would get me so wrapped up in some other area that I would lose the ethnic identification. If Agenda were to fold up, and *Jewish Currents* were to fold up, I don't have the energy or the will to revive them. And both of them are possible within my lifetime. Agenda is very weak, losing—hasn't got money, can't maintain an office, could easily fold, and it's area of activity be taken over by, as I said, this Jewish Peace Lobby, and there's areas of the American Jewish Congress [that] are getting more liberal, and so on. So that could easily happen. And *Jewish Currents*—the editors are all people in their eighties. If the editor-in-chief were to die, which certainly is a very realistic possibility—he's eighty-two, eighty-three, something like that—I don't know who would take over. I don't know anybody that could keep it going, raise the money, and get out every issue, and so on. I think it might struggle on for a year or two, but probably fold. That could conceivably happen in the next couple of years, most of those things. I think I would probably try and revive it [but I] couldn't even revive a *Jewish Currents* group here, 'cause there would be no magazine there. I would try to find something else to get involved in.

So I could easily see that that would stop, and I could take that loss. But political activity is never going to stop. Problems always exist, you know [laughs], no matter what. I would still try to, one or another, be involved in something, just in order to give meaning to my life. Without some kind of activity or something, I don't know what the hell it would all be about. So, that's it.

Chapter Seven

I Think I'm Still Looking for My Core

[Interview with Lillian ("Lil") Dimow, conducted at her home in New Haven, Connecticut, on August 6, 1990.]

DAVID SHULDINER: What I hope to get out of our discussion, Lil, is a sense of your evolving self, more specifically, your core self . . . . Have you considered what your core identity is? If somebody asks you what you felt was the driving force, would you have an answer?

LILLIAN DIMOW: I don't think I know. I think I'm still looking for my core. I'm very dissatisfied with my life, and I don't know why, because I've done so many interesting things. I have so many good people around me. But I've never been satisfied with myself. So I don't know what my core [identity] would be.

DS: Do you think that [your] dissatisfaction comes from a feeling that there's always a need for self-improvement, for perfection?

LD: That's part of it, that's part of it. But I procrastinate and do nothing about it. I'm a great procrastinator, really great. I don't know. I have never felt completely satisfied, except the period that I mentioned before we started on tape [she had described a late career as arts-and-crafts teacher in the public schools, housing projects, through social agencies, and in adult education programs in New Haven, which she followed for close to eighteen years, before "retiring" (from paid employment) in 1986, at age seventy]. I knew I was doing very good work then. I knew I was reaching people.

DS: You were teaching crafts in the inner city?

LD: And then in the school system. And I felt I had a lot of good results with kids and with adults. I worked with adults in the housing project. That I think was the most gratifying period of my life, where I really felt I was coming out, and I was bringing other people, too. Helping them to see good things about themselves, and helping them to produce things, which they never thought they could do or would ever do. I think I felt better about myself then. But I'd come home, and I wasn't very good with my kids. They say I'm wrong, but I don't think I was that great with them.

DS: Sometimes, you know, a person like yourself who seeks perfection rather than simply being complacent or accepting of the way things are is never satisfied completely.

LD: I don't think I was seeking perfection. Not in my kids. Maybe in myself, I don't know. I'm really not sure. But during that period I had a lot of gratification, a very, very, good feeling. And that went on for a long time.

DS: This may seem like a sort of leap, but I know that you and Joe [Dimow] come from [similar] political backgrounds and family [backgrounds]: old Jewish socialists instilled with a sense of values and also a sense of great dissatisfaction with the way things were in the world, the need for change. I'm wondering if, looking back, your wanting to reach out to these inner-city kids, through creative channels, might have been motivated by the same impulse that led you to become active in movements for social change?

LD: I'm sure that my background, and my family background, had a lot to do with my ability to work with these people, adults and children. I was very lucky in getting into that work, because it would never [otherwise] occur to me to do it. But a social worker who knew me (and didn't know me very well) just felt I should be working with people. And when the pilot program started at that housing project, she was determined to get me involved. She's the one who made such a change in my life. I owe so much to her. She saw something in me which I wasn't aware of. She pushed me on. She had so much confidence in me, she scared the pants off me [laughs].

DS: She recognized something in you that, looking back, you also recognized in the way you were brought up. Maybe we could look back at the period. What I'd like to have you do, Lil, is tell me what your family was like, what kinds of values, and what kind of outlook, you were raised with.

LD: Well, my father was a constructional ironworker a good part of his life, until the Depression, when he lost his job. He'd been a blacksmith in Poland and came here. My mother was a dressmaker most of her life. In fact, she was a dressmaker in Poland and had two or three women working for her. But she was in the Bund [the Jewish Labor Bund, a revolutionary socialist organization]. My father came to this country to avoid the draft into the Czar's army. Our family gradually grew to four daughters. My oldest sister was born in Poland. She came to this country when she was about four years old, with my mother. My father had already been here for about three years. It was a very hard-working existence for my father and my mother. I spoke [about this] not too long ago for Agenda.

DS: New Jewish Agenda?

LD: Yeah. It was on a panel, and I remember saying something to the effect that when I hear the sound of a sewing machine, I can see my mother at her sewing machine. It was the usual thing: She worked 'til all hours of the night. And, of course, we had a boarder, in the five rooms we lived in—and the six of us—and she took care of his food, his laundry, everything. It was a very hard existence. And my father worked very hard. But at the same time, my father loved music, and as soon as my mother could save up enough—you know what a *pushke* is?

DS: A collection [box]—

LD: A collection for charity. My mother always had a *pushke* for charity, but she always had a *pushke* for the family also. So the first thing I remember her getting was a Victrola. And my father would— just about every Saturday afternoon—he'd come home from work after lunchtime and get washed up and cleaned up and have something to eat and go down to the music store. And he bought a record almost every week, always opera. And we grew up with that.

The next thing my mother had a *pushke* for was a piano, and we got a piano. My older sister took piano lessons. My younger sister (I was the third one) was very talented. I don't remember how old she was, a toddler, it seems to me. After my older sister had her lesson, she'd go and sit down and play some of the stuff. It was amazing. She was very talented and she is a musician. She struggled.

We all went to commercial high school because my father felt that if we had office skills we wouldn't have to work in a shop. So, we all had office skills. But my younger sister wanted very much to study music. There were times when the piano was in terrible shape. My parents felt they didn't have the money to have it tuned or repaired. I'd walk with her three or four miles to someone's house where she could practice on the piano. She's very talented. She'd go in the library and get music. So we grew up with a lot of music.

We grew up hearing a lot of Yiddish stories and Yiddish poetry, both from my father telling us the stories and his friends [who] would come to the house. My father was a socialist, a communist. The Jews in New Haven, the Workmens' Circle Jews [a socialist, fraternal organization], split off or the other way around, the left-wing Jews split off from the Workmens' Circle group [reflecting a rift between supporters and nonsupporters of the Bolshevik Revolution that occurred in the socialist movement as a whole], and eventually bought a building called the Labor Lyceum, I don't remember when. They had a Yiddish school, [an] after school, for the kids, which I never got to [go to], because it died just when I was old enough to get there. But my two oldest sisters did, and my oldest sister can still read and write Yiddish, in addition to speaking and understanding. I can speak some, and I understand it quite well, but I never learned to read and write. They hired teachers. They had a violin teacher, a piano teacher, [and] a dance teacher. We learned ballet there [and] we had recitals, all of us.

This all evolved. I tie it all together. I said at [a] panel discussion that New Jewish Agenda had this past year [that] to me this was all part of *Yiddishkeit*, and *Yiddishkeit* has always been very important to me. The other thing [is that] I grew up constantly hearing, *Alle mentshen zaynen glaykh*—all people are equal. I thought everyone grew up like that. It was a long time before I learned that it wasn't so. We learned that unions were good, workers were good, and bosses were the enemy. It was a lot of struggle, but a lot of warmth, in the house. I don't know what else to tell you.

DS: It seems that your involvement in politics was so closely tied to your involvement in Jewish affairs—maybe not the Jewish community at large, but certainly the Jewish Left community. *Yiddishkeit*, to my mind, symbolizes that integration of [left-wing] politics and [Jewish] culture. Were your political comrades at that time predominantly Jewish? When did you join the [Communist] Party, by the way?

LD: Oh, god, I really don't remember. I was a Young Pioneer [the Party's children's group] and then a member of the Young Communist League—the YCL [the Party's youth group]. And at some point—I can't remember if it was just shortly before I was married or shortly after I was married; let's say I was twenty-five, twenty-six, maybe even a little younger [when Lil joined the Party itself]. I wasn't in the YCL that long—it sounds too old to have been the YCL [laughs]. But for a while I was in both [the YCL and the Party]. But I remember distributing leaflets at Winchester's (Winchester Repeating Arms Company). I must have been nine years old.

As far as the Young Pioneers [are concerned], I can't remember too much. I think it was mainly the people around the Labor Lyceum, which was Jewish. But I think once I was in the YCL, there were some others. But most of them were Jewish. More of the members were Jewish. And then, I don't know when, the IWO —[the] International Workers Order—[was formed] which had ethnic groups. There was a JPFO, Jewish People's Fraternal Order, there was a Ukrainian group—because these I was familiar with here in New Haven.

DS: These were all mass organizations that were affiliated with the Party?

LD: There were a lot of Party members active, as far as I know. The IWO was a fraternal organization, with insurance, and death benefits, and that sort of thing.

DS: Sort of a left version of what the Workmen's Circle did for the Jewish socialists? [The IWO was, in fact, the counterpart to Workmen's Circle (WC) formed by those who split from the WC during the period mentioned by Lil above.]

LD: Basically, I think, yeah. I'm sure there were a lot of intermingling of CP people and non-CP people there. It seems to me that there were a lot of Party people in it.

DS: Now, were you active at all in the Jewish People's Fraternal Organization?

LD: Not really, except it seems to me at one point I was taking care of records, but I'm not sure. But I was a member, and I had insurance—

DS: Through the IWO—

LD: Yeah.

DS: One of the [things] that we're looking at is the political thread of your developing identity; the other would be your working life. Maybe we can trace [them] at the same time.

LD: That's another reason that I think I did join the CP a little later, because I started to work nights in a bakery when I was still in high school. I was a senior in high school. I worked six nights a week. I had Monday off; nobody was around on Monday. And I remember that I kept saying all the time, "As soon as I get out of here, I'm getting into political (left political) activity." I was very close friends with the family who owned the bakery, and I am still very close friends with the daughter of the original owner, who is a couple of years older than I am. She's my oldest friend—I still say that. Completely apolitical. Has a pretty good sense of feeling about people—all kinds. Very Jewish. Religious to a fair amount, goes to synagogue every week and all. Knew my background—all of them did in the bakery, the owners—they all knew who my father was. On Legion Avenue, Sunday morning, the left-wingers would meet on one street corner, the right-wingers on [another]. Everyone knew who everyone else was. I remember (this is long afterward) one of the Workmen's Circle people saying that my father was the only honest communist in New Haven [laughs].

So, I was working in the bakery, and I wasn't involved in anything. I'd go into work three, four o'clock in the afternoon and work (especially Saturday nights) 'til twelve, one o'clock sometimes.

Sundays I came early in the morning and went almost a whole day. I worked extremely hard. But I liked the people.

DS: Now, how long did that job last?

LD: Well, it could have lasted forever, but I wanted to get a bookkeeping job, and I did eventually get a bookkeeping job.

DS: As a result of commercial school?

LD: Mm hmm.

DS: So you got out of [the bakery] and went into bookkeeping, then. Was that a day job?

LD: Yeah. But, after Joe's Smith Act trial, I was downtown looking for a job. I bumped into the wife of one of the bakery owners and the daughter who's still my friend. They asked what I was doing. I said I was looking for a job. So the mother asked, would I be interested in going back to the bakery. I said I'd go back. She said she could talk to her sons. And they called me. I went in to talk to them. Their greatest concern was who would take care of the children.

DS: How old were the children then?

LD: Carl was about four, and Joan was about seven.

DS: So they were young.

LD: Oh, yeah. And I went back to the bakery.

DS: In the fifties, now, this was.

LD: Yeah.

DS: All this time, though—you said when you [first] worked in the bakery it was virtually impossible to be politically involved. When you got the bookkeeping job, would that at least free [your] evenings and weekends for political involvement?

LD: Right.

DS: So is that when you renewed contact and [your] involvement with the Party took a new phase?

LD: Well, that's when I became more or less involved with the YCL and the Party afterward.

DS: So you were still young enough to be involved in the [YCL].

LD: And I knew a lot of them. A lot of them would come to the bakery. I'd be working there, you know. I knew them from the time I was a child, in the Labor Lyceum and all, and [their] parents knew each other.

DS: What was it that brought you to see your political ideals represented in the Party? I wonder if that experience for you is different to the extent [that] you virtually grew up with it. It became synonymous with your ideals without even reflecting on it until, when you were in the YCL, you had already in a sense internalized it. Am I—

LD: No, I think you're right. I think you're right.

DS: Was there a period during, let's say, your early years in the Communist Party that you ever recall reflecting on other alternatives, just as a way of gauging your own sense of who you were or what your involvement in the Party meant?

LD: I don't think I thought about other alternatives. The only thing I ever did think about at times was why I didn't spend the time going to school.

DS: Now, did that have to do just with the fact that you needed to bring income into the family?

LD: You mean, my working.

DS: Your not being able to pursue your education, was [it] choice or necessity that drove you?

LD: It was little of each. Necessity—I had to work. There's no question about that. We all did at that point. When I graduated at high school I knew—I cried at graduation, because I knew that was the end of my—

DS: —formal education?

LD: —formal education. I wished I could have gone further. But I also knew that my high school education wasn't enough to go to college. I didn't have the right credits, or anything.

DS: You were active in the Party until at least, what, the late fifties?

LD: When did Khrushchev's papers come out, [19]56—

DS: [19]56—his denunciation of Stalin?

LD: Yeah, about then. It was about [19]57 when Joe and I left the Party. [19]56, [19]57.

DS: Now, during that time, from your earliest involvement to the late 'fifties, were you always working; that is, did you always have paid employment that you were—

LD: Yeah.

DS: So, in a sense, you had to balance your work (paid employment), your work with the Party, and raising kids, all together.

LD: I wasn't working at the time Joe was arrested [under the Smith Act in the early 1950s] and the others also. I don't think I was working.

DS: Were you active in the Party?

LD: Well, I worked in the Party office until I was in my ninth month of pregnancy with my daughter.

DS: A paid office worker?

LD: I wasn't paid, but I worked there. Once I gave birth to a child, that was the end. After all, giving birth to a child means that your brain stops functioning also. I was so turned off, it was dreadful. It was absolutely dreadful. Here, on Monday, I'm cranking the stupid mimeograph machine, I'm cutting stencils, I'm doing work. And on Friday, and I have a child, I can no longer even think. It was disgraceful. It was really disgraceful.

DS: What you're talking about now is—

LD: I'm talking about the Party's attitude—

DS: —toward women.

LD: Yes.

DS: Since you raise it, I think it would be important if you could give me a sense of how you saw the Party's attitude toward women evolve. Had you seen before that [any] indications of a problem?

LD: I have said—and Joe has criticized me on this, but I'm going by *my* experience—that some of the men I knew in the CP were the worst male supremacists I had ever come across. Joe would say, "You don't know male supremacists. You haven't seen them in the shop." But I'm going by what *I* know, and my experience, and in my experience, they were pretty awful. Joe was unusual, he really was unusual. But it seemed to me that women were put down dreadfully. It's almost as if it was without thinking, that it was so ingrained that women are an inferior breed—at least that's the way it came across to me anyway. I'd get very annoyed at times. He was out at meetings every night, and I was taking care of the baby and had nothing else—nothing. I wasn't told anything, even. And I was criticized.

DS: For speaking out?

LD: No, there were women who criticized me 'cause I was stuck in my house. I wasn't criticized for speaking out. When I spoke out, they took it.

DS: Did they recognize the problem, though, when you pointed it out to them; did they acknowledge it?

LD: Some did; most didn't. Most felt I was making a big thing out of nothing.

DS: One of the longstanding problems in the left movement has been its progressive stand in certain areas and yet its—

LD: Blindness in other areas.

DS: Yeah, backwardness. We could say, in a sense, Marx was right, that no matter how progressive your politics are, you're still a product of your own culture.

LD: That's true.

DS: But that does raise an interesting question. Do you feel, since you were committed to socialism and still consider yourself committed to socialism, the Party's attitude did not dissuade you from your political ideology? Where do you think that discrepancy came from, the Party's point of view? Was it policy or simply that they reflected the prejudices of this culture?

LD: I think they reflected the culture. I'm pretty sure it wasn't policy. I don't think it was. Why should it be? There were some women in leadership. Not a lot, but there were some. I don't know, I wasn't happy with some of it, but I don't really remember too much, either. Not that I was any big shot. [I] never wanted to be, either. But when I had my daughter, that was really something.

DS: Part of the problem, too, being that the vision of the future that the Party had, a very compelling one, was ostensibly a reflection of that credo you grew up with, that all people are free—

LD: —are equal.

DS: —are equal. That's an important difference, there—all people are equal. I certainly have known others to have rejected socialism because they felt its practitioners were imperfect. Did you ever feel

[that] you were able to separate between the behavior of individuals and your own beliefs; or did that have an impact on your own sense of yourself, your own being?

LD: I think at times it bothered me. At the period when my daughter was born, there was no question about it, it bothered me a great deal. Yet I knew most of the people and knew they were good people. I just thought they looked at things wrong. And I would let them know, I'd let them know how I felt about it. I criticized a great deal.

DS: You didn't drop out of the Party, though, then.

LD: Right.

DS: It was specifically a political [issue]—well, gender is politics, too, but it was a—

LD: No, it was a larger—

DS: —political issue.

LL: —political issue that did it.

DS: One of the other issues that comes up is: Given the experiences you've had, and the changes that you have gone through personally, but also the changing times, do you feel that your own vision of socialism, your own ideological vision has changed, in any fundamental way?

LD: I don't think that my vision has changed. I certainly know that it wasn't socialism in the Soviet Union or in East Germany or in Czechoslovakia or any of these countries. That was a big disappointment. I think that the Soviet Union calling itself socialist or communist or whatever during that whole period until Gorbachev caused more harm for socialist movements than anything could have. That was very disappointing. I've never regretted being in the Party. I feel that with all the turmoil, with all the problems, with all the crises, I think I became a better person for having had the experience of being in the Party. And I've never regretted it. I've never felt bitter. I laughed sometimes. We had very little furniture, Joe and I, and I was constantly saving to put a down payment on a living room couch. Every time I thought I had enough for a down payment, and that we could swing it, there was another fund drive, and that was the end of my couch. This went on for years [laughs]. We had some pretty rough times. I don't know how much I should go into.

DS: Just what you feel like. I am less interested in specific [potentially awkward] details, more interested in your evolving sense of self. What fascinates me, partly because I share some of that background, growing up in an atmosphere of socialism, of *Yiddishkeit*, [that] culture. Growing up in a political culture is a unique experience that few of our contemporaries, either your age contemporaries, or mine (maybe more of your age contemporaries than mine) shared. By the time I grew up, it was a much more unique sort of experience to grow up in a political culture, whether it was the left Jewish community or the old [left, like] the Coops in New York City [cooperative apartments in the Bronx owned and run by Party members], or something like that. It does create a unique perspective.
  One of the issues that I'm raising [is]: Being only forty, I can only guess what it will be like when I'm in my sixties, but I was really curious to know if you felt that age had brought with it any kind of change or sharpening, deepening, or reflective character to your sense of political identity?

LD: I don't know. I really don't know.

DS: Part of the problem [is, I realize], having talked with many older persons, [that] age is in some ways an artificial category. You are who you always were, and that's why I always hesitate a little in isolating it as a separate issue. One of the ways it comes up more conventionally in this society is through the issue of retirement. Now, would there be a time when you felt that you had "retired," whether it was from raising children, from working, or from—

LD: I did. I retired from working.

DS: —paid employment?

LD: Paid employment.

DS: When was that?

LD: Four years ago.

DS: At that point you were sixty—

LD: Seventy.

DS: Right, you had already turned seventy.

LD: At just about my seventieth birthday I said, "That's it, that's enough." I was still working for adult education, teaching classes at an assortment, a group, of senior centers, going from one to the other. I always had to remember, this is Monday, which one am I at? The same with the schools. I had been out of the school, maybe two, three years. I was still working for the Children's Museum, [which] had opened a satellite program at the Outpatient Clinic at Yale-New Haven Hospital. I had helped them set up that program, and I was working at it a couple of days a week, couple of mornings.

DS: And again, was this teaching craft?

LD: Yes. Right in the clinic itself. In the lobby, sort of.

DS: Essentially art therapy.

LD: Well, it was mainly—a mother would come with two or three children, and one was seeing a doctor. I would try to involve the other kids, to keep them from running around. And it was highly successful. It's still going on. I decided to leave that mainly when I learned that my sister Doris learned she had cancer, and I felt I wanted to be available when she needed me. I got a very good person to replace me in that job. I wouldn't have left them flat, 'cause I was too fond of them. And that's still going on. So, I stopped working for adult education and continued teaching the same classes at West River Senior center as a volunteer, plus doing other things sort of art-oriented there—posters, their calendar, that sort of thing.

DS: I was wondering: at that time, did your political involvement change in character, or time—

LD: You mean, at the time I retired?

DS: Yeah.

LD: No, no. At that time, I was doing whatever I could to help the New Haven Peace Center, and I was involved in New Jewish Agenda, and in Women's International League for Peace and Freedom. I don't think it changed anything. I just continued what I was doing.

DS: Was there more time? Were you working part time in those final [years]—

LD: Yes.

DS: Yes, so that you had some time—

LD: Yes, there was a transition, gradual [to] part time.

DS: Right, so the actual impact of quote-unquote "retirement" itself was—

LD: No, I felt I was busier after I finally retired than before.

DS: Oh, so there *was* maybe a stepped-up amount of time or intensity, then, in terms of your political involvement?

LD: Sort of. Today, I picked up the paper today and saw that it was the anniversary of Hiroshima, and I couldn't believe that I wasn't involved in doing something today. But I don't think there's anything going on. I don't think there are any meetings. I haven't heard of anything. We haven't had any mail or anything. Last year we had some Japanese staying with us here overnight, who were speaking in the city—last year or the year before. That was the second time that we had Japanese staying here. So this seems very strange to me, and I feel a little out of it. But I'm sure there's nothing going on.

DS: Which is very surprising, because it's such—

LD: It is very surprising.

DS: —an important day in the peace movement.

LD: Yeah. But I think that's where the peace movement is these days.

DS: Yeah, it's ironic that with *glasnost* and—

LD: Yeah.

DS: —and *perestroika*, the movement doesn't know quite how to react.

LD: Gorbachev knocked out the peace movement in the United States [laughs].

DS: We had alluded to it a little earlier, around the issue of gender, that the Party clearly had some problems in terms of [its] position, or at least in terms of [its] principled relationships with women in the Party. Do you feel that at any time [that] conflicts you may have had, of whatever nature, with other members of the Party, whether it was leadership or cadre, caused you to rethink your thoughts politically?

LD: I don't know that it changed my feeling about the Party. It changed my feeling about certain individuals in the Party. I really don't think it changed my thinking about the CP. I had never hesitated to criticize. I didn't feel that difference. If I had a disagreement with one individual, I just told them how I felt or what I felt. But I don't recall that it made a difference to me. The time I felt a difference about the Party itself was after the Khrushchev papers came out. And then I definitely felt that something had been drastically wrong. I felt that we had been lied to, and that bothered me a great deal, because I always had the feeling that if comrades were going to lie to each other, how could they be comrades?

DS: The feeling was that the American Party had knowledge of what was happening, and withheld it?

LD: I assume that, I don't know if I was correct or not, but I assumed it. And that's when I left.

DS: There's another question that I wanted to address, which is slightly different, and it has to do with the character of your relationships. Whether you were on good terms on some issues or bad terms on others, this was a group with whom you were very intimate, whose shared experiences were very intense and ongoing for a number of years. Did you ever feel in some way that it was like being in a family?

LD: Oh yes, very definitely, very definitely. There was a tremendous feeling of warmth, of taking care of each other—and we did. We really did. We could rely on almost everyone else we knew for help for anything. And it worked, it really worked. That period I mentioned [the late 1940s and early 1950s when the Party was hounded by the federal government] was very unusual. But I attribute it to fear, and I can understand fear. So that I felt hurt, but I didn't feel resentful about individuals. If you're scared, you're scared, you're not going to do something. And unfortunately we were put in that position, to be scared.

DS: Well, certainly the whole McCarthy period was a threat to not only people in the Party, but anyone with progressive ideas.

LD: Right, right.

DS: Ironically, suspicions that were generated unfortunately affected a lot of people on the left, as well, who now had to consider the possibility that comrades of theirs might have been informants.

LD: Yeah. There were people who'd see me coming and cross the street. It bothered me, and I felt sorry for them. And yet, on the other hand, this was after the arrests (the Smith Act arrests) at the same time; these people from the bakery, they weren't afraid. The first one who came to my house after Joe was arrested was the daughter of the bakery owner. She saw the paper early in the morning, and she said, "This is a pile of crap," she said. "He's never even been arrested for a motor vehicle violation." And she was the first to come to the house. Those who understood the politics got scared.

DS: When I raised the issue of the family-feeling of the Party, and I got a very affirmative response from you—

LD: Yes, there's no question about it.

DS: —and I wanted to pursue that a bit. The other side of that question is, When you left the Party, [were] there any feelings of separation or loss did you go through?

LD: I didn't have it as much as Joe did, because I was involved with the housing project where I was working, and working with people there, and that filled me with a lot of the same type of feeling for people that I had had in the Party.

DS: And this was the tenants' organization?

LD: No, it was where I was starting to teach classes with some of the people in the housing project, and I was there, sometimes three, four nights a week. I worked nights, mainly, a lot there. Then I started work afternoons with school kids, also. But a lot of it was at night. So, I was very busy, so I didn't have that feeling of loss as much as Joe did. And we did still continue to see a lot of the people.

DS: So you didn't necessarily sever relationships with everyone in the Party.

LD: No, no.

DS: Are you still friends with them?

LD: Yes, yes. Some we are. Some severed relationships with us. But some we are still friendly with. We like them, feel warm towards them, always have.

DS: It's interesting. Some have spoken of the separation of the Party leaving a sense of loss that was never fully—

LD: —filled—

DS: —filled.

LD: Joe has that, I think, much more than I do.

DS: Why do you think that is? Does it have anything to do with the sense of engagement that—

LD: He did more, he was involved more. Physically, he was involved more than I. And in the meantime I really got very involved with this new career of mine, and I was getting, as I said, a lot of reward and a lot of satisfaction from it, so I didn't feel the loss. At the same time, I also didn't feel the anger that a lot of other people had, the resentment.

DS: Do you have a sense why that was, why you didn't feel that [way]?

LD: Because I still feel that I got a great deal out of the Party. I learned things that I don't think I would have learned elsewhere, including the continuation of the feeling that all people are equal and that we should work to help other people. If nothing else, we learned how to run a meeting.

DS: Organizational skills are no small accomplishment.

LD: Absolutely. And we had some wonderful relationships. So, I was never sorry.

DS: I want to ask you a question [but] I'm not sure how to frame it. Do you feel in any way that the fact that the Party or members of the Party didn't have as principled a set of relationships with women might have had anything to do with your feeling less of a sense of separation, the fact that there was maybe a distance that was created by some of the alienating things that happened?

LD: No, no, I don't think so at all. I'm not sure how much I was aware—that's wrong, I was aware of male chauvinism. But I didn't feel it as a Party policy. I felt it was strictly individuals. And if I had something to say to them, I said it. I criticized them. No, I don't think that had anything to do with it. I don't think so. I don't recall, but I don't think so. I just used to tell them they were a bunch of male chauvinist pigs.

DS: Now another thing that comes up is [that], as you had explained, in a certain sense it was serendipity that brought you in touch with a woman who drew out the creative side of you and made [for you] a late life career [referring to her work as arts-and-crafts teacher, which she began in her early fifties].

LD: It lasted a long time. She'd moved into the area where we lived, and the way this came about [is]: I had enamel on copper. It was the only craft I knew. I had learned it at the Jewish center, as a matter of fact, when our kids were going there after school for swimming and stuff like that, and decided to sign up. Actually, I think I went at night. But I took a course. I signed up for ceramics and enamel. Didn't know what enamel was. And I took to it like a duck to water. I just loved it. The teacher realized that I was taking to it very well, and he lent me books and that sort of thing.

The social worker had moved into the area. She knew me slightly. A community council had formed in our area. We were very involved in it, as a matter of fact, [in the] PTA and neighborhood community [council]. They were trying to set up some adult education, and she suggested that I teach a class there. I thought she was crazy. I had never taught anything in my life. She convinced me to try it. Then it occurred to me that what little I knew was more than what the others knew, and to this day I'm proud of what I achieved there. Because I had this group of women meeting one night a week, and when I started working at the housing project—I gave that up, I couldn't continue that, 'cause I was working at night there. [I] had a full time bookkeeping job.

DS: Oh, you still had the—

LD: I had a full time bookkeeping job [laughs].

DS: Were you politically [active]? Well, you were active in the housing [project], so you were, you had quite a [schedule]—

LD: And two kids.

DS: And two kids.

LD: So, I started to teach that class, and when I left it, I left them able to handle it themselves, except to call me occasionally if they needed materials, or if they had any specific questions. So I think that was a really great accomplishment. I felt very good about that. And when I started at the housing project, it was one night a week, I think it was one night a week, with a group of women, with enamel and copper. It was supposed to be for six or eight weeks, and at the end of that period they wouldn't hear of my leaving. So Edith, the social worker, had a conference with me and said, if you could only teach something else. So I went to the library and went through a million books, took some books out, figured out things I could do, improvising so it wouldn't cost much. And I started to teach other things.

I was doing workshops for students from Yale and from Southern Connecticut State [University] on how to work with inner-city kids. Plus various crafts. Edith was the director of adult activities, which took in a prekindergarten nursery. I did workshops for the teachers of the nursery.

This wasn't immediate, but it evolved. I taught them not only what to do with kids in the pre-kindergarten school there, but things they could teach the mothers to do at home with the kids, with stuff laying around the house—boxes, cans, scraps. And at the same time I was working with this group of women who gradually started to bring their daughters. If anything came up, if they were late in anything, the next day I met with the social worker, 'cause I didn't try to be a social worker, and I didn't try to work out their problems. We also started—once a month we'd either go out for pizza or we'd bring food there. I'd bring a *lokshen kugel* [noodle pudding], and we'd have coffee and stuff and just talk, instead of having a class.

And then the director of the youth program asked me if I would draw up a program for the kids—youth, actually, young teenagers. So I drew up a program and presented it him, and he was very excited and very pleased. But he offered me less per hour than I was making, and I refused. But I had—what's the word—tempted him with the program, 'cause I'd really lined up a good program. So I ended up working with the director—the woman who ran the senior group of women, and the young mothers group, through all the kids ages, and nursery school. I was working the whole gamut, the whole thing. By this time, I guess I gave up my bookkeeping job. And that place was my home away from home.

DS: So, in a sense, as you said, to a certain extent, you were able to find a form of engagement—

LD: —right—

DS: —social, cultural engagement—

LD: —exactly—

DS: —[that] made that transition smoother.

LD: Right. I was still, in a sense, doing political work.

DS: So, then, you really did see a connection, in some sense.

LD: I don't know if I saw it then. But it felt very good working with people and very, very gratifying.

DS: Looking back on it now, would you say there was some connection [between] what the Party was about in terms of its involvement in the community and finding various modes of community outreach [including] this work?

LD: Right. I think so. I felt it was. I don't know if I realized it then. I know I realized it afterward, that I was continuing what I had been doing, in a sense. In fact, I felt I was doing more than I had done previously, because I knew I could see that I was affecting their lives, where I never felt that before. Here, I knew. I'd come there, and I'd sit down on the steps of the administration building. Kids would come over and sit down and start telling me who was sick and who had a baby, and all. I knew everything, and the kids all knew me. It was a wonderful period in my life.

Then when that ended—as I say, it was a three-year pilot program, it was from the National Mental Health something Commission. The man who was the director of the youth program said [that] wherever he goes, I'm going {laughs]. He went into the school system, and that's when I started in the school system, the after-school program. Interestingly enough, the director of this pilot program was a woman. She was interviewing all of us, and I was petrified. What am I going to tell her? And Edith said to me, "Just tell her the truth." She was determined to get jobs for us. She was writing this down: name, marital status, kids, school, education. I said "commercial high school." She said, "And—?" She says, "Lillian, now c'mon, where else did you go to school?" I said, "Well, I did take one craft course at Southern, but I realized it was mainly [for] teachers who needed six-year certificates or something, and I knew so much more than they that that was it."

Incidently, the teacher I had there at Southern sent me students to work with. She felt I was very good. From the housing project we had a—it's near Wooster Square Park, which is a small park, and we had an exhibit in the park. We had tables. I don't remember how many tables, but I remember we had three hundred feet of clothesline, with stuff hanging on it. I had exhibits from all ages, plus I had—with some of the kids I had been working with after school I wanted a theme. What should we call it? I always had a lot of discussions with the kids. I never went into a project without discussing it with them—also teaching them words.

DS: Oh, vocabulary building.

LD: I had all the kids designing something. We were going to have a cover on the program. I did screen printing with the kids. One of the kids drew a bird, [a] very impressionistic sort of bird, and she said "art is fun." And that became the cover. Also, we did posters with the same thing. It was wonderful. All the schools in the area, including a parochial school that was there, had the posters. Stores put posters in. And when we had this program in the park—there were four corners with entryways into the park (it was just a block, a small block). I had kids with guestbooks [at each entryway]. It worked out beautifully.

DS: It sounds like there were a lot of applications of your organizing skills—

LD: Right, right.

DS: So, there's a real continuity.

LD: Right. So then from there [to] the interview with this woman. She says, "What are you talking about?" something like that. "With all this stuff you've done, how did you learn all this stuff? Where did you learn it?" I said I kept a week ahead of everybody [laugh]. Because what happened. The kids would do something, and I'd get very excited about something or other, and I'd go upstairs and show it to Jane (the office was up on the third floor [and] we were in the basement). So they were always going up and showing her things. Before this exhibit, almost a year before, some of the women I was working with were very proud of some of the things they had made. We were making lamps out of whiskey bottles and wine bottles, among other things. And they wanted to show it.

So gradually in talking I said, "Let's have an exhibit." And that really grew. We had an exhibit on three floors of the building—two floors of the building, in the basement, and on the main floor where there was big hall. We had speakers. We had someone from each group explaining how they made what was on display. It was fantastic. They all talked about me, and I was ready to go through the floor. I was called a genius. I felt terrible because [my daughter] Joanie wasn't there that night. But Joe was, and [my son] Carl, I guess, but he was small. But Joanie was involved with—it was on a Friday night and she was involved with a small political discussion group, and she didn't want to miss it, and I didn't want her to, but I was sorry she hadn't been there. Anyway, so that was really something. But then, that final thing was the one in the park. After that I started to work in the school system, and wherever I worked they assumed that I had several art degrees and probably a social work degree as well [laughs].

DS: And what you had was a degree in political experience.

LD: And I just never told them. Edith was the only one who actually knew my background. It was a wonderful experience. Then I worked in a number of inner-city schools and I got the kids really proud of their work. I always, always displayed everyone's work. I never said that one person was better in art than anyone else, and I wouldn't allow them to go into competitions with any of our work, anything that they did with me. I was opposed to competition. I wanted them relaxed, and they were. And what happened also was that gradually, in addition to the regular kids I started, in two schools, [working] with emotionally disturbed kids. They gave me the worst problem kids in the school. And the teachers said they felt a difference in the kids. So, I had a wonderful career, it was very good. I was very lucky. I was very, very lucky. Because, to be able to do something that you like, and that's rewarding—how many people have that opportunity?

DS: I was curious if you might have felt that since you didn't have formal education beyond high school, and yet nevertheless went into, later in life, sort of a second career that was a very rewarding one—

LD: Third.

DS: —actually, third career, excuse me [laughs], that perhaps the growth and experience, just the organizing experience, dealing with people, you got in the Party, do you think that made a crucial difference?

LD: I think it made a difference. I think it made a difference. I felt that I had learned a lot in the Party. I learned how to study, I think. I don't know where else I would have learned it. I had one experience when that program was ending. There was a principal who came to see me, principal of the school. He was the principal of the first community school in New Haven. I had some slides that he wanted to see, of the program on the green there, and I showed it to him. He pleaded with me to go to this school and get a degree. He said, "I don't have to tell you"—something to this effect—"I don't have to tell you how many teachers I've worked with." He had a big school, and he'd been in other schools. He said, "What you've got in your small finger all of them put together don't have." And I said, "I can't go to college. I've got to work. I want my kids to go to college. That's more important at this point. He said, "Go and get that *farshtunkene* piece of paper." Because, it hampered me, not only in getting other jobs, but salary-wise. I was paid peanuts. I had no Social Security deductions. I wasn't on any pension plans. They got away with murder with what they paid me. But I loved what I was doing.

Actually, what happened also toward the end, I got a call through Gerry Tirozzi, [the present] state commissioner of education—I think he was a principal in New Haven at that time. Anyway, they were setting up an alternate—it was an overflow school, actually, so they were renting rooms at various places. He was meeting with the man who was going to be the director, and they both felt they ought to have an art program. They both told me this, after he called and made an appointment for me to come up.

I had worked in several schools by that time, Winchester School particularly. Gerry said, "I know a woman who would be marvelous with these kids." This other man who was going to be the director said, "I know a woman. I worked with her once in a summer program at Winchester. She was great with the kids." Both together, they looked—they said they looked at each other. Both said, "Lillian Dimow." So they called me, and it was all set up for me to start, when I got a call from a friend, asking me to take a bookkeeping job in her program. And at that point I decided the salary was pretty good, I'm going to earn some money for a change, and get some Social Security. And I called Gerry, and I told him—I left word, he called me back and I told him who I was, and he understood. I stayed in that program just about nine months, and there was so much dirty politics involved in it. This friend of mine who was the director, they were cutting her to pieces, and it bothered me terribly, and I decided to quit. I called Gerry's office and I left word that I was available, in case he knew of anything. He was superintendent of schools in New Haven at that time, that's what it was, 'cause I met him down at the Board of Education. He called me back, and he said, "When do you want to start?" I said, "On what?" He said, "The job I told you about. We didn't hire anybody else. It's still waiting for you."

DS: And that was the—

LD: That was an overflow. They didn't have room for the kids. Actually, I can't remember how long I was in that program, but we were in three different places. One was a wonderful school building, an old school building. Then out of that they started—and this was the last school job I had—they started what they called an alternate middle school. It was the worst problem kids in all the seventh and eighth grades in the city of New Haven. We had a total of about sixty kids. I *loved* it. I absolutely loved working with those kids. I had wonderful experiences with them. And there were days when I was the only white person in the program. It wouldn't occur to me until I was on my way home. That sort of thing. It was marvelous, just marvelous, [I] really loved it. I didn't push the kids—I never did anyway. You don't want to do the work, stay at the back, and do what you want, but you have to behave. If you disturb the class, out. I had a very good relationship with the kids. At Winchester School, where I was for some years, I had some teen-age black kids helping me. I trained them to be group leaders for after-school work, and I pushed them to go to college, become teachers, anything. And I still bump into some of these kids. Wonderful. Anyway, so I was very lucky.

DS: Now, you're still politically active today?

LD: New Jewish Agenda, to a certain extent, Women's International League for Peace and Freedom, to a certain extent, but not terribly involved.

DS: And, of course, still teaching craft.

LD: We have a series periodically, in fact. Marilyn [Braginsky, director of the West River Senior Center in New Haven, the first senior center where Lil had taught enamel-on-copper classes] just spoke to me the other day about setting one up again for the fall, so I'll probably do that. Of course we don't know if we're going to have that center at the end of this month [some senior centers and branch libraries in New Haven were being closed as cost-cutting measures; West River remained open]. So I don't know what's going to be. But anyway, so that's it.

DS: Now, you actually did have an opportunity, though, in recent years, at least to attend university courses.

LD: I went to an Elderhostel this summer, early this summer, but that's all. A good part of it was, I was scared, because my own education was so lacking in background that I would need to go to college, that it scared me. I don't know if they would take life experience as credit. And I decided, oh, it's enough. So I don't have a degree. My son gave me a degree once—a doctorate. I can't remember what discipline it was in. It was during the crazy sixties. He knew some kids at Yale. I don't know how they got a hold of it.

DS: It was like a facsimile of the Yale doctorate?

LD: It was no facsimile.

DS: Really.

LD: They printed our names. He got a doctorate for Joe and doctorate for me. It's someplace up in the attic.

DS: Of course, you also have over the years been involved in the World Fellowship—Association, is it? [WF hosts a series of summer institutes in New Hampshire where political and social issues are discussed with specialists on specific subjects.]

LD: It's a place, not an association. It's just World Fellowship. It had been World Fellowship of Faiths, I believe, to begin with.

DS: But essentially what is it—like a conference site and camp?

LD: Yes.

DS: How long have you been involved with that?

LD: Well, I'm not involved, except to go. I've never been on the board or anything. I really don't want to be. But Joe has been very active in that. We've been going there every summer for, let's see, well over twenty years.

DS: What is the age range? Are there mostly older or younger people? Is it a mix?

LD: Very mixed, very mixed. There are three or four generations, actually. The age can be anywhere from infants to in the eighties. It's very good, it's a wonderful place, and I like it very, very much. But I haven't been involved as such. The involvement is to be on the board and I really haven't been asked if I want to run for the board, and I never wanted to.

DS: You have been involved in the discussions on current issues that are raised?

LD: If I go, yeah. I don't always go to the discussions, but I just like going there and meeting people, wonderful people. We always meet very nice people.

DS: People who share a general political outlook, do you think?

LD: To a great extent, but not necessarily.

DS: You mean, not necessarily a specific political outlook—

LD: Right.

DS: —but at least a general progressive outlook.

LD: Yeah, progressive. Yes, [those] interested in people, interested in peace, interested in the world, I'd say. Actually, I worked for the previous directors, who lived in New Haven, and had their office in New Haven over the whole winter season, when they were planning and all, and I worked for them.

DS: What kinds of things did you do?

LD: Typing, cutting stencils—I worked in the office. I knew them very well before I worked for them. But I'll give you an example of male [chauvinism]—horrible. I was leaving, I don't remember why, I think I must have gotten another job (this was part time) and I suggested someone else for that job. Her husband said, "Are you sure she's capable of doing it?"

DS: Just out of the blue?

LD: Well, I been criticizing him for a long time for being a male chauvinist, and that was—he learned, he learned a lot. I don't criticize him anymore. He says I still do, but I don't.

DS: See, I think that in some ways, you're more than modest about the ways in which you've been able to impart your vision and experience to others, who have benefitted from it. I remember once before [that is, in a previous conversation] your talking about an experience you had when you sat in on a women's studies class. I was wondering if you might want to speak to that, about the ways in which the younger students benefitted from a whole world that was not even open to them through their instructor until you participated.

LD: Well, I don't think I was the only one. There were other older women there, too. And we were all, to a certain extent, critical of her.

DS: Of the instructor?

LD: Of the instructor. Well, we felt she wasn't a good teacher. She had tremendous knowledge, there was no question about that, but I felt she was a very poor teacher, and the other older women also felt that. She used films a lot, which was fine, they were very good films, but we never discussed them. She'd give us a reading assignment, and we'd get in the next session and she'd read that assignment out loud, and we'd never discuss it. Well, that's very poor teaching. But I'd speak up. I would criticize her, but to her, not in front of the class. But the other older women all felt the same way about her. I'd bring materials into class.

DS: Was this at—where?

LD: It was at Southern.

DS: Southern Connecticut State University?

LD: Yeah. Joe was taking some course there—one, I guess, at the time that I went—and then we were going to take more but somehow or other we couldn't coordinate it. Since I don't drive, it became a hassle. But we took courses at the senior center.

DS: Course offered by the University—

LD: By South Central Community College. We had two marvelous semesters of art history—that's the first time I had studied art history [laughs]. And I brought materials in every week. Joe's brother asked me what I was doing there. He said, "What do you do there?" I said, "I show off." But I had a lot of materials. In fact, I gave the instructor a lot of slides that I had no use for at all anymore. And we had a very good anthropology, cultural anthropology, course. And Joe also took psychology, I think. I didn't take that, and I was sorry I hadn't. We're slated to have something else this fall, and I can't remember what, but also, as I say, we don't know whether we're going to have that center. But some of the other centers have classes also.

DS: I was wondering—you had mentioned this in earlier conversations, but what was the specific contribution you made to the women studies class, to the younger students? Did you make a presentation?

LD: Actually, I didn't. Because I wasn't taking it for credit, I didn't feel like doing it. But I know I brought some material on Emma Goldman and gave it to one or two of the younger women who were going to do papers on her. I don't know, I can't remember specifically. I was very unimpressed with the class, mainly [with] the teacher.

DS: Were you able to interact with any of the younger students, though?

LD: A couple of them who were also young mothers and working, and having problems, and looking for scholarships, and stuff of that sort. So some, but not an awful lot I don't think.

DS: Now [as] we wrap things up here I'll ask the question I asked in the beginning and see if you have anything different to say about it, and that is: Do you feel now that, if somebody asked you identify yourself, describe something about yourself, what do you think you initial response would be?

LD: Well, I think I would say I was a retired art teacher, for one thing. That was what I did the longest and I think was the most important of all my work. I usually say I'm a retired art teacher. I don't know—voice the question again.

DS: Well, in terms of your personal beliefs, if somebody asked you what you felt was the most important thing that you wanted to be identified with, your primary identity.

LD: Still, *alle mentshen zaynen glaykh,* that all people are equal, and that it would be nice if the world were a better place where all people *could* be equal.

DS: So, would it be safe to say that your overarching sense of yourself is rooted in some fundamental way in your political upbringing?

LD: Oh, I think definitely, I think definitely.

DS: And would you say your sense of commitment to socialism is different?

LD: No, not really.

Chapter Eight

I've Always Had a More Individualistic Approach to Things

[First interview with Jacob ("Jake") Goldring, conducted at his home in Bridgeport, Connecticut, on June 22, 1990]

DAVID SHULDINER: Jake, what I'd like to do to begin this interview is to ask you point blank: In your lifetime, what would you consider to be the one identity that you'd most like to be associated with? If somebody asked you, "Who are you?" what do you think would be the thing you'd most want to be remembered for?

JACOB GOLDRING: Well, that's pretty hard to pin down, but I would think that it's the general overall feeling and activity that I've devoted to social issues, on many different levels, and many different aspects.

DS: And by social, would you specifically mean social activism?

JG: Social activism, absolutely.

DS: So, is it safe to say, then, that you might consider your political identity to be—not the only, but perhaps the most important?

JG: Well, my political identity was certainly a very important part of that. At certain times, it *was* the most important. Certainly, in the last two or three decades, it has not been the most important, although it has played a role. I don't know how further to define that, but in the thirties, forties, and fifties, it certainly predominated my activity, and gave it a certain kind of meaning for that period of time, and a perspective that my other activity fitted into.

DS: I assume now that you're speaking of your political identity as synonymous with your activities, the activities that dominated your life at an earlier period, let's say, when you were predominantly a political activist?

JG: That's correct, when I was not only a member of the Communist Party, but I was [also] the chairman of an area of the Communist Party.

DS: That was in Bridgeport?

JG: Well, I was in Bridgeport—Fairfield County. I was also a treasurer of the Communist Party, and yet I was also engaged in activities of a broader nature that the Communist Party was an integral part of. For example, I've always been interested in housing. As chairman, in the thirties, of the Communist Party of Stamford, I was involved in a coalition of a lot of community people interested in trying to procure affordable housing for people. People accepted me, taking into consideration my political views, and were willing to work with me as part of that coalition. For example, I was able to work even with the president of an important corporation in that area, again, as long as we both agreed in the direction we were moving in trying to get housing into the Stamford area. So, my political activity was the focus of all of this other activity.

DS: Let's look at that for a minute. One of the other things I'm exploring is the ways in which that form of identification first appeared and developed. More specifically, I'd like you to talk a little about where your political outlook [might have come] from. Did it come from, initially, family or co-workers?

JG: I think my political outlook came partly from those sources, but [it] also [comes] from the problems I was confronted with when I began to grow up and mature. For example, as a kid of thirteen, during the summers I went to work on the tobacco plantations around Hartford. I lived in Hartford.

DS: Were you born in Hartford?

JG: No, but I grew up in Hartford. I went to school in Hartford. I actually was born in Springfield [Massachusetts]. I can recall at the age of thirteen, participating in a strike, along with young people like myself—[age] fourteen, fifteen—on the tobacco plantations. I graduated high school in 1932 [from] Weaver High, in Hartford, with no jobs available of any kind, not the McDonald's type or any kind of job. So, I would say that those factors influenced my political orientation, along with my family. My father was a socialist, a member of the Workman's Circle, and I would say certainly that there was some family influence.

DS: Did your father talk about his political activities with you, try to influence you in any way?

JG: He didn't try to influence me, but I knew. He made it clear that he was a man who supported, for example Norman Thomas for president [on the Socialist Party ticket], that kind of thing. So that his political views became known to me, and they were a factor. My father was also a trade unionist, a member of the Bakers and Confectionery Workers of America. He worked in a number of the Jewish bakeries around Hartford. Hartford at that time had a substantial Jewish population. I took part in picket lines with my father, when he was on strike. So, those influences definitely were a factor in my development.

DS: Now, as to the ethnic factor, were you taught or aware of Jewish traditions being imparted to you in the home, in the family?

JG: Yes, to a certain extent. My family sent me to Hebrew school. I was *bar mitzvahed*, as a thirteen-year-old would. A little of Jewish history was taught to me. But I would say that I never became imbued with that background in any deep manner. I would say that in that sense, I would differ from [Joe] Dimow, who has more of a feeling for Jewish tradition and history than I do.

DS: Did your parents, for example, send you to a Workman's Circle school?

JG: No, they didn't.

DS: I was wondering if there actually was one in Hartford.

JG: I don't recall. There was a Workman's Circle center, in the north end of Hartford, on Main Street. I was there many times, but they never sent me to a school as such. But in Springfield, I had gone to Hebrew school for several years. I had that much background.

DS: Now, what has been your principal wage-earning trade?

JG: I would say that my principal wage-earning trade has been as a carpenter and a contractor. Early in life, in high school, I showed a great deal of dexterity and ability to work with wood—manual training. And while I did very little in that direction for a number of years while I became a political activist and a full-time organizer for the Party, later, in the the late forties, I began to move in that direction, and I again became interested in carpentry. I started working in the field and became what I feel is a competent carpenter and from that developed into a small-time contractor. Then out of that grew an interest in a kind of concept that I had, which became my principal occupation in the last decade or so [before] I retired from the construction field. And that is, people began to ask me, as I developed a sense of what a house consists of, and how it's made, created— people began to ask me in the 1950s: "We're going to buy a house, how about looking at it for me? Not to appraise it, but to tell me what it needs, what's wrong with it." Out of that, I developed a home inspection business, in which I would write up a technical report of a house, that is, its structural integrity, what this house might need in the coming period of time. This was a time also when a guy like Ralph Nader was awakening in the American public a deep sense of wanting to know what they're getting. So that this began to grow very slowly, along with my contracting, and one supplemented the other. I might look at a house for somebody, and they would say, "Gee, we want to put on an addition, will you do it?" So [it] served that purpose.

But eventually this grew to the point where I couldn't do both. I tried to have both businesses continue by having someone run the contracting, but it [didn't] work out. So I began to devote all my time to the inspection business and counseling people on housing.

And eventually I was able to develop a staff and inspectors, and that came into full bloom. But my construction has always been at the center of that overall approach to housing and the structural integrity of housing. So, that's what I retired from—an inspection business.

DS: You also were a carpenter. Did you "retire" from carpentry per se—or do you describe it that way—at a certain period?

JG: Well, I never really retired from it. I did odds and ends. I did a lot of things around this house. I designed this house to fit the lot— exactly what I needed. It was also my place of business during that time—the inspection business, because I had outgrown the other house [I'd lived in] and I thought that that business served best if worked from home. So I've always done some carpentry. I have a love [for it], a feeling that you create something. Say you put on an addition or you build a house, you can say, "Well, there it is, I did it." There's a sense of having accomplished something, and it's tangible, it's right in front of you. So I've always been able to do a little bit of that, not necessarily for any financial gain, but just to satisfy my own desire to do things.

DS: Would you say, then, that a very important part of [the] expression of your identity is the craft, of carpentry?

JG: Well, *now* it isn't, but certainly for a number of years it was. Many people had heard of what I was doing, my work, and they wanted me. I was well recommended to them, so they would want me to do work for them. So, for many years it certainly was the most important thing that I was doing, in many ways. And [it] led to the stage of becoming a contractor, and still performing that work—not just one that ran a job, but actually, physically, [doing] some of the work— and then eventually getting into inspections.

DS: And so you continue to do some consultation around contracting as well as home inspection?

JAKE. Yes. For example, in my retirement (if this is what you would like to hear), two or three years ago, I did [consulting for] an outfit in Bridgeport that administers several million dollars of state funds

in social work that administers a whole number of programs, such
as detoxification—you know, alcohol, drugs, counseling. [They]
owned seven or eight buildings in town where they do this work or
where some people lived. [They] asked me to look at a number of
[them]. They had heard of me, [of] my consulting work, [and] asked
me [to look] at a number of buildings for them: Which had the
greatest potential, say, as a halfway house? They were interested in
acquiring it. I was able to pick out what I felt was the best building
for them. Then I was able to get them an architect, 'cause they had
difficulty finding one who was able to draw plans [for] gutting the
building [and] redoing it inside for their purposes. They had to get
three bids, [and] I [was] able to find them an outfit that I had heard
of, doing alterations in town. That outfit gave them a bid that turned
out to be the lowest. Then from there, they asked me to supervise
the work and to decide how much money to release weekly to the
outfit, so that they would not overpay as they went along. I was
able to spend six or eight months getting that project resolved for
them. And they were very delighted and very happy with that work.
It turned out [that] the results, from what I believe and what they've
told me, were excellent. So they want me to go on with another
project. Well, I felt that I should—I'm in retirement. I was willing to
do some, but I just didn't want to become totally engaged.

DS: What's fascinating to me, Jake, is that your remarks were spurred
by [the question] of your identity and activities [that reflect it]. You
speak of retirement, and yet you're describing a tremendous amount
of activity related directly to what has been your main wage-earning
occupation. Let me ask you, then, at what point, what year, you
would use the term "retirement" in relationship to your activities?

JG: I decided in the early eighties that I had inspected so many
homes—I estimate that I have been inside at least seven or eight
thousand homes in Connecticut, which really means spending
several hours at the house, writing up a technical report, testing
everything in the house I could. As a matter of fact, I even secured,
after extensive study and examinations, including [an] oral [exam],
a termite license, so that I could say that I'm competent to find
termites, or not find termites, as well as anybody else in the state.
But I decided that after inspecting at least seven or eight thousand
homes (I *myself* had) that I should pull out, that I'd had it. I don't

know if you want to call it burnout. I was about sixty-seven then, and since any inspection entails climbing up on a roof, you can't inspect it [without doing so], and a roof is an integral part of a house; sooner or later I'm gonna get hurt at that age. So, in [19]82 I sold the business, and that in a sense marked my formal retirement—in mid [19]82. That would be eight years ago on July first.

DS: Now, we'll focus a little later on in our conversation about what has principally occupied you during your retirement [from wage earning]. But what I'd like to do [now] is look at your wage-earning work, that is, your work as a carpenter, and the sense of identity you had surrounding that, and your political work in the Party or in other venues. I'd like to get a sense of how those two elements interacted. One thing I'd like to ask you is, Were you ever involved in any trade union activity in your profession, in carpentry?

JG: No. I was inv¡olved in trade union work when I worked in shops that had unions. This was in a period prior to World War II and after, for a while, like General Electric in Bridgeport. I was involved with the U.E. [United Electrical and Machine Workers Union]

DS: What job did you have?

JG: At General Electric I had several jobs. One of them was, I worked on the assembly line in the home-laundry section making laundry machines. And I was a union steward, and very active in the United Electrical Union, and that was one of the biggest locals in the state of Connecticut. During the war—I had entered G.E. just before [WWII]—well, in [19]41 or [19]42 [it was] one of the biggest locals, about four or five thousand members, with a very strong Communist Party group in the shop.

DS: Now, did you join the Party before you came to work at G.E.?

JG: Yes, I was a member of the Party, and I'd been an organizer for the Party, prior to my going into G.E. I joined the Communist Party in 1936.

DS: What were the circumstances surrounding that; what motivated you to join at that time?

JG: In 1934, after being out of school for two years and finally doing some odd jobs, including working in the forests of Connecticut in the Civilian Conservation Corp—

DS: Oh, so you were involved in the CCC.

JG: —yeah, I was involved in the CCC in several places in the state and developed a feeling for woods and trees. That's why you see at this house [Jake's home] where it is right now, all surrounded by trees, and having a certain woodsy kind of location. Anyway, in [19]34, I entered the University of Connecticut, at Storrs. I became very involved in the student movement.

DS: What were you studying there?

JG: Well, I didn't know what I wanted to study there, but I seemed to have an ability in math, and gradually I became a math major. So that [in a] sense evolved on its own. Finally, in four years, in [19]38, [I] graduated with a bachelor in science with my major in math and my minor in social sciences. I took a lot of history, in addition to my math courses: history, sociology, some psychology, that kind of thing.

DS: Did you have any particular career goal in mind at that time?

JG: No, but I felt that at least I was equipped to teach math when I got out of school. I never did use it directly, but certainly in my work in the construction field, in an overall sense my training was very useful.

DS: But you hadn't thought of being a carpenter at that particular time?

JG: No, I had not. I became so absorbed in the growing Congress of Industrial Organizations—the CIO—while I was at school. It had come into being, in [19]35, [19]36.

DS: Let's discuss that. You were involved in the student movement. Was it as a student that you were exposed to the work of the CIO? And then what was your subsequent relationship with the CIO?

JG: Well, yes, as a student I became interested in the trade union movement. I was in Hartford regularly while at Storrs [at the university], and I saw workers were organizing, were developing trade unions, in places where they had never existed before. John L. Lewis [first president of the CIO] came along in [19]35, [and] brought all of this together and set into motion this vast trade union movement. I felt, more and more, at Storrs, that this is what I would like to become a part of.

DS: Were you working to support yourself at the time you were in school?

JG: Yes, I was. I worked weekends in Hartford. I had a job all through school working for H. P. Kopplemann, a newspaper distributor in the Hartford area, working Saturday nights, which gave me enough money to just about feed me during the school week. I worked on the student part of the WPA at Storrs, after school.

DS: What kind of projects did the WPA have for students?

JG: Well, they had any number of projects there. Some of them were physical, clearing land, let's say, for an athletic field; others were part of various academic projects going on. There were both, under the National Youth Administration, the equivalent of the WPA. So there were a number of possibilities where a student could supplement his income in order to continue in school.

DS: Your joining the CCC, how did that fit in—what time were you—

JG: Well, I was in the CCC in [19]33 into [19]34, partly.

DS: Did you take time off from your studies then?

JG: No, I had not started. There was a two-year gap. I graduated high school in [19]32, and I didn't get into Storrs until [19]34. So there was that gap. That's when I was in the CCC. My family put away the twenty-five dollars a month that I received and with that— a hundred plus—I was able to enter Storrs. The matriculation fee then was seventy five dollars a year. There were no other fees. Otherwise, I would have not been able to go. We were that poor.

DS: So the WPA, in a sense, was responsible for providing work that enabled you to save up to get to school.

JG: To stay in school—actually to eat, to have a room, [and] to buy some books. My family really was not able to give me the financial support. Then working summers on various jobs, and that way I was able to get through school.

DS: Let's talk more about student politics.

JG: Sure. We were able to develop a fairly substantial student movement at Storrs, and I emerged, I guess, as a leader of it. We became a part of the American Student Union, nationally. We had what is called a Social Problems Club at Storrs.And there were several faculty people that were interested in what we were doing. We brought speakers down, we held discussions, we held forums, that kind of thing. And we participated in whatever student movements there were elsewhere. I would say there were as many as forty or fifty students that were interested in that kind of thing, out of a very small student body. Storrs then only had maybe between a thousand and twelve hundred full time students. So it was a very small school, to the point where you got to know just about everybody on campus. You had that intimacy that is missing, I suppose, now. It was a very valuable four years in the sense of not only training me as an organizer, a youth organizer, but also developing my interests in many different things going on, and then also training me academically to fit into various things that I did later. I never directly used my math or other things, but it awakened in me a vast interest and ability to fit into a whole number of situations later. So it was an invaluable kind of period for me.

DS: Now, when you graduated from the university, did you have at that point a conception of where you wanted to devote your energies?

JG: Oh, yes. When I graduated, there was an organization in the state of Connecticut that John L. Lewis called Labor's Nonpartisan League. This was a political offshoot of the labor movement, an effort to get the labor movement into politics. It consisted of [a] state organization, organizations in various congressional districts, and largely trade unionists that would get their locals involved in the political campaigns. [It was] not aligned with any political party, that's where its name arose: Labor's Nonpartisan League. I was asked by some of the officers if I would be interested in a job with Labor's Nonpartisan League.

DS: This was what year?

JG: This was 1938, and I said yes. That job was [in] Fairfield County, right here. And so I came down [to] this area, into the Norwalk area, found a room, and began to work with Labor's Nonpartisan League, forming chapters of it, meeting with them. And a very important election campaign was evolving then for the gubernatorial campaign in the fall. At that time you had, as you do now (there are many parallels), Jasper McLeavy, who was the mayor of Bridgeport, a socialist, running for governor; Ray Baldwin, a lawyer, running for the Republican Party; and Wilbur Cross, professor of Shakespeare, for [the Democratic Party].

DS: [This was] also a period of [the] stepping up of your political involvement in the left, in terms of the Party. When exactly did you join the Party?

JG: I joined the Party while I was a student at Storrs, in 1936.

DS: Now, what was it that drew you specifically to the Party?

JG: Well, my sister had joined the Communist Party. She had some influence, certainly, on me. But I also felt from what I could see and read that the Party was very much involved in furthering the trade union movement, in furthering the New Deal, in working indirectly for the reelection of Roosevelt. So that I felt that the Party was the most cohesive and the strongest organization I could see, in a political sense, that was moving in a direction that I was interested in. So that I joined the Party, although I never met with anybody or had any chapter or branch meetings to go to while I was at Storrs. There was no branch of the Party at Storrs. So I was just a member at large. But after I got out of Storrs, I became more and more involved in the Communist Party.

DS: Now, was it members of the Party that directed you towards joining [Labor's Nonpartisan League]?

JG: Well, yes. There were several Party people very much involved in the Nonpartisan League, and [they] suggested that that might be a place where I might fit in. So I must say that they certainly were the ones that encouraged me to move in that direction.

DS: Right. But, of course, you had already embraced the goals and the political line driving the Party, so it wouldn't have been at all out of the ordinary for you to take up this particular work.

JG: No. It certainly was a natural step in [my] development, absolutely.

DS: Now, this gets to a very important issue, the development of your sense of identity. So far, we've been talking about a natural evolution of your own sense of self. When did you see changes taking place, maybe a disparity between your self-identity and what was happening with you in the Party?

JG: It's very hard to say when. In many ways, I've always had a more individualistic approach to things, and my own views about things that didn't coincide with the Party's. I can't say that they were overwhelming, no, that would be misleading. But on many things, I felt that the Party tended to be—in approaching things, it approached from the "all, or nothing at all" view. It just seemed to go overboard, to get totally involved in something to the exclusion of everything else. And I disagreed. I've always had the view that trade union leaders, Party leaders, should be required, so far as one can, every five or ten years, to leave their position and go back to work to get a sense of reality. I've always felt that [was] missing somewhere, and that applies to me as well as to people that I was working with. On a number of things, I always—again not fundamentally—but I always voted either alone, [or at least] against a vast majority, on some issue I felt they were not approaching properly. But in general, I agreed with the overall postion of the Party. I don't want to misstate.

I did begin to become uneasy a bit with the [Hitler-Stalin] Nonaggression Pact in 1939, in the fall of [19]39. At that time I was at the Party national convention. I went to Chicago with a number of people from Connecticut, in late August of [19]39, when that very thing broke out—World War II, and the Soviet Union signed the Nonaggression Pact while that convention was in progress. The whole uncertainty, and the kind of flip-flop that I felt was going on —[party positions] didn't seem to quite make sense or explain what was happening. And it's coming from guys like Robert Miner or Earl Browder and others who led the Communist Party at that time. But I didn't make any break. I didn't disagree fundamentally. I was just uneasy. I certainly remained a devoted Party person during that period of what was called the "phony war," you know, before the actual invasion of the Lowlands took place, which was a year—a year or two later.

DS: A "phony war" because many people felt that it was—

JG: Well, it was a kind of stalemate. After Germany invaded Poland, and the Soviet Union came into Poland from the other side, and Poland was divided, as well as the Balkan States, and that became— it stopped, any military activity stopped.

DS: There was a perception that the United States wanted to see the Soviet Union fight, and possibly even fail, on its own.

JG: Well, there was the idea that we should try to drive Germany toward the Soviet Union, not the other way. So there was a lull, a period [where] nothing happened. And that period became known as the "phony war." Now, during that period the Party developed all kinds of theoretical ideas that, to me, were somehow not really in keeping with the situation. For example, after practically a decade in which Hitler had been in power, well, since [19]33, and the Party had developed the whole United Front Against Fascism, and the dangers of fascism, some people were writing theoretical articles that actually Britain is the main danger in the world, not Germany— our theoreticians like Robert Minor and others. Somehow, it just didn't jibe, what we had been doing all along and what made sense. Then everything became rectified, exactly, I think, forty nine years ago today, June 22, 1941, when the Soviet Union was invaded by Germany. Now, first they had come through into—the spring following the Nonaggression Pact—they had come in through Holland and Belgium, and into France, and [had] set up Vichy France [the occupation government]. And then again there was a lull, while they were gearing themselves for—June 22 [when they] invaded the Soviet Union.

DS: So, in a sense, history rectified what many in the Party felt was a mistake in terms of supporting the Nonaggression Pact.

JG: That is correct. Then, of course, [the Party] said, "Well, that bought them time." We began to rationalize—it made sense, you see. The Soviet Union had a better chance to prepare to defend itself.

DS: Which [implied that] the attack [from Germany] was inevitable.

JG: Yeah. So, this was the way in which we were able to justify that period, in looking back after[ward].

DS: This is important, too, in [that] there was sometimes a lot of struggle between your sense of yourself and your beliefs and principles and the sort of muddying of the waters through various historical twists and turns [and] the Party's responses to them. I would like to ask how long it was that you did, in fact, continue [with the Party], in spite of whatever doubts you may have had. How late did you continue with the Party?

JG: Well, I was a member of the Party until around 1960.

DS: So, you survived the McCarthy period.

JG: I was a Smith Act defendant, along with Joe [Dimow]. Before that, in the fifties, I had been away [for] a period, what we call "unavailable," working underground for the Party as a Party organizer. During that period, in the late forties and into the fifties, is when I went into carpentry. I used that "unavailability" period as a Party organizer on a part-time basis in order to develop a skill, and a trade, and that's what I wanted.

DS: What year did you first become a carpenter?

JG: Well, in 1949, the Party asked me—in Connecticut, right after the [19]48 arrests of the national leadership—in [19]49, the Party decided to place people under other names, in other locations, and get them out of political activity—what they called an "unavailable" period. I was against that and I voted against it. I felt that we were adopting a tactic and strategy that maybe was suitable in Tsarist Russia, but just didn't seem to have an application here. I felt we were just rigidly following what the Soviet Party had done in its early days. Nonetheless, when it was voted that we ought to do it, and I was asked, I did it. I went to work—I left the state, took on another name, [another] identity, and went to work in the construction field for the first time, in 1949, as a laborer on a housing project. And then from that I began to get into carpentry, which I felt I had a certain affinity for [which had] shown itself in high school. So, I began to move in that direction. Occasionally, I would come back to Connecticut, and by [19]54 I was back in Connecticut as a Party organizer while also working on construction, carpentry.

DS: Working full-time as a carpenter?

JG: Working full time as a carpenter, right.

DS: Now, during the years between—let's see, you graduated from the University of Connecticut in 193—

JG: [19]38.

DS: —[19]38 until 1949. During those years, how many of those years were you a full-time organizer for the Party?

JG: Well, there were three and a half years in which I was in the armed forces. I was in the Air Force in World War II, and during, certainly, those three and a half years, I was not in any political activity. During that period, the Party had no form of organization for members of the armed forces. Prior to that period, I worked for one or two years in shops, like General Electric, so that I was not a Party organizer while active in the Party. I'm trying to figure out exactly how—probably from [19]38 to [19]54—let's say, half or less than half [of that time] was I a full-time Party functionary.

DS: But it could have been at least forty to fifty percent of that time.

JG: Yes, that's correct.

DS: What I'm getting at here is, what work you were principally involved in, whether it was explicitly political or whether it was strictly wage-earning work?

JG: My wage earning was important for me to make a livelihood, but my whole purpose that made my wage earning fit into—you know, [gave] me some meaning—is that I was involved in political or trade-union work with it. So I've worked, not only at General Electric, I worked in the brass industry. We had a big brass shop in Bridgeport, Bridgeport Brass, which had about four thousand workers. I worked there for a while. I worked in several shops in Bridgeport, the longest being in General Electric. I entered the armed forces while I was at General [Electric].

DS: And, as you say, when you were at G.E., you were also active—

JG: Yes, I was very involved in the trade-union movement there, as I was [at] the Bridgeport Brass. I worked in a steel plant in Bridgeport for a while, trying to help organize a local there.

DS: Now, in your trade union activity at that time, were you under the advisement of the Party? Was your work as a trade-union organizer autonomous or was there a clear sense that what you were doing was a part of the overall Party program?

JG: Oh, there was a clear sense that it was an overall part of the Party program, absolutely. It isn't as though the Party directed me, but it's just that I felt that this was in integral part of my whole ideology and my whole outlook.

DS: I guess what I'm getting at, Jake, is that, as I'm sure you're aware [that], in terms of one's self identity, [there] are two ways of relating to that. One is simply [on the level of] trade union consciousness, in which the trade union movement was an end in itself. For you, I get the sense, what you're saying is that as a Party member the perspective on trade union activism was part of an overall project—

JG: Yes.

DS: —a component of what the left movement was all about.

JG: That's right. It was a part of an overall perspective, in that the immediate gains that you are able to achieve for workers fitted into the long-term idea, that you're trying to convince them that socialism is the solution for them.

DS: Your sense of identity during that whole period—from the thirties right into the early sixties—was dominated by your association with the Party. What I'd like to now do is to discuss as much as possible, and even as subjectively as you care to, what your feelings were, [about] your sense of self-identity during that critical period, and following that period, when you left the Party. First of all, what was the reason and what were your feelings at the time that you quit the Party?

JG: Well [hesitation], in the late fifties, going into 1960, thereabouts, the Party had already been split. There was a serious split in the Party in 1957. I guess the Party had been so battered, plus the Khrushchev revelations on Stalin in [19]56 that occurred while we were on trial for the Smith Act, and that resulted in a certain division, even here, in our political thinking. It didn't manifest itself until the late fifties. More and more, I was unhappy with not only what had occurred in the Soviet Union, but the role of the American Communist Party. I have always felt that the American Communist Party has never taken a position independent of the position of the Soviet [Communist] Party. And I don't mean that they're under the dictates of the Soviet party, but they're afraid, politically, to have an American position toward something. If the Soviet Union has a critical attitude toward Israel, we must have it here. That's been the attitude of the American Party rather than what's in the best interests of the American people, in its approach, say, to an issue of international scope. So, these things became more apparent, more manifest, certainly, as time went on. And I was unhappy with some of my colleagues in the state leadership here and their approach to things. So, by 1960 I had begun to break away, for all of these reasons.

DS: How did you feel about leaving at the time? You obviously had many friends, associates, comrades, that you had worked with very closely for many, many years.

JG: Well, I felt unhappy, let's put it that way. I felt frustrated, I felt somewhat embittered at times, [but] not because I had been a member. That's one thing: I know a number of people that felt, oh, they wasted their time, they were misled by the Party. I personally don't feel that. I feel my time in the Party enriched me, made me better equipped to do things, to understand things, even though I disagree with a lot. Some of the finest people, I felt, that I have ever met were in the Party. Not that all Party people were great people. But there was a certain idealism, a certain integrity, a certain feeling in your relationship to other people, that I felt was missing on the "outside." And it is not to be found in other political organizations.

Certainly, when I left, I continued to maintain a good relationship with people in the Party, to the best of my ability. And I was very friendly with those people that remained. And right up until now, I would say, I've never been—certainly in the period of [19]60 to now, thirty years—I've never been pro-Party or anti-Party. I will not join a red-baiting kind of attack on the Party. But I don't favor the Party's approach, and I'm not a member. That's been my position. I've spoken on this on several occasions, before groups that have asked me to, and they want to know about the McCarthy period or something and how do I feel now. So, I've always made it clear that I'm not pro- or anti-Party and that the people I met in the Party were very fine people—most of them.

DS: Now I'd like to ask you a slightly different question, and that is, During the time between your leaving the Party and now—we're talking about close to thirty years—have you ever felt a sense [of], shall I call it loss, or a feeling that something was missing in terms of your own feelings and aspirations?

JG: Well, yes, to be perfectly honest. Not necessarily the Party as such, but certainly, after spending at least—well, from [19]36 to [19]60—twenty-five years or so, in which one is totally involved, there is a loss. But I've also felt in the last number of years the loss of anything to substitute for it. There's nothing there I feel that I can relate to in a political sense that had the same amount of meaning for me. I still feel that I believe in socialism, as a future course for mankind [sic], but I don't see or feel that I'm part of any socialist movement. That's missing.

DS: Now, during this period, beginning in the early sixties, were there times when you actively searched out for those organizations or groups where you might possibly, if not substitute, at least regain at least some sense of that belonging or shared commitment to political goals?

JG: Well, to a certain extent, yes. And at the same time, I might say that that coincided [with the time] when I began to devote much more time to the work I was doing of carpentry, of construction, where I began to take hold of it a little better and began to give a little more attention to that direction, while trying to find an orientation where I might fit into something politically.

DS: The carpentry wasn't exactly a substitute for political work—

JG: No.

DS: —but did you feel at least that it compensated in some way?

JG: Yeah, I felt that it compensated in some way. As I said, you get a feeling that if you do something of a construction nature, the results are there; there's a certain sense of satisfaction, of being creative, of having accomplished something. And that, to a certain extent, may substitute for the inability—[for] being frustrated politically, not being able to do something in a political direction. At the same time, it was a period of the complete isolation of the Left, and partly the decimation of the communist and the socialist movement in America, and a serious decline in the trade union movement. So [it] wasn't just the Communist Party, but really the whole Left was isolated after the McCarthy era, you see. And even things of a very accepted nature, like the broader aspects of the New Deal, were under attack. We're in a period of history where the Right begins its ascendancy and tries to isolate all the accomplishments of the previous period. At least, that's the way it [looked] to me.

DS: So, during this period following your leaving the Party—but still keeping inside of you the ideals that, as you saw it, the Party had once stood for—you found yourself involved in your work. At least that gave you a sense of accomplishment, and the results were [laughs] somewhat more tangible, anyway, than—

JG: —that's right—

DS: —the political activity can ever be [where] it's always difficult to see—

JG: —absolutely—

DS: —really tangible results. Were there specific organizations or activities of a political nature that you did involve yourself since that time?

JG: Well, yes, for example, the peace movement in Connecticut. I became quite involved with that, over a period time, and came in contact with a whole new group of people. Again, very fine people, particularly coming into the eighties. Right here in Bridgeport, around the Catholic Diocese, there was a group of social activists, some [of] whom were full time organizers for the Catholic Church, that were very concerned and involved in a whole number of social issues in Bridgeport. I became involved with them, including the peace movement. I worked to the point where I became the chairperson of our local SANE/Freeze group. We took part in a whole number of movements on a state scale: Hiroshima Day, with a demonstration downtown; the June 12 mobilization, 1982—

DS: For nuclear disarmament.

JG: Yes. Then [there was] a national organization called Jobs for Peace [of] which we had quite a chapter here, largely as a result of the social activists in the Catholic Church, a very fine group of people. Almost from the start, I made it clear to them—and they wanted to see who I had been—what my political activity had been in the past, so there would be no misunderstanding that I was trying to infiltrate or do anything or take over. And I had very good relations.

I became active in the housing movement. For many years I've been interested in housing, not only as a craftsman, but also in trying to obtain housing for people that can't afford it. I was part of the housing movement of Bridgeport going way back to [19]38, [193]9, that brought some of the first federal housing into Bridgeport. And through the years I continued some of the things in that direction. In the last six years, we've set up the Housing Alliance of Bridgeport.

There's a great deal of homelessness around. There are serious housing problems around. So, I've been able to remain very active in many ways. Now, politically, on various levels, around the lake here [Jake lives on the shore of Forest Lake] we have an association of about two hundred and fifty that belong to the association, that pay an annual dues to belong. I've been the vice-president of the organization. Now, have they been involved politically? Well, we're a nonpolitical organization, but certainly we try to swing the vote of the Lake for various city officials that will further the interests of the people of the Lake area as a whole. So I've been active in city politics, in the Democratic Party, more or less.

DS: Clearly, then, although you left the Party close to thirty years ago, your sense of political commitment didn't diminish. [It was] just that you had difficulty finding avenues for expression that could, let's say, provide the same sense of purpose or meaning—

JG: —that's correct—

DS: —as the Party did. Well, now we get to another interesting issue that I want to bring up, and that is [that] in a very real sense, you could say that your leaving the Party was itself a form of retirement [laughs].

JG: Well, yes it was—from a certain kind of restricted activity in certain directions to one where one functioned in a much different manner. So, it was a retirement from one but into another milieu.

DS: Now, in a similar fashion your retiring [follows] from construction, that is, formally giving up the contracting business yet still not completely retiring, in the sense that you take odd jobs, but certainly retiring from that full time occupation. What were your feelings then, when you retired? Did you see or experience any kind of change in your relationship to the political community, other things in your life at that time?

JG: Well, certainly I was hoping that [in] all of my activity maybe something could form that would move in a socialist direction so my activity would be integrated with that. But nothing really materialized, so that [in] that sense, I feel isolated, in that I'm not part of any broad socialist movement around. I read all the political organs, more or less, let's say the *Guardian* [self-described "independent radical newsweekly"], *In These Times* [a democratic socialist newsweekly], the *Daily World* weekly [official Communist Party paper], the *Nation* [progressive news and analysis weekly]. I follow things closely, as much as I can, but I don't feel that I'm a part of anything on the left.

DS: Even though you're involved in these different broad-based activities.

JG: That is correct. What's missing I feel is that there's no real left activity.

DS: Now, you were still active in different organizations, housing or peace, while you were still working as a contractor?

JG: Partially, right. But that engaged a lot of my spare time. Then, when inspections began—and I was one of the first to do this kind of thing in the state of Connecticut—I was in on the ground floor, and it eventually took off. I was helpful in forming a professional organization, called ASHI, the American Society of Home Inspectors, and I became the tri-state president of the [ASHI] and that functions now. I'm a retired member from it. My objective was [to] move this organization in the direction of not just being a professional organization, from the point of view of inspecting a house, but [of] being concerned with the whole housing situation in the country.

DS: Even then there was—

JG: —even then—

DS: —a political perspective that you had.

JG: It was a political perspective. I would meet up with people and try to move this organization to a more responsible feeling for what I consider is one of the basic components of the whole American economy: housing. Over sixty percent of the people own their own homes. Of course, they're mortgaged up to the hilt, but still that's a very important, basic thing for people here. Housing embodies—

you consider what's in any house, a major part of the whole American output of consumer goods, whether it's the lumber or the concrete or the actual contents of the house, so that housing is an important and integral part of the American economy. And the striving for a decent place to live is an important kind of idea on the part of newly formed—you know, young people—families. So I felt that this was a basic thing that fitted in with my whole moving toward socialism, with no contradiction.

DS: This is interesting, Jake, because when we began this conversation and I asked you what you felt your dominant political identity was, you said [that] at one time it was involved with the Party, and then it was involved in construction, and maybe now it's something else. I think, perhaps, you might have been looking at that [question] in terms of "what is my predominant activity?" In terms of what your underlying and fundamental belief system is, it seems like everything you've done, whether it's political organizing, carpentry, contracting, or whatever, the underlying, fundamental belief still seems to [reflect] a conviction in the political process, in [particular] the socialist movement.

JG: That's correct, I would say it is, it is.

DS: So in a very real sense, then, the dominant [aspect] or core of your identity has always been political in some sense of that term.

JG: That's correct. Even from the point of view of the most immediate politics, right here in the city [of Bridgeport], of, say, influencing the mayor to do something in a certain direction that would help housing. [During] the last administration, I was appointed on a Housing Advisory Committee, an official city commission, to advise the so-called Common Council. So everything is in that direction, whether it's, as I say, immediate politics, how to make the Democratic Party more progressive, pushing more toward the Left, again, with that concept that socialism is the way I feel we should move eventually.

DS: Now, we've alluded to your post-quote-retirement-unquote activities, in terms of the various political involvements—peace movement, and working with church groups and on housing issues, et cetera. How did your political activity (or did it) change in a significant way when you retired from contracting?

JG: Well, I would say that it just gave me more time to be able to do these things. It didn't change in any significant way; I just became more involved, furthered what I was doing.

DS: Did you feel differently about the relationship between your political beliefs and your actual involvements than you did, let's say, when you were doing contracting, in which the relationship was a little more indirect? I mean, did your feelings or attitudes change as you became more politically [active] again?

JG: Well, I also felt that the whole situation was changing in the country, politically, for the better for a while, so that it enabled me to participate more fully. I don't know how else to answer that. I would say that—certainly [in] the late sixties, seventies—I feel that [in] the Left a new youth movement developed, a black movement, [a] civil-rights movement. What had preceded it in the forties or fifties maybe was isolated, but something new had arisen, so that there [were] opportunities for moving ahead.

DS: And of course, you were, as you say, involved—even as you were working as a carpenter and contractor—in different kinds of activities. But by 1982—was [that] when you retired?

JG: —right—

DS: —as you say, there was still some momentum, so that [there were] both political considerations, since you always have been motivated politically (and found that in retirement you had more time to devote), but also the [fact that the] historical moment was right. There was still—

JG: There was still a momentum, and that momentum was furthered by Reagan [and] the Cold War, which had reached a new [level of] danger of nuclear war on a world scale. The peace movement was thriving when I retired, and I was able to become more effective with it. I would say at the same time [that] since I left the Party, I've also been able to give more vent to my overall interests in art. I'm not an artist, but [I have an] interest in museum attending, the history of art, of music, of architecture. All of these things [I had] a better chance to explore after I left the Party (particularly before and during retirement), as avenues for me to further my interests.

DS: So your [interests] in matters cultural were given new channels, partly because the all-consuming commitment—

JG: —that's right—

DS: —to Party activities, was no longer—

JG: Party activities were all-consuming, and you don't get the opportunity. You're just caught up in it [and] you don't get the opportunity to really develop your interests in these other directions. But, let's say, in the last twenty years, my wife and I have belonged to the [Yale] Repertory Theater, the Long Wharf [Theatre] series. We go to concerts, we've gone to just about every important museum in the country, we've gone to Europe. I mean, these are our focal points of interest. And my wife's interests are very similar to mine. She was also part of the Party apparatus when I was. So we've had this opportunity to explore things that we didn't have the time to get into before.

DS: So, in a way [it's] fortunate [that] you were able to grow together.

JG: Yes, I would think so.

DS: One thing I did want to ask, since we had discussed it earlier was the character, if any, of your cultural involvements, specifically ethnic, cultural involvements. Now, you said that as a child you were—your father was a member of the Workmen's Circle and you did go to Hebrew school for a while. Were there any other periods in your life when you were involved in any kind of Jewish cultural activities, before or after retirement?

JG: No, we never have been involved. We don't have a New Jewish Agenda group [the left-liberal organization in which Joe Dimow is active] here. Bridgeport's lacking a cultural base, an atmosphere, say, that New Haven has or maybe even Hartford has. We don't have a university [actually, there's the University of Bridgeport, but it's relatively small and isolated]. We just don't have it here. Even along Jewish lines, we've never been involved in the Jewish community center to speak of. That consists largely of [a number of] middle-class and upper-middle-class Jews in the greater Bridgeport area, and we have not been interested in that sort of thing. We may go to some event at the center, but we haven't been participants.

DS: At any time in recent years, or earlier, would involvement in specifically Jewish political activities have been something you would have been interested in, even if opportunities presented themselves organizationally?

JG: I don't know, and I would doubt it. I've never been oriented in that direction where I've been interested in Jewish activity as such.

DS: Now, would that be just because of your lack of exposure, or would you attribute it to [the] internationalist outlook of the socialist movement? How would you define—

JG: It may be partly due to a lack of exposure. It may be that if there were a New Jewish Agenda group here, there would be enough interesting people that I would want to—you know, who had a broad outlook on Jewish affairs, that I might participate with. I'm a member of the New Jewish Agenda in New Haven, but we don't go, we don't participate, except when they have some special events.

DS: And what was it that motivated you to join New Jewish Agenda?

JG: Well, to a certain extent, their outlook, which is not the narrow, sectarian outlook I feel most Jewish organizations may have toward the Middle East situation. My wife and I have never been particulary interested in observing Jewish culture as such. We certainly brought up our only child, our son, to feel that he's Jewish. For a while he attended, in New Haven, a *shule* [Jewish school] on Jewish history—

DS: A secular Jewish school?

JG: Yes, along with the Dimow kids and other children. But he never expressed any interest, say, in becoming confirmed at thirteen.

DS: What I'm getting at, Jake, is [that] since we're trying to explore various aspects of your identity, I just wanted to make sure that I didn't neglect the ethnic factor.

JG: Absolutely.

DS: It seems that, in your case, your sense of Jewish ethnicity, while you recognize [it]—at least in terms of wanting your children to know their background—that perhaps it was not ever an essential element in your overall political outlook.

JG: No, it never was. Though maybe, as you were saying, if there had been a group here with some remnants of the Left—the Old Left, like the Dimows, or Sid Resnick—I don't know if you've met him—

DS: Yes.

JG: —and others, it may be that we would [participate] much more. But there was nothing left here. For one thing, the Bridgeport Party never had a large Jewish membership, as the other [Connecticut] parties had [such as] Hartford and New Haven, where it may be that as much as forty or fifty percent of its membership may have been Jewish. That was not true [in Bridgeport]. So there is no such group of people left.

DS: Right. So a primary motivation for connecting your ethnicity and politics is if there were a large enough number of politically left Jews—

JG: I think I probably would have been a part of that.

DS: Right, because you would have felt at least some—

JG: —identity with them—

DS: —identity—

JG: —that's correct—

DS: —because of a common ethnic and historical experience?

JG: That's right.

DS: Again, [is it] sufficient, but not necessary in terms of your core political identity, that that identity could be sustained apart from any specific ethnic or cultural identification?

JG: I don't know

DS: That's interesting. It's difficult, sometimes, to separate those things out; those become issues like "what if?"

JG: Right.

DS: As a way of concluding this conversation of ours, do you feel at this point that your core identity—your sense of self, what gives you purpose and meaning—would you say that that driving force in your identity is still the political?

JG: Yes, I think the driving force in my identity is still political. I really feel that way; I feel that everything that I try to do, while it has an immediate sense, is part of a larger picture. And without that larger picture [there would be something missing. Yes, I believe in doing things that better people's lives, including my own. And these people I work with are good people, also, making their contribution in a genuine way. But by having a long-range picture as well as an immediate goal equips me with a more rounded outlook.]*

DS: The larger purpose.

JG: That's right.

*[NOTE: Jake sent me a written request to change this concluding remark (hence it is bracketed). The statement he initially made says essentially the same thing, but he referred to "the good people" he works with as "do-gooders." He did not intend it to be pejorative, but was apparently concerned that it might be taken that way.]

Chapter Nine

Those Influences Remain, and They're a Part of My Heritage

[Second interview with Jacob ("Jake") Goldring, conducted at his home in Bridgeport, Connecticut, on July 6, 1990]

DAVID SHULDINER: Jake, I indicated to you that I wanted your response to the initial interview. Let us begin with your critique, what you felt about the initial interview, what you thought needed amplification, what you thought was missing.

JACOB GOLDRING: With my limited experience with oral interviews, I thought that on the whole it was a very good interview. I thought that your questions and follow-up, in an effort to delve into my answers a little more thoroughly, was very competently done. I might throw in a few suggestions—I don't know if you can call that a critique—[about] where there might be more amplification. For example, it seemed to me that one might have asked, near the beginning, a little more [about] not how I came to join the Communist Party [but] why I became interested in socialism. I think, since some people didn't and some did in that period, why did I? That might have been amplified a little bit. Or, for example, in the current period, one of the follow-ups you might be interested in trying to do today is not only our current interest in socialism, but how does that reflect on our children? Since you were interested [in] whether *our* parents had any influence, whether we in turn have any influence on our children. Do *they* have any interest in socialism? Have we made any impact on them in any direction? Or are we disappointed, in that they haven't followed up, if they haven't. Another might be our current attitude toward what's going on in the Soviet Union, whether or not, even if we are *not* interested in socialism, what we think. What are our relations, what are *my* relations, at this moment, with the Communist Party, [of] which I was a member for so many years and an officer.

Then, for example, [you] know that in my interview I said that on many things, or a number of things, I voted alone. I think there might have been a follow-up [by] you: "Well, in what way? What were those things? Why were you a maverick?" These are some of the things that I'm posing that might have rounded it out a little more. But I don't want to take away from the relatively, overall, thoroughness of the interview.

DS: Well, these *are* some of the things that I think are important to address. And, perhaps, those are some of the things that we can expand upon this time.

JG: Alright.

DS: In fact, let's begin at the beginning of your list. Maybe we can have you talk a little more about what specifically drew you to socialism and even more specifically, why you chose to identify yourself as a proponent of socialism.

JG: I had read the books of Upton Sinclair, of Lincoln Steffens, people of that nature. Muckrakers, people who had somewhat of a social psychology. When I got out of high school in [19]32, it seemed to me that certainly conditions in the United States were such that any intelligent person would begin to lean in that direction. There seemed to be no solutions to the problems of the country. There were no jobs to be had. There was no opportunity for me to go on to college. There was absolutely no employment of any kind, in even the minutest service industry. I felt that [in] the United States we had a great country, we had the resources—the coal, the mines, the natural resources, the forests, the land, the brains—to produce a decent standard of living for every man, woman, and child. And here the people around me in Hartford were devastated. Everybody, every single homeowner on the street that I lived [on] in Hartford was dispossessed of their home, foreclosed by the banks—everybody, without exception, which will give some idea of the devastation that existed. Our parents—my father worked a little bit, being a baker. People at least ate bread, so that he continued with partial employment.

But everywhere, many of the men, if not all of them, were unemployed, as well we younger [folks]. More and more, I began to drift in the direction of feeling that harnessing our resources in a logical way *was* the answer to our country's problems, since there were no other solutions being proposed. And the country was drifting from [19]29 on. So this led me in that direction. When I entered Storrs in [19]34, and became caught up in the student movement and, intellectually, began to read a little more about socialism, Marxism, I began to move more and more to what I felt was the only organization specifically trying to do something with people's [problems], and that was the Communist Party.

DS: Now, we had talked about the particular attraction that the Party had for you in the beginning, in our previous interview, in terms of its goals, its organization, and your basic support of its overall aims. But, as you pointed out in the last discussion and have highlighted in your critique this morning, clearly you felt that although you embraced the overall outlook of the Party, you were often at odds with specific programs. You indicated an interest in elaborating [upon] some of those specific reasons; maybe those will help us get at the particular sense of identity that you had as reflected in what was often [a] kind of a maverick stance within the Party. When do you feel was the first time you had a serious minority position within the Party?

JG: I don't know if it was the first time, but I remember very much differing with Party people, say in the Stamford area, on the approach to such issues as welfare. I remember a big fight that I had with state Party people. A black leader in the Party, from California, originally— Pettis Perry, his name was, who had hardly any public education, had learned to read and write largely by himself and eventually became a leader of the Party—accused the Party of white chauvinism, almost everywhere. The Party had not properly addressed the whole question of discrimination against blacks; [it] had paid lip service to the whole thing, of this whole question of chauvinism. He came to New Haven, at a state meeting. And I [said I] felt it wasn't so.

Everybody else cowtowed to Pettis Perry, said how right he was. They beat their breasts—"How terrible we were"—and we agreed, we had driven blacks out of the Party by [our] methods of behavior. I took exception to that. Of course, I was ganged up on, 'cause I felt that we tended to adapt to every little criticism that might be made in order to avoid really dealing with it.

Another time, for example, when things began to [be] difficult in this country, in the late forties, after the arrest of the Party leadership in [19]48 the Party decided, probably by [19]49 and again acting on fears, which indicated that they didn't know what they were dealing with—this was a reaction that had not been thought out—they decided that all gays and lesbians had to be put out of the Party, that they were vulnerable. They were people who the government could use as informers very easily, by telling these people that they would expose them to the public. And at that time, of course, gays and lesbians were what we might call "closet" people. They were not known to the general public. *We* had admitted them to the Party on an equal basis, certainly. We generally knew who they were. Some of them were very fine people who had risen in the Party ranks. One in particular was a leader of the Party in Norwalk. We voted about fifteen to one, if I remember correctly, to put them out of the Party. I objected, I was the one vote. And I tried to cite—well, if Walt Whitman had been a member of the Party, could we have put him out of the Party? Here was America's great poet, who was a homosexual—so what? That didn't make him less of a person. And he was a great man. There were other very fine people, and that could not be our criteria for putting people out. Well, I was outvoted, and the Party proceeded to expel—not expel, but drop—all people in that category. These are a few instances of what I mean.

Another one was—and I may have mentioned [it] earlier—when the Party, following the tactics of the Soviet Party as though this were Tsarist Russia, when our Party leadership was arrested and other state Party leaderships were arrested—that the leadership of the Party all over the country should go underground. I was absolutely against that—and I was completely outvoted by the Party leadership—'cause I felt that certainly [it] would be a mistake, that we were still a country with certain rights and freedoms, and that we should be able to speak out to the public, and that we were playing into the hands of the F.B.I. and the Right *precisely* by going underground, which would further their attacks on the Party by saying we *were* secretive. These are some of the instances that I can cite in which I disagreed very vehemently with the Party.

DS: Now some of these objections, it would appear, were based on differences of opinion you had around tactics. But some of them seemed also to be based on [differences in] fundamental principle. I'm wondering what you felt when you were so obviously outvoted on matters that seemed to you, and maybe to others, matters of principle [that] were not to be compromised.

JG: Well, yes, they were matters of principle, without any question, but I felt, again standing on principle, that I for one could not just desert the Party at that time of crisis. That would never enter my mind, [that] I would leave under any such conditions. In effect, it would be as though I was running away from something because there was a little pressure being applied. And since I agreed with the overwhelming part of the Party program, I felt I could not justify, and I *would not* want to justify, leaving the Party at that time. I had no such desire, even though I had been outvoted on a principled manner.

DS: Nevertheless, this dilemma, to a certain extent, remained unresolved until finally you felt the need to make the break. If there were fundamental principles or principled positions around which you disagreed with other members of the Party, what was it that provided the breaking point? What, in your opinion, made your differences strong enough in the early sixties so that you felt finally compelled to sever your formal relationship with the Party?

JG: Well, I would say there were several things. There were not only a whole accumulation of unresolved questions, both theoretical and practical, but I also felt that there had been certain specific maneuvering in the Communist Party of Connecticut that would tend to isolate me—some very specific things [such as] in voting [Jake indicated, in the first interview, that he was the sole dissenting voice on a number of occasions in matters being voted on within the Party.] I have shied away, and I say this very honestly, from being the Party chairman. It may be psychological, but I am afraid of being in that position. Not a physical fear [but] a fear. It may be I don't feel competent, that I could hold that position, or a position like it.

Now, there was a vacancy in the job of the secretary-treasurer of the Party. A fellow named Mike Russo had left (he had gone to another area) and a vacancy appeared. I didn't want it; I didn't want that position. I'm not saying that in hindsight; I just didn't. At that time, I went away on vacation for two weeks, and when I got back, the Party chairman had called a special meeting of the state committee and [had] elected a secretary-treasurer, deliberately in my absence, thinking that I would be the one that would get the position and [that I] wanted it. The mere doing [of] that created a deep antagonism in me, for that kind of attitude and procedure. And [it] put me in a position where I began to further question the manner in which we were operating. When I left [on vacation], no meeting had been planned, but one was especially called for [in] my absence, and this was done. Later on, other things were done of a similar nature that I was unaware of. And these precipitated, along with my theoretical disagreement, my leaving the Party.

DS: So, you would say it was a combination of both disagreements on principle but also behavior that, in your estimate, was really uncharacteristic, one might even say unwarranted, behavior for a person or persons who claimed to hold beliefs and principles of collective responsibility.

JG: In my opinion, it was not a democratic way of proceeding and therefore, I felt that [much] further estranged from continuing [membership in the Party].

DS: It seems that very often, regardless of what one claims to hold to in principle, there [often] are contradictions in people's behavior. People claim to be in favor of socialism, and yet their interactions do not necessarily reflect those principles. I was wondering if, perhaps, your reluctance to hold a position such as chair of the Party came from your reluctance to have to, as the chair, publicly defend either principles or the behaviors of other Party members that, in your private thoughts and feelings, [you] profoundly disagreed with?

JG: That may be part of it, no doubt. It's also a lack, on my part, of self-confidence in being able to perform in that kind of position. And therefore, while I'm willing to be part of a collective leadership, I am not willing to be one of the two or three top leaders.

DS: Now, was that maybe a disagreement that you had, in terms of the Party structure, that perhaps there wasn't a sufficient collective responsibility taken?

JG: That is part of it. I might just cite, as it comes to my mind, another instance. After 1956, when Khrushchev spoke on the Stalin aberrations, [on] when Stalin had been in power, and the many deaths that he had caused, the Party here in America broke into two groups, basically. There was to be a [19]57 convention, which would be preceded by conventions in the various areas, including Connecticut. I was more heading the left group, those who wanted to see a strong Party in the United States, not one too amorphous and split up. And Sid Taylor headed a right group. Interestingly enough, the left group had more support than the right group.

DS: The right group's position was what?

JG: The right group's position was of a much greater reform in the American Party, where it moved more to the right, as far as I could describe it. Nationally, it was led by guys like Johnny Gates, who had been the editor of the *Daily Worker*, and Steve Nelson, who was a part of that right group, as against (the names escape me) those who were the leadership nationally. I felt that [rift] would lead to the dissolution of whatever organization there was to be [at] this 1957 national convention, and we held a convention in Connecticut to determine who the delegates would be. At this convention, I would say, the left could have predominated; it had a majority of people at the convention in Connecticut. But at this convention it was proposed that we try to adjust our relationship and send people from both groups, which I heartily agreed with.

In the voting, I refused to vote for myself as a delegate, and [missed being] elected by a couple of votes. I even insisted, and supported the plea, that [because] a couple of people had not arrived who I knew would support the right [that we] wait until they get here. I [was] anxious to see that an amiable, balanced [group] go to the convention. As a result, only one group went to the convention, even though the other could have had a part of that. So that, again, I felt there was, if you want to call it, treachery, in that there had not been this compromise carried out that had been agreed upon. That embittered me, and I felt that I was being duped into this kind of united feeling that didn't exist. So all of these things, I would say, hastened my leaving the organization, [in] that I couldn't agree with the manner in which it was operating.

DS: Essential to maintaining a set of principles, of beliefs, it would seem, is a community of support, even if there aren't always agreements on matters of strategy, tactics, principle, what have you. At least there's a sense that you have collective responsibilities and goals.

JG: Right.

DS: During [the] time of your membership in the Party, were there times when you felt a sense of wavering or doubt in your beliefs or [in the] principles of socialism, because of the discrepancies of behavior that you saw [in] fellow Party members?

JG: No, that I don't think I ever wavered on [that]. I've always felt, and I do now, that we have to move toward socialism in some form. Not the Soviet model—one can argue on whether it's an application of socialism or not—but that here's no solution in the world, aside from socialism as the next stage, that's going to solve some of the very basic problems that the world is confronted with. And not merely poverty, but the whole nature of the possible outbreak of a terrible third world war, with nuclear destruction for one thing; the whole impoverishment in much of the continent of Latin America [and] Africa; that the United States is always engaged in some form of maneuvering, jockeying, even sending troops to various areas, and not even as part of the Cold War that existed in that period.

So, I've always felt that we've gotta establish socialism, and particularly here in the United States [where] we are able to achieve a level of manufacturing, of science, of development that will enable us to harness the various forces around [us]; [Socialism] will not only give us what we need, but [it would] take the belligerency out of the foreign policy of our country, which otherwise becomes more and more rambunctious. *That* I never lost faith in. But whether the Party was the right instrument, *that* I began to question. And knowing the turbulent history of all kinds of parties on the left in the United States, I realized that this process was unresolved and would continue to go on, and that the Party was not the solution.

DS: Another question that you raised, and [that] may be appropriate here, is your feelings about the continuity of your own identity in a period where there isn't any organizational network and political community that really provides the [kind of] support that the Party provided for you. When you grew up, you even had your parents who were involved already in the socialist movement. Do you see your children growing up in an era where you cannot provide [guidance]? How do you deal with the dilemma that you cannot offer your children the same organizational direction, let alone set of principles in which they can see socialism, not just as an ideal that you continue to support, but as a program that an organization or organizations are articulating, that you could introduce to them?

JG: I would say that, interestingly enough, our son grew up (we have only one child) in a period [in] which I was heavily involved in the Party (he was born in [19]54). In his early youth, he certainly heard of and asked about what we had been doing, because he was inquisitive enough to sense that it was an unusual kind of thing. And insofar as we could, we told him about it. But he grew up, of course, in a completely different milieu than ours; therefore, there was no effort on our part to imbue him with a sense of the necessity of becoming involved in socialist kind of activity. But rather, we felt that we created the environment for him to feel [about] social matters a little more keenly than the average child, and we feel that he has.

[Now that] he has grown up (he's about thirty-five), he's not involved in any political activity of any kind, but he chose a field of work that may reflect his upbringing. He chose a field of medicine. He's not a doctor, but he's involved in hospital administration. To a certain extent [that] may be due to the kind of upbringing he got, where one has more of a feeling toward people, toward humanity in general, and toward our past background. And this may be kind of a compromise on his part, I don't know. His attitude toward many things going on, I think, is a reflection of his early training with us. I think he has a keen understanding of developments that go on, even while not [a] participant in any way. I don't know how that's reflected on the part of my colleagues Joe [Dimow] and Sid [Resnick] and their children—I don't know. But my wife and I still retain that feeling for—we gauge all kinds of contemporary events going on, from the point of view [of] what we consider a Marxist approach to things. And it's almost imbued in us to look at things from that angle.

As far as—I don't know what else you asked me there—relations
with the Party after we left? [actually this was a question Jake had
posed]. They've been cordial. We don't see the leadership of the Party
very often. I think they make a point, maybe, to avoid us, I don't
know.

What's interesting is that the Party in Bridgeport—and it's one of
the ways in which Bridgeport differs from Hartford and New
Haven—if you want me to go on, I will [DS nods affirmatively]. All
three cities have almost the same number of people. They may differ
by a few thousand from year to year, with Bridgeport generally
considered the biggest city [in] population of the three, with maybe
a hundred and thirty-five thousand—and the 1990 census may show
it a little better, and Hartford and New Haven between a hundred
twenty, twenty five [and] a hundred thirty thousand, somewhere in
there. But of the three cities going back, Bridgeport always had the
biggest Party—Communist Party. It also had—of the three cities,
the Party [in Bridgeport was] based in the shops, in the industrial
sector.

It also had the least number of Jewish people in the Party. Only a
minority of the Party was Jewish in Bridgeport, as compared to
elsewhere. It had a branch of the Communist Party in General
Electric, of forty to fifty members alone. And it had branches in a
whole number of shops in the city. It had helped organize some of
those shops—into the United Electrical, Radio and Machine Workers
[UE], or the Mine, Mill and Smelter Workers Union, and a whole
number of unions. And [we] were able to recruit a number of these
people into the Party. It also had in this Party, interestingly enough,
several leaders of the followers of Father Coughlin—the Coughlinite
movement. I don't know how familiar you are or have heard of Father
Coughlin.

DS: Well, he was a racist—

JG: —right—

DS: —preaching—

JG: —but he was a radical. What [attracted] people to him, say in
Bridgeport, [was that] he condemned the piling up of the wealth on
one side and the poor people on the other. And while he used anti-

Semitism as a part of gathering that following, that tremendous following, by his radio talks, several leaders of the Coughlinite movement in Bridgeport were workers in shops. And as the trade union movement developed, the Party came in contact with them and was able to convince [them] of the erroneous nature of Father Coughlin and what he stood for. These people joined the Communist Party and were leaders here in the Communist Party, and [were] very honestly concerned. This was not just burrowing in, trying to get in. They left the Coughlinite movement, and they were very fine people. They were very sincere in their desire to try to do something. So, while we had one of the biggest Parties of the three cities, if not the biggest, it was characterized by a differentiation, as I've tried to indicate.

Now, I would say, the reverse is true in some ways. There is no Communist Party in Bridgeport. It is completely gone, to the best of my knowledge. And I'm involved in enough movements around to know that [if] I would meet up with somebody who is a member of the Communist Party, I would sense it, I would gather it. Well, first of all, I was on a committee, up until a couple of years [ago], and I was able to work effectively with many people in trying to keep the shops from leaving Bridgeport, organizing programs so that workers who were left out after a shop [closed], would have some kind of training in order to move into something else. So, I would know if there were Party people involved. It was virtually absent. I've been involved in the housing movement—the Party isn't there. Basically, there is no Party here. There *is* a Party in New Haven; I run into it, I know it's there, because I have to go to New Haven occasionally on various activities. There's a Party in Hartford. So, that's an interesting kind of contrast.

The other thing about Bridgeport, which makes it a much different city: It certainly has close to the number of Black people or Hispanic people that the other cities [Hartford and New Haven] have, maybe a few less, but it's lacking in a whole number of things that these cities have. For example, it doesn't have any kind of a cultural (and I mean it more in the artistic sense) base. It has nothing compared to New Haven and Hartford. We don't have a single bookstore in the whole city of Bridgeport. We don't have a single movie house in the city of Bridgeport. We had a porno [theater] downtown up until a few months ago [which] just converted into a regular theater that gets second movies, after they've made their first round, but nobody'll go downtown. That's the only theater that exists. We don't have a professional drama group in Bridgeport. New Haven—I go to New Haven to go to Long Wharf; I go to the Yale Repertory. We have nothing. Hartford has the Hartford Stage [Company]—it has something going for it. We have no chamber music in Bridgeport— we have to go to New Haven. We have no traveling symphonies. New Haven has a series, Hartford has a series, coming to the Bushnell—we have no series. We [do] have a Bridgeport Symphony Orchestra, like New Haven and Hartford, our own little group.

But the city is a different kind of city somehow. It doesn't have the intellectual [and] the cultural kind of base that one finds in the other cities. It's a very interesting phenomenon. The one university we have is in a virtual state of bankruptcy—the University of Bridgeport [It has subsequently been bought by the Unification Church]. It's, in effect, almost collapsing, compared to the schools that exist in the other cities. These are very interesting differences. And the caliber of people—I'm not trying to be a snob, I don't mean to imply that. I'm very active, for example, in the group around the lake [on the shores of which Jake lives]. This is middle-class over here. I'm not a working-class person now; I was. And I'm on the board of directors. It's a very active group. And I've helped—I've been the vice-president; they have wanted me to be the president. And all of this I attribute, by the way, to my background in the Party, which equipped me better in dealing with these things. A year or two ago, at a meeting of the board of directors—I was the vice-president—I said, "Fellas, there's a wonderful show, just the thing we'd like to see, boats," (which we have in our water) "sailboats, seashore scenes, at the Yale Art Gallery, open to the public, free: [Winslow] Homer, [John] Sargent, [Thomas] Eakins—American artists, just the thing you'd like to see." Well, they didn't laugh at me, but they practically did. This is not their milieu. This is not their thing, you see. Well, I sense that they think that I'm highbrow and they're not, you know, that kind of thing. Anyhow, I just want to give you an idea of the different kinds of atmosphere one has to operate in.

DS: You intrigued me with a remark that you had made at the end of our last conversation, after our taped-recorded conversation was done, in which you alluded to this whole question that you've just laid out about the difference in locale and the effect that that might have on political and cultural developments. I'd like to take that a step further and ask you if you feel—and try to think in terms of the entire scope of your experience in Bridgeport—do you feel that the particular locale and the milieu, as you describe it, of Bridgeport has had any effect on your particular ideological development and involvements?

JG: Yes, I think it's had an effect. I lack here (I and my wife, really) a group of people who are not necessarily left or socialists, but who one can sit down with [and] really delve into some of the problems, political problems, cultural problems. I'm not saying that such people may not exist, but I haven't met up with them. As a result, I said to Joe [Dimow], about six or eight months ago, look what's happening to the Eastern European countries (this was last December, January): Germany, East Germany, Czechoslovakia, Hungary, the Soviet Union [Jake is referring to the "democratization" movement in Eastern Europe]—we've got to sit down and discuss this with other people. Let's get their thinking: What's going on; what's happening to the Communist Party and socialism? And as a result, we did have such a meeting. We called people around the left, and people we thought would be interested, just to [discuss], with no conclusion in mind, but just a place to sound off. [The unanticipated breakup of the Soviet Union was to begin scarcely more than a year after this meeting.]
    There's no possibility of calling such a meeting here [in Bridgeport] alone. It doesn't exist. And just as we don't have a [New] Jewish Agenda, we don't have the remnants of a socialist Party, following Jasper McLevy [socialist mayor of Bridgeport from 1933 through 1957]. After Jasper died, the Socialist Party actually disappeared, excepted for individuals, and that is true of the Communist Party, by and large.

DS: In Bridgeport.

JG: In Bridgeport. And in much of Fairfield County, not just Bridgeport. At one time there was a good-sized Party in Stamford and a Party in Norwalk. There was once a branch of the Communist Party in Darien, Connecticut. And that we understand. But the Party as such has disappeared from the entire county. I'm amazed. And not only that, but Fairfield County was once really the intellectual kind of place for many important people to come to, out of New York and elsewhere.

Now the county is virtually the center of big business in the United States. When I say that, I mean [that] probably in this county there are more members of the Fortune Five Hundred, more companies for the county's size, than any other county in the country, which is an interesting kind of phenomenon. So [with] the flight [of intellectuals] out of Bridgeport there's nothing there of this nature. There's no left. This is the point I want to make.

As I say, I go into New Haven, and I can see the presence of the Party. Even ten days ago, I was in New Haven. I'm a member of an organization that gives out money.

DS: Oh, a foundation that gives grants—

JG: —a foundation, that's right—

DS: —that gives money to grassroots [activist] organizations.

JG: Originally out of Boston. I'm on the New Haven board of that, and we give out money. Our hearing night was about ten days ago. And as far as I know, no members of the board are members of the Party. They're all progressive people, you know, very socially conscious people. But I heard certain things said there about a member of the Party in New Haven. I know the Party is around [laughs], there's no escaping it and their attitude toward it. They're not red-baiters, on the [foundation board]. And I've been in Hartford, and I know that there's a left in these places, you see. So that's what amazes me, the difference that appeared now in the cities. I just wanted to dwell on it for a few minutes.

DS: But it is important, Jake, to the extent that, in order for you to feel complete—that is to say, to feel that your core identity is reflected in your activities and pursuits—you have to, at least from time to time—

JG: —touch base with somebody—

DS: —outside of Bridgeport.

JG: Right, right.

DS: So, apropos of your whole raising of this issue, it clearly is important to understand the difference, in terms of your own personal development, that a specific set of local social and historical conditions can make.

JG: Yes. If I were buying a house today, for example, in need of a new location—of course, I wouldn't leave this house, because of not only having lived here many years, but [I like] where I am—but if I had to pick up, it certainly would be a place [much] like New Haven, where I would feel there are people I can deal with, and talk to on a different basis, on primary [issues]—socialism, as one of the things. So, that is definitely missing.

DS: A community base, a group within which—

JG: —that's right—

DS: —you can feel at home.

JG: Right. That, plus the lack of a cultural atmosphere in the city, whereas New Haven would have what I feel is an integral part of what I would like to be doing. And as I say, all through the year we go to New Haven once or twice a week, to go to various affairs, as these things are missing largely in the city here.

DS: It's clearly a factor. One other issue I want to raise is the whole issue of retirement and age. And what I'd like to try to get at is the relevance that you might feel, if any, that your retirement and your coming of retirement age may have had on your beliefs, your feelings, your activities.

JG: Yes, well, of course, while I functioned as a businessman and head of this inspection agency, my political activity, my participation in various community groups, was at a much lower ebb. I was too busy running the business, very honestly. After I got out of it, of course, then I began to expand very rapidly into a whole number of things. My retirement, I felt, gave me an opportunity to pursue various things that I wanted to do. That included various community activities. Also, in a way, indirectly, artistic endeavors, which I had never been able to [do] and which grew along the way. For example, the artist of that picture [Jake points to a portrait hanging on the wall], and a number of the pictures here, was the chairman of the Communist Party of Connecticut, Mike Russo.

DS: The sketch we see here?

JG: Yes. That's a head of Beethoven. He also did, and I'll show you, several other pictures here. That's a still life, on the wall, of his.

DS: Of three pears [on] a cabinet.

JG: That is correct and [it is] what might be called an impressionist painting. And I include a large one or two in the other room that are fairly impressive. That nude on the wall that you can see at an angle, that's his. He's a very competent artist who, as a young man—he was born in Bridgeport [and] grew up in the city— at any early age, won an honorable mention in the *Prix de Rome* for a statue of Christ that he had done. He never got to Rome, only because the thirties had broken out [laughs]. Mike was left stranded with his artwork. In the [19]34, [19]35, Mike joined the Communist Party—a very dynamic kind of guy—and he became the Chairman of the Communist party of Connecticut by the late thirties and lived in Bridgeport. Right now, he's living in Massachusetts and paints full time. Oh, he's an older guy now. He's about eighty one or two. His wife, Bridgeport-born, I believe, also was very involved in the Party with Mike. Mike is not in the Party now; neither is his wife. Mike devotes—he's not involved in community affairs of any kind— almost all of his waking days [to] painting. And this has been true for a number of years.

 Anyhow, some of my artistic interests sprung from that acquaintance with him. I think he awakened some of it. And one of the things I did—many musicians [who] come into the house here took a look at that print of Beethoven and [asked], "Where did you get it?" because so many of the pictures of Beethoven are so dull and routine, they depict no real character of the man. And Mike has always been fascinated with Beethoven. I would tell these people that came in, "Well, Mike Russo drew it." "Where can we get it?" Well, I had it on loan, even, a couple of times. People offered to but it. So I finally—only a few years ago, [19]85, [19]84, [19]85, [19]86— I decided that I would duplicate that print. And so I did. I had one of the finest companies in the state, that does work for the Metropolitan Museum of Art, make some copies for me.

DS: Reproductions?

JG: Reproductions. And then, using a list of people that may have known Mike at one time or another, I sold the reproductions signed by him and got enough money to cover its costs, which ran into a few thousand dollars. Then, on his seventy-fifth—

[After the tape ran out Jake described a gift of $1,000 he made to Mike Russo on his seventy-fifth birthday, proceeds from the sale of the reproductions.]

DS: It seems, Jake, that in your description of Mike Russo—for the last several minutes we weren't talking about you at all, and yet, we were, because I see very strongly in you a sense that a full picture of your identity would not be complete without that cultural component, that you see [that] there is a real relationship. Here, in fact, was a fellow Party member with whom you shared an interest in the arts, who was himself an artist. Would it be correct to assume that, for you, there is a real strong link between your political outlook and your cultural outlook?

JG: I think that that is absolutely correct. I would like to tell you about another cultural link, not only with Mike, but with others. Mike, himself, also [was] a very fine piano player—he just was a very talented guy—and never pushed it. [He] preferred sculpture and painting, but had, from his very early youth, an interest in music, of serious music, that was very deep. One of the shops in Bridgeport was Columbia Records. Bridgeport was once the heart of the record industry. Decca Records was in Bridgeport—[it was] one of their main plants. Harriet [Jake's wife] worked at Decca Records. We had Columbia Records, where Columbia pressed all of its classical music, in Bridgeport. And we organized a UE shop at both places. Harriet was a member of the UE at Decca Records in 1940. And one of the guys that we recruited to the Party at Columbia Records was a record presser, pressing classical records. And this guy would walk out of the plant—it was his way of getting at the company—he'd press some records, walk into the men's room, strap them to his back or his chest (he was very flat-chested), and walk out [daily] with, say, two or three records, daily, out of the plant. He'd call Jake Goldring: "Jake, I've got some"—not to sell 'em, but to give them, knowing our love of music. So, without a nickel to our name, Mike and I were able to build up little record collections. We were always jostling with one another [over] who should get the next record, or this one— one of [the] Beethoven quartets, or whatever. And over the years, in the Party, and among people, we were able to build up a feeling, a love, for this whole field of serious music. And I think Mike's influence [was] certainly among those that helped that along. These interests are what we've carried on, even in a period of—without the existence of the Party. But I mention that to show the relationship.

Even the nature of our interests, the kinds of things we like to read—I'm more of a nonfiction reader. I'm nearing the end now of a book which I find fascinating—most people would find dull, I realize—a biography of Jackson Pollock [American artist, pioneer of abstract expressionism], which I think is fascinating. It's basically a history of art in the United States in the mid part of the century, from the thirties—including the WPA art projects—right up through the end of the fifties, a vital period. But my interests stem from all of these influences. And part of them are Party interests that I want to give credit to, even if I am not a Party member, and even if I feel they're working wrong, incorrectly. But those influences remain, and they're part of what I feel is my heritage. Because, as I said earlier— a couple of weeks ago—I don't take the attitude where I condemn the Party. I don't condemn the Party. I don't say that it was a waste of time or that I did the wrong thing. Rather, I take the attitude [that] it enriched my life, even though I disagree with it, what it's doing. It was a wonderful period to be with people, and I have no regrets for the fact that my interests in certain directions are partly attributable to the Party.

DS: It's a vital part of your development—of your developing identity, [of] who you are.

JG: That's right.

DS: I think it's a great way to close this second conversation—

JG: I might even say, for example, [about] my relations with Joe and

Lil [Dimow], that's a vital link. We share a lot, we're friendly. We may go to concerts together. We do certain [things together]. We may go to an art show. Lil calls us [and says] "Yale's showing something." So, we have a social relationship based on these factors now as well as our general outlooks.

DS: But the general outlook is, in a sense, the link—the thing that brought you together—the [political] base.

JG: That is correct. I might just say one other thing that's important, as far as certain differences that exist. See, I'm a bit older than Joe— not a lot, say, six years, five years, whatever it is—but during these five or six years (and Joe will experience this later) people have died. Three people have died in the area, that I *did* have some communication with. So I'm getting to that point where people are passing away, and I'm outliving them, and there's a loss. There's no substitute for that loss. So that, to me, is an important factor that accounts for some differences of why this area appears to be more barren.

DS: So age is also—

JG: Age is a factor, at this time, at this time, 'cause we're at the age where, let's say—well, a man, a male, has a life expectancy of almost seventy-two. Well, I'm a bit above that, and many of the people have died already that were in that category.

DS: So, maybe it's a combination of, as you say, both chronological age and also social [sociohistorical] age. Thirty or forty years ago, chronological age itself might not be a factor if there [were] a lot of younger members of the Party, or in the movement as a whole, that you would have something in common with, that would transcend the age barrier. [But] now you are talking about your age cohorts who are among the few remaining people linked to that time when there was an actual community, a political base—

JG: —right—

DS: —here in Bridgeport. So that chronological age wouldn't have made as much of a difference then, as it—

JG: —as it does now, right. And it doesn't make a difference *now*, as long as people are alive [laughs]—

DS: —even though it's not only some of your contemporaries dying, but [also] the diminishing of the political network, [that] leaves you still with certain byproducts of it. In this case, you were just talking about the cultural byproducts.

JG: Absolutely.

DS: But that becomes maybe even more important or intensified, would you feel?

JG: That's right, that's right. Absolutely. We, together, have more and more sought the substitutes that would give us something that would compensate for this difference. We just came back from an Elderhostel in Italy, sponsored by Trinity College of Hartford. And its whole direction was [that] we were with people, some [in] our age brackets, some younger, some older. Art, architecture and music—that was the [subject]. Why were we interested in this? Because of our interests that had been fostered all along by our association either with people, with the Party influence, et cetera.

DS: Plus the fact, too, that one of the attractions of Elderhostel is that you can not only share an interest with other people, but with your age contemporaries who have gone through, perhaps, a lot of the same experiences—maybe not politically, but certainly have gone through those eras that you experienced, and from which, perhaps, their interest [in] or exposure to art comes from.

JG: Yes.

DS: So it still provides some link—not certainly the same, like you say, somewhat of a substitute, but—

JG: Right. But the fact that we all had an interest in these specific topics brought us together. At least we had some thread that could [provide] some means of communication with them.

DS: Plus a common historical experience.

JG: A common historical experience, right.

DS: Well, I think [that] quite a lot of insights have come out of this second conversation; in particular, I think, some understanding of the way in which [the] particular circumstance of your own development—physically [within a particular physical/geographic setting] and socially—have had an impact. [They are] also aspects that one might not necessarily consider in a study of political identity: the outside (often considered outside of it, but certainly related) cultural and intellectual interests that are clearly linked, certainly as you see it.

JG: I might just add that in the late forties, I was in charge of the *Daily Worker* for the state. And I had to go into New York—this is anecdotal, but it might be interesting for you to hear. I had to go into New York to deal with the *Daily Worker* office. And while I was there, they took a stack of drawings off the shelf and said, "We're about to discard these. Would you want them for any reason?" These were cartoons that would appear in the *Daily Worker* on various current events as they occurred. And I said, "I'll take 'em." I took 'em back, and I looked at 'em, and I put 'em away, in the attic, or on a shelf somewhere. In 1983, [198]4 I read of a show of American art at UConn [University of Connecticut], at the Benton Museum, and I wrote to the director that I had some drawings of artists of that period, and on my way through I'd like to stop off and show 'em to him. And I did. Well, these drawings were all political drawings. I never hung them on my [wall] as art [though] they are art, in a way. A number of them were [William] Gropper [leading social realist painter in 1920s and 1930s], original Groppers, and other artists [whose] names momentarily escape me.

   The director of the museum at Benton took a look and he said, "Gee, these are very interesting. I know of Gropper—I never met him or anything—he's dead, of course. And this is all political art. Let me see what they're worth, and we'll carry some insurance while you entrust them to me. Let's put down a thousand dollars." I said, "Let's make it two thousand dollars, a little more. They may have a little value." So, he sent them into New York [and] had them appraised by an American art expert. He called me up a month or two later, and he said, "I can't believe it. These drawings are worth twenty thousand dollars." I said, "I can't believe it either."

Well, I donated them to the museum, practically all of them. I kept one that I wanted. That one I gave a few years ago to *Jewish Currents*, to Morris Schappes [editor] to sell for funding. That one dealt with Nazi tanks in the Soviet [Union in] World War II. Anyhow, that would indicate—the fact that I even held them—I had that interest in art that just seemed to—well, this is art, even though I don't want to hang it, I just want to hold on to these and eventually somewhere somebody might want 'em for some historical use.

One day, I found out where Gropper lived, in the late fifties, early sixties, in Westchester [County, New York]. I rang him and I identified myself, and I said, "Mr. Gropper, I have what appears to be some drawings of yours. Your signature is on 'em. They're originals." He said, "I'd like to see 'em. C'mon down." I went over there, and Gropper took one look, and he said, "Where the hell did you get these?" So, I told him where I got 'em, and he was incensed. He had been practically the *Daily [Worker]*—he had been doing at least a cartoon a week for the *Daily Worker.* And he said "I want them." So I said, "Mr. Gropper, you can have 'em, but I want one of your oil paintings, in exchange." Well, needless to say, that deal was never cut. He said, "I don't want you to release those. That's a period of time that pretty well is over, and [they] do not reflect fully what I feel now." He said, "Let me tell you. One day I was in the office—I was in the building that houses the *Daily Worker,* and I went up the elevator, and I got into the office, and there was my drawing on a big stool. They were stepping on my drawing to reach an upper shelf. That's how they regarded art." I said, "Well, Mr. Gropper, I'll take good care of them. And I don't intend to release them just to exploit them in any way whatsoever." So, when this show arrived at UConn, I finally gave them—after the show was over. So they have them there, so sooner or later they'll have a show that illustrates that period and will show these.

DS: I'm glad you shared [this anecdote] with me, Jake, because it illustrates two things: the link between art and politics that you saw very clearly—

JG: —I don't know if I saw it, but I sort of felt something—

DS: —and yet at the same time, ironically, the lack of regard, at least on the part of certain individuals, for the artistic output of—

JG: —that's right—

DS: —one of their own—

JG: —that's right—

DS: —comrades.

JG: They were ready to throw them in the ashcan, a whole pile of drawings. They had used them, and that was it.

DS: I thank you once again, for this opportunity to talk with you and bring out some links in [aspects] of your identity that aren't often drawn out—the political, the cultural, and the personal—and the tremendous variation that [can] exist even among those people who hold to the same ideology.

JG: You're welcome.

Chapter Ten

It Was an Episode, a Long and Good Episode in History, and It is Ending

[Interview with Sidney ("Sid") Resnick, conducted at his home in New Haven, Connecticut, on August 17, 1990]

DAVID SHULDINER: What I'm interested in is a sense of [the] development of your self-identity, [in particular] political [identity]; how your professional life as well as your political organizing life related to that, and as you grew older, if you felt that there were any changes in your sense of identity [and] your activities that might be considered related to age. This is, ostensibly, a study of retirement, the aging process, and political identity. I've focused on the lives of individuals who are still politically committed and active, to see what that process is like, through the different stages in your career—life's career.

SIDNEY RESNICK: I'm not retired fully, you know. I work thirty hours a week, still.

DS: Right. And [for those] people I've spoken to—it's similar. Their activities are at just as high a level, although maybe what they're getting paid is at a lesser level. Joe [Dimow] has raised this before, when he said he had retired in terms of paid work, but in terms of occupation, what has driven him lifelong is his political work. And if anything *that* activity has not diminished.

SR: You have more time for it.

DS: Yeah. So, we'll be looking at that, too. First of all, what I want to do is not get so much a history of all your activities in the Party, but to really get a sense of where your personal development led [you] to eventually join with and become active in the Party for so long. So, maybe we should begin with your family background. Where does your family come from?

SR: Both of my parents come from cities in the Ukraine. My father was not a political person. He was, I would say, a backward person, in many ways. He didn't read very much. And he and my mother never got along and eventually they split. My mother was the leftist in the family. She had brothers who were in the revolutionary movement. She never knew herself which revolutionary movement, and I don't think it was the Bolshevik movement. I sort of suspect it must have been what they called the Socialist Revolutionary movement, in Russia—the SRs. One of her brothers was an organizer. He died in another city; he died from sickness. He was very well known in the city, and the fact [is] that he was honored, and his death left a big impression on the family. So I think that my mother got a lot of, some of, her left background from home.

Then when she came to this country (she was in New York), she worked in a garment factory [as] a blouse maker. And she was one of the earlier members of the International Ladies' Garment Workers Union. She was on a strike with them several times, several strikes. She used to tell me how she would try to collect dues from workers (I think it was a quarter a month); how they would give her a hard time; how one time she went to the president of the union (Schlesinger was his name) and cried to him that she couldn't get the dues. So, she was very attached to the trade union movement. I think the Russian Revolution made a great impression on her—the October Revolution. She always— still—had visions of the workers taking over the Winter Palace, and that kind of stuff. Even in her later years, when she was sort of critical of the Soviet Union, she never was completely negative. You had that feeling about her. And I think I got some of my left backing through her, left thinking through her.

Also, she was a reader of the *Freiheit*, the Communist, Yiddish paper. I was able to read Yiddish at an early age, because she sent me to a Yiddish school. I used to read the paper.

DS: Was that one of the Workmen's Circle schools?

SR: No, that was the IWO [International Workers Order].

DS: Oh, this is already now in the twenties—

SR: The thirties. . . . You know, the IWO split from the Workmen's Circle, for left-right reasons [right-wing members of the Workmen's Circle opposed the Bolsheviks; left-wing members supported them, eventually seceding and forming the IWO]. The Communists, since 1922, had a Yiddish daily newspaper. And it was a very mischievous, feisty newspaper at the time. It had a lot of good writers. Many people read it who were not particularly communists, but they liked the spirit of the paper, or the literary level of the paper. It was, I would say, on a higher literary level than the *Forward*—

DS: Which was the social—

SR: The Social Democratic paper. I mean, they were more careful of their Yiddish. They avoided Anglicisms in the Yiddish language, that kind of stuff. And they had a great respect for Yiddish as the language of the Jewish working people.

DS: Now, in your home, was there a heightened sense of Jewish identity that you were raised with?

SR: Okay, well, you know, at the time, it was like the most normal thing in the world. I went to a Yiddish school, an after- hours school. The organization that was connected to the school, my mother belonged to it. I used to attend their meetings at night.

DS: That [was] the IWO?

SR: That was in between the IWO and the Workmen's Circle. It was the *Sholem Aleichem shules* [schools named after the famous turn-of-the-century Yiddish author]. They were not quite communist, but they were not quite Social Democratic either. That's where I went when I was a kid. And then I grew up in the Depression years. I was born in 1922, so I remember the Depression years very clearly. There were neighbors and friends of my mothers who were communists or leftists, and I used to go to their meetings. Then I moved to one area of the Bronx, the south Bronx, [where] there was a Pioneer group, Young Pioneers. These were mostly kids from the neighborhood. Some of them I knew from school, or some of them I knew from my Yiddish *shule*. We used to have meetings, weekly meetings, where we would discuss world politics, things like that. We'd go to demonstrations, like for the Scottsboro Boys, May Day demonstrations. We used to have little blue shirts with red bandannas. Sometimes we'd have picnics and there would be large numbers of us. So it gave us a feeling that we were a big movement. And these were just children.

Then there was the Young Communist League, which I joined, I think, in 1939 or 1940. A big influence on my life was that after I graduated the elementary Yiddish school, which was of this non-communist, non-Social Democratic school, I went to the communist school system, the IWO school. That was a high school, and we met Saturdays and Sundays. I would say it was a Party- line school. The teachers were CP members, and the whole orientation was pro-Soviet, and so forth. Most of the students were very bright kids. Some of them were better students than I was and went on to big careers, you know—professors and things like that. The school met on Fourteenth Street, near Union Square. I used to look forward to the school because it was interesting to me. I liked my friends there, and it was part of the whole revolutionary élan at the time—[the] spirit of the time. So that was a big influence in my formation. I had several teachers that I [not only] greatly respected, but I [also] really liked very much, because they were friends and comrades. So that was a happy experience, and it meant a great deal to me. And then, after I finished this high school, we had higher courses to qualify to become a Yiddish teacher. I went to those courses, but I never became a Yiddish teacher. I went into the army, in [19]42.

When I came out of the army, I joined the Party in my Bronx neighborhood. Because I was with a group of very young guys who [were] veterans—you have the aura of being a veteran—I became an area leader and a soapbox speaker, for several years until the Party tapped me to become what they called a "colonizer." They offered me various places to work, such as in a steel mill. The Party had a big organization in New York, and it had very little elsewhere. So they wanted people from New York to go and settle in other parts of the country. [Is] this familiar to you?

I selected Connecticut, and I went to work in a brass mill in Waterbury. I didn't stay there very long. First, the work was boring to me. I worked nights, and I disliked it very much. And this was in 1948 when the presidential campaign with Henry Wallace was on. Even though the Party wanted me to work in the brass mill, they also wanted me to work in the election campaign, because they had so few people, and so few people who wanted to take a lead in things. So the Party was torn in this contradiction, because to work in the brass mill you had to lie low and not be a public political person. And if you worked politically you couldn't work in the brass mill, because you would be—firstly I didn't get into the union. I didn't spend enough time there to be qualified as a union member.

So, within a few months, the Party's position on me changed. Rather than work in the mill they wanted me to work politically, which was fine with me, because it was more interesting to work politically than to work in a brass mill. In 1948 I worked in the western part of the state—it was the fifth congressional district then. There's still a fifth congressional district, but it's not exactly the same district. It included Waterbury, Torrington [and] Ansonia—the three big brass cities at the time. The Communist Party had a few members in each town, and they were the core, also, of the Progressive Party, the Wallace Party. One of the leaders of the Mine, Mill and Smelter Workers in Thomaston, Connecticut, ran as our candidate for Congress [in] the fifth district. He and I used to drive up and down the valley in a truck, and we'd hold little meetings and rallies, and he would speak. I would speak and play records. We did [that] for the whole summer. We had a couple of candidates in Waterbury. We had a black candidate and an Italian woman who ran for state representative. We ran this campaign, and by the end of [19]48 the [Progressive] Party had received a very small vote, and it sort of disheartened people.

And at that time the Cold War was on, getting stronger. The Communist trial was getting stronger [Sid is apparently referring to the harassment of the Party under the Smith Act] and I decided to stay in Connecticut. I moved down to New Haven from Waterbury. I worked in the Connecticut Party from [19]48 to [19]68. I was a youth organizer for the Party, then I was an organizer for the *[Daily] Worker*. I was still considered the organizer for the Waterbury section. I was on the state committee of the Party, with Joe [Dimow], with Jake [Goldring], [and] with my neighbor downstairs [in the duplex in which Sid presently lives]. He was the chairman of the Party then, until we were arrested in [19]54.

DS: This was under the Smith Act?

SR: Under the Smith Act. We were arrested for violating the Smith Act, conspiring to violate the Smith Act. This was on Memorial Day of 1954. We went to trial later, the following year. We had a very long trial. There were eight of us defendants, and we had several stool pigeons who were members of the Party who we knew, friends of ours, who testified against us. But the guy who testified against me was such a fool and [an] idiot, that I don't think the jury believed him. So, when the verdict came in, one of the guys was freed, they had a hung-jury decision on me, and the others were convicted. Now the guys who were convicted, the six of them, they went to the appeals court, and the appeals courts reversed the decision. When they reversed the decision on them I was also freed.

But, at that time I was still working with the Party. I stayed with the Party, [though] the Party had then become very small. I think at one time there may have been twenty members in the state. I was in charge for a while [of] a group in Hartford. We even had a little youth group in Hartford.

DS: What year was that?

SR: That was in the early sixties, the late fifties, early sixties. The anti-Vietnam war movement was developing then. As this movement developed, it had a great impact and [offered] a great lesson for us. During the Korean War, and in other situations, the Communist Party always thought that [if] it would organize it would inspire others to do things. Very often we would say or think [to ourselves] that we were responsible for this or that thing happening in the peace movement and so forth. But as the anti-Vietnam War movement developed, we saw that it was developing without any effort from us. We had no input into it. We didn't know who the people were. There were people coming forward that were motivated by either pacifist views or peace views or democratic views or civil-libertarian views or religious views, who came forward from everyplace. There was no counting them. The Party could take no credit for this, because this was already far beyond the influence of the Party. It made me realize for the first time that in social movements the CP, which always boasted that it's responsible for this, and responsible for that, inspired this, inspired that, that really it doesn't inspire everything. That even in situations where, say, children of communists were involved, where they did it on their own, that the Party was not the direct instigator of all these things. This was a very important lesson for me, because you realize after a while that no political organization has that much power and influence to serve as that source of inspiration, that there were many other currents which fed into mass protests.

Now, I stayed with the Party. We had a branch of the Party in New Haven, we had a branch of the Party in Hartford, this is what I know. There may have been one or two little groups in Bridgeport. I did a lot of work for the Party. For instance, before I was arrested, we tried to put out a bulletin, a state- wide bulletin, Connecticut bulletin, and I was mainly responsible for that. Then we put out a page for the Weekly *Worker*, a Connecticut page, and I used to be responsible for that. I had to get it into the mail on Sunday night, so that they would get it in New York in time to print it, and it had a lot of articles on Connecticut. I was like the pinch-hitter. We had then a leadership of the [Connecticut] Party that consisted of four people: there was Jake Goldring, there was Sid Taylor, there was Bob Eakins, there was me. We were like the active core of the Party. This is already after the trial. One of the defendants who was freed, Al Marder, was not active in the Party at all during this period. He was in business and sort of stayed away from politics. And Joe had left the Party. So there was the four of us. I stayed with the Party until [19]68.

I left the Party for a combination of reasons; I would say there were three. One was the Party's attitude toward Israel. I thought the Party was wrong in completely condemning Israel as the aggressor in the 1967 war. Now that was a sore point in the Party, because the American Party wanted very much to be on the Arabs' side on this conflict, and it regarded anyone who wavered or disagreed with them as being subject to Zionism—Jewish nationalism. I was opposed to the Party's stand on the Six-Day War, and I favored the *Freiheit's* stand; the *Freiheit* broke with the Party over that issue, too. I was with the *Freiheit*, I knew the editor of the *Freiheit*, I knew other writers on the *Freiheit*, and I started little by little to work with the *Freiheit*. I used to translate for them, because they needed an English translator. So I worked for the *Freiheit*.

Then, in [19]68, there occurred two very disturbing things. One was a party-manipulated rise in anti-Semitism in Poland, which at that time was run by a Party leader called Gomulka. He was in rivalry with another Party leader, and both of them resorted to anti-Semitism against each other. As a result of that, it ruined the Jewish community in Poland. Many of the Jews left, and many of the Jewish communists left. It was a big blow. Here, I was talking to people in the Party and saying there's anti-Semitism in the Polish Communist Party. You guys admit it. What do we say about it? What do we do about it? And these guys'—the Party guys—position was [that] Poland is a socialist country. It's under attack from American imperialism. What they're doing may not be right, but we should not add to their difficulties. This was the classical, traditional answer that they gave. So don't criticize it. And because the *Freiheit* criticized them (and I wanted them to criticize) they were angry at us. So that was the anti-Semitism.

And then, later that year was the end of the Prague Spring, when the Soviet Army moved into Czechoslovakia. Now, I would say that many of the communists around here sympathized, at least for a while, with Dubcek and the Czech communists. However, when they saw that the Soviet Union moved in, then again the old rationale: "The Soviet Union is defending the socialist camp, it's fighting against America, we should not criticize them," you know, that kind of stuff. By that time I was no longer on the state committee. I left the state committee of the Party after the Six-Day War, June [19]67. That summer I left the state committee. I left the Party, I would say, in August or September of [19]68. And I've never been back. [Now] I work for the *Freiheit*, I work for *Jewish Currents*.

DS: When did you begin working for *Jewish Currents*?

SR: Well, the *Freiheit* and *Jewish Currents* both took the position that Israel was not the aggressor in the Six-Day War. The *Jewish Currents* editor was also a former communist who had left the Party earlier. I think he left in the [19]56 period, when the Party really split and dwindled to a smaller outfit; he left then, also mainly on the Jewish question [and] the Khrushchev revelations. So the *Jewish Currents* and the *Freiheit* were, in a way, allies, because both of us came from the Party, both had a socialist outlook, and both shared similar positions on Israel and the problem of anti-Semitism in the Soviet

Union. We wanted the American Party to be more critical of anti-Semitism in the Soviet Union. And they said no, we don't want to be more critical, we don't want to be public about it, because we don't want to hurt the Soviet Union—you know, that sort of stuff.

So, I began to work with both, because, first, the *Currents* consisted of people that were more my age, whereas the people in the *Freiheit* were the generation ahead. They were my mother's generation, the people in the *Freiheit*, like [Paul] Novick, who died last year, he was ninety-six years old. And all his peers, they were in their eighties and nineties when the *Freiheit* folded. So they were at that time in their seventies, you know, sixties and seventies, in [19]68.

DS: You were in your late forties?

SR: Yeah, late forties, that's right. I preferred also to work with the *Currents*. Now these were not organizations, they were publications, and we were trying to get subscribers, to raise money for them. Occasionally I would contribute articles or translations. I'd get a lot of translating work for the *Freiheit*. As a matter of fact, Novick, who was the editor of the paper, and was an extraordinary man—a Jewish Marxist, left-wing leader, and I would say a very competent journalist—I was his main translator for many years. All his reports that he gave in Yiddish, his main reports, I translated.

DS: For the English-language section of the *Freiheit*?

SR: For the English language section of the *Freiheit*. And some of his reports were put out as pamphlets that I translated. For instance, he did a critique of Irving Howe's book *World of Our Fathers*, and I translated that, and it was published in English. It was published as a pamphlet. He did a critique of the Polish communist position at the time when there was the anti-Semitic wave in the Communist Party there [in the late 1960s]. He had several articles, and I translated them, and they were put out in a pamphlet. That was a service I did for the *Freiheit* and for Novick. I'm glad I did, because if I didn't do it, nobody else would do it for the money they paid, which was next to nothing. They couldn't get a competent translator. Competent translators, if they were around, either were not sympathetic to the *Freiheit* and were not willing to work for it, [or] were certainly not willing to work for what the *Freiheit* was willing pay them. In me they had the lucky combination that I was with the *Freiheit* and I think I was a competent translator.

So, every week for seventeen, eighteen years, I weekly had something in the paper, sometimes an article of my own or very often translations by Novick of an article by the associate editor, Suler, or translations by the editor of the Soviet [Yiddish] magazine in Moscow, Vergelis, and translations of Israeli communist leaders, whose articles I had in Yiddish. I felt I was performing a service, because I was able to bring the writings of these Jewish communist leaders of different countries to the very limited English readership of our paper. I was glad to see that a couple of the things that I translated turned up in books. Like, there was a book, *The Left and the Jew*, by— [gets up to search for book]

DS: Liebman, *Jews and the Left* —

SR: Yes, *Jews and the Left*, by [Arthur] Liebman. He has one of my translations of Olgin.

DS: Max Olgin?

SR: Moishe Olgin, or Messiah Olgin, who was the founder and first editor of the *Freiheit*. Novick took over from him in 1939. Olgin was a great Russian Jewish intellectual.He was a Party liner (this is in the thirties when Stalin was there), but when he had the opportunity, he diverged from the Party line and explored new approaches. For instance, he was one of the first, or the very first, person in the Yiddish Left movement who raised the question of cooperation (this was during the Popular Front period), of Jewish communists with Zionists and rabbis in the fight against fascism. Now, this was unheard [of] 'til then, because rabbis were [seen by the Left as] our enemies. And he raised the question of our cooperating with them. He was, I would say, still hesitant, and it was hemmed with all kinds of qualifications. But the point was that in the fight against fascism, Jews have to join together, unite—we must unite with Zionists, Social Democrats, too. So, this was an innovation that Olgin introduced. Now, he introduced it under the impact of the whole Popular Front concept that swept through the Western communist parties, but he nevertheless did it. I translated some of his articles of that period. So I was glad to see that it was picked up by a guy like Liebman.

I stayed with the *Freiheit* almost to the end. Near the end, I had a quarrel, not so much with the paper as with another writer for the paper who misrepresented something I said about East Germany. I asked Novick for the right to reply to him. Now, this other person was a very well known Yiddish cultural movement leader in New York, then and now, and Novick didn't want to get involved in a polemic between us, because he felt it would not end soon. He was also a politician; he didn't want to antagonize his allies. So, for a while, I stayed away, I didn't write anything for the paper. But then I started writing, translating again for the paper, but not to the extent that I did before. And then in [19]88 the paper closed down, and a year later Novick died. We used to say [that] the tragedy of his life was that he wanted to die first, and the paper would continue. Instead, the paper died first, and he had to live a year with the knowledge that he survived the paper rather than the opposite. It's sad.

DS: Now, what I find very interesting about what you've just spoken about, Sid, is the way in which your political involvement and your Jewish ethnicity just seem to be combined almost naturally. Do you attribute that to your upbringing [in which] politics and ethnicity were considered almost synonymous?

SR: Let me say this. By the way, Irving Howe touches on this in his book, when he discusses young Jewish American communists, so I want to be frank with you on this. I was brought up in the Jewish movement, in the Jewish Left movement, and there were people, some friends of mine, who really wanted to remain in this movement. They felt at home in it. In *my* case, it was a little different. I was brought up in this Jewish Left movement, but I always thought that the great contribution that I would make, or people like me would make, would be in the broader American movement. So that while I was never a conscious assimilator, I would say that for a considerable period of my life, I had been following an assimilator's path. Because, when I returned from the war, I didn't rejoin any Jewish movement. I worked for the Communist Party, for the American Veterans' Committee. I worked for the Communist Party here in Connecticut. I was in the Progressive [Party], but we called it in Connecticut the People's Party. Generally in the country it was the Progressive Party. So, I worked for the People's Party, and I worked with [the] YPA,

Young Progressives of America. And the communists formed a youth organization in 1949 called Labor Youth League, and I was Connecticut chairman of the Connecticut Youth League. Now, all these activities took me away from the Jewish movement.

When I'd come from Connecticut to visit my mother I would see the *Freiheit* and read it there. And maybe I subscribed to the *Freiheit* then, I don't [recall]. I was never completely away from it. I sort of followed it, I had an interest in it. And then I had friends that I continued with [who were] in the Jewish movement. I did not work in the Jewish movement, [but] I never was completely disconnected with it, because of friendships and just because I followed it. And also, the Communist Party in Connecticut had an interest in the Jewish movement, because, say, in this city [New haven] and in Hartford, we had a Jewish following, a Yiddish-speaking following. We had a Yiddish cultural club in New Haven. We had a Yiddish cultural club in Hartford. And we had individual smaller groups of Jewish people, Yiddish speakers, in some of the different towns in Connecticut, like Bridgeport [and] Stamford. These were mostly people of the older generation. Now, we were very interested in maintaining contact with them, because they were a source of support for us, [including] financial support. Some of their children were in the movement, but most of their children were not in the communist movement, but they were progressive people elsewhere. You know, they worked in other organizations. By the way, this was different among the Jewish communists in Connecticut than of communists from other ethnic groups.

DS: Speak a little about that, [about] how it was different.

SR: It was different in this way. During the thirties, there were several ethnic groups working in Connecticut, communist ethnic groups among the Lithuanians, the Russians, the Ukrainians, Hungarians, and to a smaller extent among Italians. Now, to my knowledge very few of the children of these ethnic groups remained with the communist movement. I think it was because the children felt that this was a bar to their acceptance—their American acceptance—that their parents were foreign-born. And they associated the communist movement with being foreign, too.

DS: So, in other words, it was both the politics of their parents, as well as their ethnicity [that] they considered a hindrance.

SR: Right, right. Now, I had a chance to observe this very closely the year that I lived in Waterbury and worked with the Progressive Party, because in Torrington, Ansonia, and Waterbury we had groups of foreign-born workers, either Russians, Lithuanians, Ukrainians, and Italians, who were, I thought, for the most part, wonderful people. Very fine people. And many of them were leftists from the old country. Some of them became leftists in this country, working in factories, and so forth. Very devoted. Not politically knowledgeable in any way. They accepted what the Party said. They didn't read very much, except maybe some of them read literature in their native language. These people had their own organizations, and the party tried to be the unifier, the coordinator, of everything. Sometimes they respected the Party, sometimes they didn't.

For instance, I learned for a fact that there were many Russians who were in these left-wing movements, not because they were left, but because this was a Russian nationalist expression to them. This was their way of defending Soviet Russia. I found this among Russians: The class, the social angle, was less important to them than was the national angle, of defending Russia, defending Soviet Russia. This was also true of some Ukrainians. They thought that the Ukraine under the Soviet regime was coming into its own as a cultural, independent force or national force, and this is what attracted them, not so much the general politics. So, some of them, with this type of view, didn't have any particular love for Jews in the Party.

[The] Russians had a big group in Waterbury, I would say a few hundred people. They owned a building on North Elm Street called the Russian Hall, which had two floors, the basement and the first floor, which was a meeting room. And the Party would have its meetings there, too. Some of the Russians resented us. Now, part of it was it was the Cold War, but part of it was, too, that they were not happy to see Jews, Jewish communists, in the place. What they saw was that the representatives of the American CP were young American Jews, and they knew that in the city there were several other American Jews, born in Waterbury, who were very middle class people, who had nothing to do with them, because these were all working class people. There were a few of them who had no love for us. So, this is one factor.

The other [factor] is that none of these people brought their children to come into the communist movement, none of them did. Most of their children were not even progressive or liberal. Among the Jews, the Yiddish-speaking Jews, they raised their children, and most of them, too, did not come into the communist movement, but a few more did than, say, among the Russians. No, I would say that a much bigger percentage among the Jews, the American-born Jews of communist parents, came into the movement, than was true of the other ethnic groups.

DS: Let me ask you something at this point: For yourself personally and for other Jewish communists, was there either a heightened sense of ethnicity or [a] different sense of ethnic solidarity among Jews than among other ethnic groups in the Party?

SR: Heightened sense of solidarity? I don't know about a heightened [sense]. Well, first, we were more sensitive, cognitive, of the Jewish question because of Hitler, the legacy of the Hitler period, the Holocaust, [and] the question of anti-Semitism in the Soviet Union, so that, I would say that there was a greater feeling of Jewish ethnicity among children of Jewish communists than there was a feeling of ethnicity amongst children of Ukrainian or Russian American communists.

DS: Now, I imagine the State of Israel would also have heightened that whole—

SR: Yes, that's right.

DS: —that whole question. I wanted to ask you about that, too, because you mentioned the Russian nationals who supported the Soviet Union for nationalist reasons. Do you feel [there] may have been some confusion about the defense of Israel by Jewish communists, a sense that maybe nationalism was taking precedence over the political questions?

SR: Yeah. You know, at the time there were some people who were aware of this. In 1948 I was in Waterbury, and I was working for the Progressive Party. I knew that the Soviet Union and the communist movement were defending Israel [the Soviet Union was among the first nations to grant official recognition to the new State of Israel, although this was revoked a few years later]. So a lot of people in the communist movement, even though they had no particular interest in Israel, the fact that the Soviet Union was supporting Israel, that sort of decided it for them. It wasn't that they were particularly vehement in defense of Israel, but as long as the Soviet Union was supporting Israel, they were supporting Israel. And it seemed at the time that the United States was lukewarm in its support for Israel, which it was for different periods.

DS: For the newly established state of Israel?

SR: Yeah. In 1948. So, the Progressive Party, for instance, took a very strong stand in defense of Israel, whereas Truman and the Democrats were more wishy-washy on it. There was, I would say, among some sections of the Jewish communists a great pride and interest in Israel. I was not among them at the time. I went along with it because the Party went along with it, the Soviet Union went along with it. And if they were for it, I was for it, too. But I didn't feel any great urgency to defend Israel.

DS: You never considered yourself a Zionist, for example.

SR: No, never, never. As a matter of fact, what prevented me from being more pro-Israel at the time was that I had a distaste for Zionists. I did not like their parochialism. I did not like their attitude that Jews are always going to suffer from anti-Semitism. This was like a built-in guarantee for them, that this movement would always exist, because there would always be anti-Semitism. There's no possibility that it would ever end or disappear.

DS: Or that the only solution to the Jewish problem was—

SR: That's right, was Israel.

DS: —a national home.

SR: That's right. And I never felt that way. Later, I felt that this was also a very one-sided view, because the Zionists had to be given a lot of credit. They prepared Palestine for the State of Israel. Were it not for them, many of the refugees after the war, where would they have gone? I sort of mellowed, somewhat, toward Israel, though I still have a strong suspicion and distaste for Zionism. I feel that the Zionist movement, outside of Israel, has been more a negative factor, that the Zionist movement—the pro-Israeli attitude that many Jews have—has created a parochialism and a chauvinism amongst Jews that we didn't have in the thirties. I thought that Jewish people in the thirties were more liberal, more progressive, more attuned, to broader social concerns. Whereas, I think that the obsession with Israel, and this whole one-sided defense of Israel, has turned many Jews in a right-wing, chauvinist direction. I feel very hostile to them for that reason.

DS: Would it be safe to say, then, that your break with the Party [is] partly attributable to the fact that they took a one-sided position on the other side?

SR: Yeah, that's right, that's right. They deny all these things. They didn't see any validity in Israel at all. They didn't give any recognition to the factor of anti-Semitism, which persists in socialist societies, and why does it persist. Nobody would want to investigate why it would persist. They would say, oh, it's due to Hitler, but the fact is that there are other reasons why it persists. One of the reasons is that Jews in the socialist countries, in the Soviet Union, occupy professional positions. Most working Jews in the Soviet Union are in the professional classes. They are better educated than many other people, percentage-wise. People from other nationalities see that Jews are a big proportional force in the arts, the sciences—not in politics, not in the army, not in diplomacy, but in other areas they are. When you're in a situation in a country where there are few positions available, and the positions that are available are proportionately held by a [large] number of Jews, this creates an anti-Semitic feeling. If the Party doesn't curb it, doesn't explain it, doesn't do anything to resist it, then it becomes a big force. Now, the CP here never wanted to recognize that, never dealt with that. Other people did, there were others who did, called attention to it. But the Party didn't want to because the Party's position was [that] socialism solves all questions—the women question, the nationalities question—it'll solve this question, too.

DS: Let me ask you about something related to what you just said. Given the tendency of many national and ethnic groups toward what you call parochialism, have you ever felt any sense of conflict or tension between the two important factors in your life, that is, Jewish culture and your political involvement?

SR: Yeah, absolutely. Any intelligent communist—Jewish communist, especially—at different times would have felt these tensions, some more, some less. For instance, when the thing happened in Poland [a campaign by the Polish Communist Party in the late 1960s to remove "Zionists" from its ranks, widely viewed as a thinly veiled anti-Semitic purge], everybody was talking—the press was talking— that Jewish communists were being singled out, pilloried, condemned, fired from jobs, forced to leave the country. And there were even Polish communist leaders at the time who were saying, "Hey, what are we doing here? What are you doing? It's wrong, it's wrong what you're doing to the Jews." When you talk to Communist Party officials at home, including the Jews among them, they would say this is being blown up by the Zionists, it's being blown up by the Jewish nationalists. They have problems, they'll overcome these problems. Don't worry about it. Let's not go public, let's not raise this in the public, and all that kind of stuff. In this situation, my Jewish concern overrode Party loyalty. And I was really pissed off at the Party leaders, that they permitted this. And there were other situations like this. Even before the Six-Day War, the Israeli Communist Party—at that time there were two Communist parties in Israel—but the more Jewish Communist Party in Israel—

DS: The one that didn't have Arab members?

SR: That's right. That was *Makai*. They were raising questions before the international movement. They said, look what Nasser is saying about Israel, that it should be wiped out. And look what Ben Bella in Algeria is saying about Israel, it should be wiped out. What right do they have to say [it]; why are they anti-imperialists? Why are they progressives if they say that Israel should be wiped out? And the answer was [that] the struggle against imperialism is the basic struggle of our time. These people are part of the anti-imperialist movement. On these questions, while we don't agree with them (some of them didn't even say that, they wouldn't go so far as to say that), we don't want to make a public issue out of it. So, if you were a Jewish communist, and you were aware that there was a state of Israel, that it was not a fascist state, it was a democratic state, and communists were a legal party there, there was a labor movement and a peace movement, and all that kind of stuff, and here anti-imperialist friends of the Soviet Union are saying wipe Israel out, naturally, this also created a tension. You felt you were in a contradictory position. I used to raise these questions. I raised these questions with guys like Aptheker, in the Communist Party.

DS: Herbert Aptheker [Marxist historian and specialist in African-American history]?

SR: Yeah. I saw then that it was a waste of time talking to them, that Aptheker and Lumer—Hy Lumer.

DS: He was the editor of [the CP journal] *Jewish Affairs*?

SR: He was the Jewish commissar for the Party. And their whole position was: the main thing is [to] defend the Soviet Union [and] fight the anti-imperialist struggle. America is the main enemy, Israel is an ally of America, and we have to go along with the Soviet Union. So these people followed this. It was part of their assimilationist attitude, it fitted in with it. But it was also their extreme devotion. All they saw was loyalty to the Soviet Union. If you felt other loyalties, other concerns, you were continually at odds with them. It was not just me, it was Morris Schappes [editor of the *Jewish Currents*], it was Novick, it was Jewish communists all over the country, who felt this way and who were continually having these tensions with the communist leadership. In the case of the *Freiheit*, the *Freiheit* declared its independence from the Party in 1956, after the Khrushchev report. The *Freiheit* then felt it was no longer going to be an organ of the Party, a Jewish organ of the Party, and it declared itself to be an independent Jewish labor and people's newspaper, [a] progressive newspaper.

DS: Now, you bring up an interesting point, because so many people in the Party left over the Khrushchev speech in [19]56—

SR: Right.

DS: —why was that not a critical enough point for you to leave the Party? What was your thinking at the time?

SR: I was associated with the group in the Party that was eventually defeated—the Gates group. These were the reformers.

DS: And Gates was—

SR: Johnny Gates, he was the editor of the *Daily Worker* then. This was a group that was defeated. People that I respected in the Party, like A. B. Magill [author of *Israel in Crisis*, a book published in the 1950s that was critical of but not opposed to the then-new state] and people like that, they that were associated with the Gates group, and we were defeated.

We were defeated primarily because the bulk of the Party membership that might have supported a reformist position was so disheartened, so disappointed, and so annoyed with what went on or felt that they were had, they left in droves. Those that remained in the Party were the two extremes. The other extreme, the very pro-Soviet extreme, they were more manipulative, and they were more aggressive. They were better infighters than we were. To them it was very important to get the franchise from the Soviet Union, and they secured it. To us, it wasn't that important. We were more theoretical, more talkative, obviously, and they were interested in maintaining an apparatus, maintaining a Party machine that would be recognized by the Soviet Union.

Eventually, Gus Hall [chairman of the CPUSA] and his crowd won. And then, in my own case, I didn't leave the Party, though most of my friends did. I didn't leave the Party because I still felt that there is a role for a radical movement to play in this country against American imperialism, that would uphold a socialist-type solution, and the Party may yet change. Of course, not everybody in the reform movement in the Party had left the Party. Many remained in. For a time, the Party was more open on these things, a certain openness that it didn't have before Khrushchev's speech, and that it maintained into the early sixties. So, I felt maybe the Party'll change.

But by 1967, [19]68, it became very evident that the Gus Hall faction of the Party was completely in control, and that it was subservient to the Soviet Union type of position, and that there was going to be no change. At that time I didn't even think that there would be a big change in the Soviet Union. You sort of felt that this was like a given, a fixed thing. I stayed in the Party.

I would also say [there were] personal factors, too. I had friends who were still in the Party, and I didn't want to leave them completely. I thought maybe the Party would vindicate itself, it would [adopt] a correct political position, that kind of stuff. So, for these reasons I didn't leave the Party. I stayed on, and I was one of the leaders of the Party in Connecticut. I attended the Party's convention in 1966 in New York. I met Aptheker and all these other guys: Lumer, and we worked with Betty Gannett. She was like the Party rep to Connecticut for many years, several years. She was a Jewish woman, too, but also a person who despised the Yiddish movement. I mean, *despised* the Yiddish movement. I would say guys like Aptheker despised the Yiddish movement. They felt it was okay for the old-timers, that's their language, let it be. But that this Yiddish movement had a right to autonomy, that it had a right to consider its own positions, this was out. I personally think that Aptheker would have been happy if the Yiddish movement, the Jewish movement, could become an auxiliary to the black movement in America. I mean, the guy is so enamored of black people—

DS: Nationhood.

SR: Nationhood, peoplehood, culture. He is so enamored, Aptheker, that the preferred role for him for the Jewish movement was to be the auxiliary to help this oppressed people achieve their freedom. The fact that the Jewish people had its own vitality, its own reason to be, its own tradition, meant nothing to him, absolutely nothing. He even wrote an article that was published in *The Masses* at the time, no, *Masses and Mainstream*, [on] the superiority of the Negro, the superiority of the Negro. The guy has abnegated himself before the black movement. I don't know if he's still that [way] today. I think he is. He has no use for the Jewish movement, no use. I would say [that] guys like Aptheker, Lumer, Betty Gannett, and several other Jewish leaders of the Party tolerated the Jewish movement, the left-wing Jewish movement. They tolerated the *Freiheit*. Then, after the Arab-Israeli war of [19]67 they fought the *Freiheit* tooth and nail. They would have liked to destroy it. And it created a lot of animosity.

DS: Sid, you [have] had a certain tenacity, in terms of your determination both to remain Jewish-identified, but also [to remain] a Marxist [and] to continue in the Party as long as you could feel [that] in good conscience you could remain. Related to that question of the tension between Jewish ethnicity and politics is a similar question, and that is: Did you at any time feel that your own belief or confidence in Marxism as a guiding political philosophy was called into question because of these contradictions that you saw among so many Marxists, [that of] their inability to deal with this relationship between ethnicity and politics?

SR: Before I answer this question, let me just also say this. This question of Jewish cultural attachment, or concern, and Party loyalty, or loyalty to the social cause—socialism—this has been a continuing problem in the left-wing, Jewish movement. The left-wing, Jewish movement is a century old. The left-wing, Yiddish socialist movement is over a century [old] now, over a century. For instance, the founder, the man we call the grandfather of Jewish socialism, was Morris Winchevsky, who was born in Russia and as a young man went to England [where] he founded the first Yiddish, socialist newspaper in London. He became a very important journalist, and he came to the United States and worked in the Jewish, socialist press, the Yiddish, socialist press, in the United States. He was one of three people responsible in the Jewish movement for the break with Daniel DeLeon [of] the Socialist Labor Party and the eventual formation of the Socialist Party. So, the man goes back quite a way. Now, *he* had this problem, he had this problem with other socialists, including Jewish socialists, who looked down on the Jewish question, [who said] "what do you need it for? It's something for immigrants. Everybody will become Americanized in the United States, and they won't even *know* they're Jewish. Why are you bothering with this?" And he said, "We are a people, we are going to be a people for a long time. We have a culture, and a language, a beautiful language. We want to cultivate it. Yiddish is a language the immigrants know." So he continually had to fight for a position. The Jewish Socialist Federation of the Socialist Party had to fight for its position, against other people in the Socialist Party who were indifferent, or hostile.

   The same thing happened in the communist movement. There was a Jewish Federation in the Communist Party for a long time, [a] Jewish section of the Communist Party.

DS: The Jewish People's Fraternal Order?

SR: That was outside the Communist Party [in the International Workers Order, a "mass-based" multicultural organization that supported the communist movement]. There was a continual hostility within the communist movement toward, I wouldn't only say just toward the Yiddish movement, but I would say to all national movements. And at different times the Party felt this was source of strength, support, we get money from them, we get children, we get support from them and that's good, but the Party never recognized that these movements had a right to their own life, to their own autonomy. They felt that they were appendages of the Party, to carry through the Party's position within this national group, and that in time, when assimilation becomes more prevalent and dominant, these people will disappear, and the need for these movements will disappear. This is the traditional, and I would often say, the unspoken position that Jewish communists and communists of other national groups have. It's only when you look around—here and there, there were groups of people, in the Jewish movement much more, but even in other movements. For instance, among the Finns, the American Finns, there was a guy who's name was Ross, I think, Carl Ross, who did a big study of the Finnish communist movement in the United States and how, in this movement, they were fighting the Party for autonomy, for their own cultural identity, and so forth.
    I wanted to say that Winchevsky and later Olgin and still later Novick continually fought for what they called a synthesis, a synthesis between progressive Jewish culture and loyalty to socialism.

DS: Internationalism.

SR: Internationalism, yeah, yeah. And they felt that there was a synthesis between the two and that you had to fight for it, but it should always be accompanied with respect for the Yiddish culture, for the Yiddish movement, for its autonomy, for its right to exist, and so forth. One of the arguments we had with the Soviet Union after the fifties was that the Soviet Union didn't permit Yiddish organizations. There was no Yiddish cultural movement in the Soviet Union. There was no Jewish movement at all. You couldn't meet. If you were Jewish, you couldn't have a movement, you couldn't have an organization. At times there were Party leaders who found excuses for it: that the Jews are assimilating, they don't need Yiddish anymore. Why emphasize particularity when you should emphasize universalism, you know, that kind of thing. So these were the conflicts. Now, go back to your question.

DS: I wanted to know, given that history—[tape runs out].

   As the tape went out on the other side, you were talking about this history of trying to resolve this conflict, [to] create a synthesis between ethnicity and politics. Would you talk a little about what you feel may be a continuation of this problem, in terms of, say, generational conflict?

SR: Yeah. Now I remember what your previous question was, too. Did we feel that anything was wrong with Marxism? At the time, I never felt there was anything wrong with Marxism, if you want to put it that way. But you were worried, or wondering, whether the governments were doing—the socialist [and] communist governments—whether *they* were not committing mistakes. It never occurred at the time, say in the sixties and part of the seventies. I never questioned Marxism itself. I questioned the actions of communist governments, but not Marxism itself. I felt maybe the communist governments weren't applying Marxist thinking correctly, you know, that kind of thing. I would say it's only since Gorbachev that I feel there are questions about Marxism itself, about Leninism itself, that are legitimate to raise. For instance, to me, [there's] the whole question of the intrusive nature of a communist government, it's desire to control every aspect of life, including culture, recreation—not just the workplace, not just the politics, but every aspect of life. This is intolerable, it's absolutely wrong, it's absolutely wrong. I could see why, in the Soviet Union today, there are so many people that are so embittered—even against Lenin, who was my hero—because the Soviet government introduced an intrusiveness, a control of people's lives, that should never have occurred. So, there are a lot of questions about Marxism, about socialism itself, that you have to question now, that I question.

DS: How have you felt about this? Also, I was wondering if you might be able to look at the changes that have taken place, generational changes, because now you are a member of the older generation of the communist movement, in a sense. Do you feel there is a difference in historical perspective that the older generation has now, the older left generation, and yourself in particular?

SR: You say the communist movement. I'm out of the communist movement. I look at the communist movement, and very often I think, their role is spent, they're finished. It could be that something may happen and they may find a new *raison d'etre*, but as far as I can see, much of their role is diminished, and they're now going to play the role of any other small, radical party in America. They're going to be no different. They don't have a franchise from the Soviet Union anymore. Of course, the Soviet Union isn't interested in giving out franchises. Maybe they'll get a franchise from Castro, I don't know. I can't speak for these kinds of people. I know people of my generation who left the Communist Party, having differing views on what socialism is. In the *Jewish Currents* we had a forum, "Are you still for socialism?" Different people say, "I'm for socialism, it's how you define it." And I would say the same thing. I was brought up under [this] system. I very often tell this to Jewish immigrants from the Soviet Union who've come here, and they think that everything's so wonderful about this country—

DS: The new Jewish immigrants?

SR: —yeah—and they think everything's so wonderful. And I tell them what this capitalist society means to a person who's a working-class person, and that there are terrible problems in this country. They're not aware of these problems because all they see is the middle-class suburb, [and] they think they're gonna be part of it. They don't see that there's big pockets, big areas of people that are deprived and hungry and ill-educated, and really deteriorating. The whole population is deteriorating. They don't see that. So, very often I find I'm arguing with these people. "Look, this is also part of America that you've got to see, part of capitalist society," I would say, depending on what your definition of socialism is, [because] everybody has his own definition.

In a way, I think this is a time of sorting things out, of waiting. The whole communist, socialist movement has proved to be wrong in many of its assumptions, in many of its accomplishments or lack of accomplishments. We didn't understand many things. And even though I'm outside the communist movement, in a sense I share some of these faults, and some of these negative things that happened because at one time I had supported them. Even after I left the communist movement, I still didn't see the full depth of some of the things that were wrong.

To me, one of the enduring accomplishments of the communist movement, for which I feel very grateful, is its sense of internationalism. See, the communist movement did inculcate a sense of internationalism in people, respect for other people, an interest in other people's culture, and this to me is a very important thing. I meet people today, let's say at Yale [where Sid works in the Law Library], young people from other countries, and if I know the country they're from, like Greece, let's say—we have a person from Greece—just from remembering what I read in the communist press thirty years ago, I can talk to them about Greek politics at the time. And they're amazed: "How do you remember this, why do you know this?" And you knew because you were in the communist [movement], and the whole struggle of every country against imperialism was something that you wanted to follow. So, it created a great respect for other people, a desire to learn, which people [who are] not communist or socialist don't have.

I remember the second time I saw Norman Thomas [longtime leader of the Socialist Party in the United States]. It was after my Smith Act trial, and he spoke at Yale. I'll never forget this. I was sitting nearby, and I think I was the oldest guy in the audience at the time, there were all young students. And people asked him what he liked about the socialist movement, what he liked most about it, and he said the same thing. He said this, that it's the sense of internationalism, the sense that you're part of an international struggle against injustice, against capitalism, exploitation, you know, all that; that people in other countries were your allies, brothers, that you worked with them. See, this is an important accomplishment of the communist movement, of the socialist movement. It touched me that even Norman Thomas felt it. This is one of the good things that the communist movement accomplished. But this was done with the accompanying of so many bad things that you wonder [if] the price [was] worth it.

DS: Even so, there was a sense of solidarity, and I've heard it described—tell me if it's appropriate in your case—a sense of almost family, or home. [Actually, Sid alluded to it earlier in the interview.] Did you feel that when you were active in the Party?

SR: Oh yeah, oh sure. I mean, the Soviet Union was like the homeland. It was the country of the Revolution, the first country that made the revolution, Lenin's country, the country that suffered so much to build socialism.

DS: Did you feel that same kind of sense of family or home with your comrades here, in the American Party?

SR: Until I began to question the Party politically—

DS: In—

SR: —in the late sixties, I would say I felt that, too. I accepted a lot of things that the Party said, even though I didn't think they were the wisest things. Maybe they knew better than me. There's always somebody who knows better than you why certain things are done, and you just went along and accepted it. I remember in [19]49, I think it was, the Italian communist leader made a famous statement that if Italy goes to war with the Soviet Union, the communists in Italy will defend the Soviet Union. And then communist leaders in other countries said the same thing, they will defend the Soviet Union. And then Paul Robeson here, said that black people in this country will defend the Soviet Union. And William Z. Foster, the [CPUSA leader], said the American workers are going to defend the Soviet Union, and I thought, hey, c'mon, they're not going to defend the Soviet Union. Why even bring it up, there's no need to even bring it up. I kidded with my friend, "What the hell do we have to bring it up for? It's not necessary for us to say it." But I went along with it. It's just this idea of affirming your solidarity with the Soviet Union, carrying the banner, holding the banner. I would say that many communists are very uncritical. Many communists are very uncritical.

DS: So, it's sort of like defending the family, right or wrong?

SR: Defending the family, right or wrong, that's right. And I'll tell you, I found another thing. Once I left the Communist Party, I started to do a lot of reading that you never did when you were in the Communist Party, not only because the Communist Party discouraged it. We just didn't have the time, we didn't have the time. You're so bound up in this campaign, that campaign, and reading Party literature, that you don't have the opportunity to read other types of literature. For instance, one of the great influences on my life after I left the Party was Isaac Deutscher, former communist, great historian of the Russian Revolution. [It] opened up a new world to me. Many of the questions that I had raised, or felt and never spoke, here the guy's writing about it. After being with this type of approach for many years, I look back at my former comrades and I try to talk to them, and I see how narrow they are. They are really very narrow people. They're very parochial, they're very limited in some ways and they also are very hypocritical in some ways. I know people, say if Israel commits a human-rights violation, oh, they're burned up. But at the same time, they kept quiet about much more massive human rights violations in other socialist countries. Never said a word about it. So, [there's] this selectivity. And a lot people take things on faith. The communist movement attracts all kinds of people, so it attracts people that are dull as well as brilliant, and inquiring as well as stolid. So, you get people like that. I look at these people today and say, hey, these were my old buddies. I can't even find a common language with them today.

DS: This raises a very interesting question. As you've grown older, and have explored a wider spectrum of alternatives, you still call yourself a Marxist—

SR: Yeah, I think so.

DS: —how is it that you think that you've changed and others have remained more rigid? I mean, there's a common assumption that as you grow older, you become more rigid, but it's not true in your case, certainly.

SR: Well, listen. It's probably the great differentiation among people that shows up in different ways. I'd also say this. This is the unkindest thing to say. There are communists in this city, for instance, guys like [Sid mentions the name of a prominent local Party leader] and some of his buddies, who have such a heavy investment, their entire life—even though they may have had qualms of their own, they kept [it] to themselves. I *know* they have qualms. But publicly, politically, they had such a commitment that it is now awkward and difficult for them to say, on many things, we were wrong. It's very difficult for them to say that. A guy like [him], I know, is very annoyed with Gorbachev, feels he's an enemy or certainly doesn't trust him, doesn't trust him. And there are a whole group of communists in this country who do not trust the present Soviet leadership. They were hoping that Ligachev [a more "conservative" Politburo member] would win. They don't know which way the Soviet Union is going.

By the way, I don't know which way the Soviet Union is going, either. And not everything that's happening there am I happy about. There are some things that people are saying there, in newspapers and elsewhere, [such] that I'm amazed. For instance, one of the best Soviet newspapers today, the most critical of the past, is a weekly paper *Ogonyok* [literally, "the light"]. And one of the writers for this paper had just been to Israel and said he's planning to write a series of pro-Israeli articles for *Ogonyok* to end this one-sided criticism of Israel. Okay, let's end the one-sided criticism, but he's going further than that. He is making a defense of Israeli policy, Israeli government policy. Hey, what are you doing? The Israeli government policy is wrong in its oppression of another people, we've got to recognize that. But there are some people who are so eager to jump into Western-type positions. They don't distinguish these things. Maybe these things will sort themselves out after all.

DS: Of course that raises a lot of these questions. The whole issue of what Marxism is has become very, very murky.

SR: That's right.

DS: But let's get back to the point after you left the Party. The lack of the political affiliation must have [left] a real gap. Obviously, politically you're still committed to the socialist movement, but without that organizational framework. Two related questions: Was there a sense of loss that you felt—

SR: Yes.

DS: —and how did you compensate? Did you feel there was adequate compensation?

SR: First, I was brought up with these people. I lived with these people for many years. They were friends of mine, friends of my wife's, friends of my children. [I] was not happy to know that they disliked me or they spoke against me. Some of them said unkind things about me. There's one guy in Hartford, who is much richer than I am, and he said that I sold out to the middle class. These things happen. But then, as time went on and I became more acquainted, I read more. I began to see the limitations of these people, and it bothered me less. It bothered me less that I was not their friend anymore. Because, for some of them I said, So what's the big deal if you're not friends with them. They're not that important or stimulating or great people. If they could cut you off, why be so sad about it? So I began to see them in a somewhat different light.

   The other thing was [that] I did have an organizational affiliation. I was associated with the *Freiheit*, I was associated with *Jewish Currents*, I was associated first with *Breira* [a precursor to New Jewish Agenda], and then with New Jewish Agenda. So, I had progressive organizations I belonged to, that I could meet with people, talk to people. I wasn't like a leaf flying around in the wind. These were compensations for me. These were not organizations like the Party, with the discipline of the Party. But I didn't miss that. I didn't miss that discipline, because I saw that this discipline was also self-defeating and restrictive, and that kind of thing. So I didn't miss it that much.

DS: Also you had the compensation provided by your increased activity in organizations that consisted not only of your political contemporaries, but [of] age contemporaries as well.

SR: Yeah, yeah, that's right. And political contemporaries. Some of these people were younger people we could work with. So I didn't really feel that great a loss. And I used to look at the Communist Party from a distance. I was interested in what they were doing. I would try to follow their press, and their articles, and things like that. And I was always looking for changes, different types of formulations. Not until Gorbachev was there any great change. Under Gorbachev, it became interesting to watch how they were scrambling to reassert themselves, scrambling to say that they knew this all along. Now all the communist leaders say, oh, during the Brezhnev period we tried to say this and tried to do this. We were opposed to this, and [were] opposed to that, like hindsight. But I don't believe these people, because they may have had private qualms, but they fought *us*. What I have against a guy like Aptheker and Gus Hall, people like that is, not that they were wrong, so much —you're in politics, you make mistakes—[as that] they were consistently wrong, they were badly wrong. But what was worse was they were nasty about it. It's their nastiness, their superiority, their pomposity, especially in the case of Aptheker. This is what gripes me more than anything else. They insulted people. Like, what's his name, Aptheker insulted the editor of the *Freiheit* on the Israeli position by saying that Novick is a colonialist, [a] *colonialist* because Israel was a colonial country. Israel wanted to be a colonial power, and Novick supported Israel, so he's a colonialist. It's this nastiness, this intolerance, this is what gets me. I just reached the point, hey, hell with these people. They're not that important. You don't miss 'em that much.

DS: When you left the Party, there was a sense of alienation from your political comrades who had failed to move with the times. At the same time, the Old Jewish Left that you were always very much identified with, committed to, was experiencing what we might call retrenchment, to the extent that the younger generation of Jewish political activists was very different and did not identify with the Old Left, [the] communist movement, [or] with Yiddish culture. I was wondering how you and your comrades in the *Freiheit* and *Jewish Currents* felt about being a sort of older generation up against some real odds.

SR: I would say there were many people who worried about it. There were people who worried about these questions, particularly the younger people, people my age.

DS: Younger people in their fifties and sixties, instead of the *Freiheit* people in their seventies and eighties.

SR: That's right.

SR: Right, right. We worried about these things. And we couldn't do very much about it for these reasons. One was that—and this is the fault of Paul Novick and the *Freiheit* group—they were so concerned in maintaining this Yiddish newspaper that it blotted out a lot of other concerns. They were so concerned with maintaining the paper from day to day, and afterward from week to week, that they never gave much thought to succession. I once asked the associate editor of the *Freiheit*, Suler, "What you people think about? Do you ever worry about succession?" And he asked me, "What does it mean, succession?" [laughs], and I tried to explain to him. If they thought about it, it was like some vague thing. Their immediate thing was raising money for the paper. And they raised an awful lot of money for the paper. The *Freiheit* raised more money—you know, it's really fantastic—no other paper this size could go to its readers and get a quarter of a million dollars a year, year after year, year after year, certainly in the whole postwar period, more than that. Eventually, so many of its readers went into old age homes and no longer had [subscriptions] or couldn't read the paper anymore because of their eyesight that the paper had to fold. This is really what brought the paper down. So there was worry about it. But the *Freiheit* editors, they should have been the ones to stimulate this. They never thought of it. They never thought of doing anything about it. They never encouraged younger people. For instance, Paul Novick never invited me to—he wanted me to work for the paper, but when I told him how much I would need for pay and for the expense of running back and forth from New Haven to New York, he said, "We'll pay you more than we pay me." So how much more was it? It was like a hundred and fifty dollars. They were going to offer me a hundred and fifty dollars a week. You see, this guy's on Social Security, so to him a hundred fifty was big pay. He was going to offer that to me. And this was at a time when pay should have been like two hundred fifty. I said I can't do it. If you have to spend forty dollars for fare a month—it'd be much more than that, because you have to pay your New York [fare] and pay to get back here. So, they didn't encourage me, or other people, younger people. And, in a sense, toward the end, they had nobody they could entrust the paper to.

DS: How did you, in turn—obviously the younger generation in relation to the *Freiheit*, the older generation relative to the younger Jewish socialists and communists—how did you deal with what still is a generation gap between the *Currents* and the people involved with [the *Freiheit*]—

SR: You said *Currents*, you mean the *Jewish Currents*?

DS: The *Jewish Currents*, yeah.

SR: How did we deal with that.

DS: Yeah. What was your feeling? [Also], to put it very bluntly, did you have any self-consciousness about the fact that you and your comrades were also aging.

SR: Yeah, yeah. I'll tell you, the same problem the *Freiheit* had, the *Currents* has. It's odd. The editor of the *Currents*, Morris Schappes, [is] a very fine man, and yet he is not struggling and fighting for succession. He had a young person [Larry Bush] who was editor for a while. They couldn't get along. I think it was the generation gap. You know, Larry Bush and Schappes. And Larry Bush went off on his own, and he didn't succeed on his own. Maybe he'll be working with the *Currents* again. But you have these strong individuals who take over a magazine or publication, put their stamp on it, and think that it can't exist in any other way but their way. This may be a problem for the *Currents*, too. Very often Joe [Dimow] and I talk about it: "Who's going to take over if Schappes becomes incapacitated?" And we don't know. There may be nobody to take over.

DS: Do you think that maybe it's not necessarily a question of Jewish ethnicity itself, but [rather] the *Currents* [generation]—your generation—and how you looked at and handled things? Do you think that it's in some sense a product of age, that your experience is not easily translatable?

SR: Oh yeah, oh yeah. I would say that. Younger people come in, I've seen, say at meetings of the *Currents* board. A lot of things they look at as very quaint. When we talk about some of the things of the past, some things that happened twenty five years ago—you know, [like] the extreme devotion to the Soviet Union—they can't understand it. First, they may even think we were fools for having been that way. [With] some of them, I have to say, it's very much like [the way] Zionists have a feeling towards Israel. Actually, the communists and the Zionists have very much in common, except that the Zionists have lasted longer. I mean, complete fidelity to the Israeli government, seeing every thing Israel does [through] rose-colored glasses. They're always right, everybody else is wrong. This feeling of aloneness, against the rest of the world, that kind of stuff. And it's very much like the way it was in the Communist movement. So, maybe some people can understand, you know, make a parallel with that.

I would say that in the American Jewish left-wing movement, the question of succession was handled very badly, or not handled at all. And we're going to suffer for this, because we're not going to have a left-wing Jewish movement, [a] secular movement, anyway, that will continue this. Maybe the time for it has even passed. The social environment is different now. It was an episode, a long and good episode in history, and it's ending. Its role has ended, or is ending.

DS: So, would you say that maybe there are two issues: One is the aging of participants in the movement; [the other is] the age itself that we live in.

SR: Yeah, that's right, sure, oh sure. There are some Jewish kids—by the way, there's another thing that may change the situation somewhat. There is, among Jewish intellectuals in this country, student youth, a certain interest in the Jewish radical past, and in Yiddish secular culture. Part of it is that many of these people are disgusted with the chauvinism of the Zionist movement or they are turned off by the religion or the religious aggressiveness, and they're looking for a socially viable, socially attached—a Jewish movement to which they can feel an attachment, an ideological attachment. For instance, a lot of Jewish kids go for Emma Goldmann [an anarchist leader active in the early 1900s]. And there is an interest among Jewish college youth today—more than before, more than, say, twenty years ago—in the Jewish socialist movement. I see people— I was surprised. There's a guy I know at Yale who is learning Yiddish in order to do a paper on the Jewish socialist movement, some aspects of it. So that there is that kind of interest. But this is going to be a limited kind of thing, it's not a mass [movement].

DS: Now, I'd like to switch just a little to a different but related subject, and that is the relationship between your politics and the work that you've done, both paid—salaried—work and your work in the Party. First of all, I wanted to ask you, how many years were you actually a paid organizer?

SR: Very few; as a matter of fact, maybe a year and a half at the most, and this was in Connecticut. I was a youth organizer for the Party, which meant that I was the labor youth chairman in Connecticut. This was an organization that maybe had sixty, seventy people in the state. We had clubs in Hartford, New Haven, New London, UConn [University of Connecticut], Norwalk, and Bridgeport. This was [at] our apogee. I was the state organizer, and I used to run around, and the party paid me. I forget what they paid me: sixty bucks, seventy bucks, something like that. At first I lived at the Y, and then I got married, so I moved in with my wife in New Haven. I was on the Party payroll maybe a year, a year and a half, from [19]49 to [19]50. Then the Party had to retrench. We felt great troubles coming against us from the government, so we cut down the staff, and I was one of the first to be cut out.

DS: Actually, then, your life as a Party organizer—

SR: A paid functionary, was very brief.

DS: —was very brief. So that, throughout your working life, then, you've mostly had to balance—

SR: Right.

DS: —regular paid employment with your Party work. What was the first paid employment that you had?

SR: Well, when I was still in New York, before I came to Connecticut, I worked in the printing trade.

DS: Did you apprentice?

SR: I apprenticed. Well, not officially, but I learned the printing trade in New York. When I came up here, I got a job in various different printing shops in the city. When I first came to Connecticut in 1948 for several months I was an employee of the Progressive Party in Waterbury. And then when I came down to New Haven in [19]49, I was an employee of the Party as a youth organizer, that I told you about. So I would do all this Party work—my Party activity was after hours, after working hours. You know, when you were younger, you had energy and you could do it. So, I'd work a whole day, have supper, and then go out to meetings, sometimes in New Haven, sometimes out of town. I'd run down to the railroad station, get a train to Bridgeport, New London, things like that—Hartford. At that time I didn't have a car, so I had to do a lot of hitchhiking around the state. People used to joke about me hitchhiking around the state. So, I used to do that.

DS: Now, as a printer, were you ever involved in union organizing, labor organizing?

SR: When I was a printer in the fifties, it was very difficult to get into the Typographical Union. And then, when I got arrested, after [19]54, I was known as a communist throughout the trade. I gave up any thoughts of trying to get into the union then. When I was arrested, I had a job with the Columbia Printing Company in New Haven. The owners of it were former members of the Workmen's Circle, so when I was arrested, they treated me pretty decently. They let me keep my job. And during the trial, in the morning and the afternoon [I would] be at the trial session, and then late in the afternoon [I would] go to work. It was all downtown. I was the only one that had a job at the time, of the defendants. And I stayed with them until they let me go in 1978 or [19]79. They cut out the department I worked in. They cut out metal type.

DS: So, you didn't retire, you were laid off.

SR: I was laid off.

DS: 'Cause they switched from metal type—

SR: —to computer typeset. So, I lost my job there. I had another job for a while, and then I realized I couldn't get any more jobs in this trade. The trade had disappeared.

DS: The old—

SR: The typesetting trade had disappeared.

DS: That you had known.

SR: I had known. Working with metal type, or "hot type" they called it. And I couldn't get a job anymore. So, then I started looking around, and I finally landed a job at Yale.

DS: And your job as Yale is—

SR: I'm a library worker. Not a librarian—a librarian has a degree. I'm a library worker, and I have a very interesting job at the Yale Law Library. It doesn't pay as much as I would have been paid in printing, but it's an interesting job. It makes up for it in other ways.

DS: Do you work like in special collections?

SR: At the Yale Law School, I'm in charge of the project of updating loose-leaf volumes that we have. We have hundreds and hundreds of loose-leaf volumes, issued either by private corporations, like [a] commercial clearinghouse, or by authors, books that are not printed as bound volumes, but as loose-leaf volumes, so that changes could be made frequently. And then there are government agencies that have loose-leaf binders. But many of the binders come from a few corporations that deal with law in specific fields, like Medicare, aviation law, radio law, and all that kind of stuff. We get a lot of material every week, stuff that has to be changed, [such as] new [legal] decisions [or] additions, and I'm in charge of this part of the work. We have several students that work for us, and I'm supposed to provide them with work, check their work. And I do a lot of the updating myself. So that's the work I do.

DS: So, is this full time?

SR: Yeah, I work thirty hours a week now.

DS: Thirty hours, that's three-quarter [time].

SR: I work four days a week. I'd like to work two days, three days, but I couldn't swing it.

DS: Then you've been pretty much full time employed throughout your working life.

SR: Oh yeah, oh yeah, yeah. In a way, at different times I didn't particularly cotton to the idea of being a full-timer for the Party. Maybe, when I was younger, I had such ambitions. But after I got married, I didn't want it, because it was too uncertain, it was too time-consuming, so I didn't want to.

DS: But let me ask you something, which I've asked others, since you've had such a long working career as a printer. If somebody asked you what you felt your primary identity was, would you immediately choose your occupation, or would you choose your political identity?

SR: Ah, now that's an interesting question that we often talked about in the Party: Are you more Jewish, or are you more communist?

DS: That also is—

SR: I used to answer [that] a person is many things. Your living is one thing, your political interests is another, and your cultural interests [are] another. A person is an amalgam of different things. By the way, I became a printer for Party reasons too.

DS: Oh, describe that.

SR: Yeah. Why did I become a printer? Because one of my heroes when I was a young kid was Georgi Dimitroff. You heard of him?

DS: The architect of the Popular Front [actually the United Front against fascism in WWII]?

SR: Right, that's right. He was the leader of the Bulgarian Communist Party, and when Hitler came to power, they framed him with burning the Reichstag. He led a beautiful defense, a very courageous defense, against the Nazi court. And then the Soviet Union traded him for another person. He was brought to the Soviet Union, and he came as a hero to the Soviet Union. He became the head of the Communist International. Now, Dimitroff's life began as a printer. He was a printer, and he described how he used to set leaflets for the Bulgarian Communist Party, set the type, and all that kind of stuff. And that fired me up. I knew of other communists from different countries who were printers or typesetters. This was a service I felt I could do to the Party, help the Party as a printer. Now, in actual fact, I really didn't use printing that much for the Party, except for the time when we were putting out our little Connecticut paper—*Connecticut Challenge*, we called it—and I set all the headlines [laughs] in my shop.

DS: Surreptitiously?

SR: Yeah, surreptitiously, yeah. I'd set the headlines, then I'd come home and cut them apart, and paste them on to the copy—the text I typed. So I used to do that. But that was really the only direct benefit, except that at different times I tried to teach people at the *Daily Worker* how to set headlines, because they were woefully inadequate when it came to printing—knowledge of typesetting, display—woefully inadequate. I used to have a lot of arguments with people, and people didn't like me for that, because they thought I was intruding into their field. But anyway, that's one of the reason I became a printer.

DS: So it wasn't your family—your father wasn't a printer—

SR: Actually, my father was, but it really had no influence on me, because I never knew what he did in printing—he was a pressman, I was a typesetter.

DS: A pressman, you say.

SR: He ran a press.

DS: Oh, he ran the printing press itself.

SR: I never worked on a printing press, but I prepared the type for the printing press.

DS: So, you were exposed to the work, but it really was the political inspiration that drove you into the—

SR: —that's right, yeah—

DS: —field.

SR: I would say that was the big factor in my becoming a printer.

DS: So, in a sense, even though your printing work was not done, necessarily, mostly for the Party—mostly it was not—still, the idea that a printer had an important contribution to make—

SR: —that's right, that's right—

DS: —to you, that was a factor.

SR: That's right, that's right [laughs].

DS: I suspected as much. Would it be safe, then, to say that in terms of your career, whether [or not] your actual work as a printer was directed by the Party, [that] the major driving force in your life has been the political?

SR: I would say so, yeah, yeah, I would say so. And I would say, in more recent years, partly as the result of changes in my own thinking, my main interest now is what I would call the Jewish movement, the Jewish progressive movement. I'm very interested in the Jewish question in the Soviet Union. I write about it, I correspond with people there, I talk about it, I give lectures about it. And I'm interested in [New Jewish] Agenda, I work in Agenda. I'm interested in *Jewish Currents*. I also contribute to a magazine in Canada, *Canadian Outlook*, a progressive Jewish magazine there. That's my main interest right now. I don't have—I belong to the DSA, but I don't attend meetings.

DS: Democratic Socialists of America?

SR: Yes. I don't attend meetings much. I'll go to a meeting of CISPES [Committee in Solidarity with the People of El Salvador] once in a while, or a peace meeting once in a while, but I'm not involved in those movements. Whatever time I have, I would like to devote to the progressive Jewish movement.

DS: Why would you say that is your principal focus? Does it have anything to do with this issue we've been talking about, the generational one; that as a member of the old Jewish—[as a] caretaker of the Old Jewish Left—do you feel a certain urgency now as you grow older to pass on this legacy of progressivism?

SR: Ah, pass on, huh? Well, I think we have a role to play for some time yet, certainly for maybe another couple of generations. I think it's important for people to know that there has been a Jewish, socialist movement, how the Jewish, socialist movement made a contribution to the general Jewish community, and to the community at large, what the role was that it played. Because many of the Jewish movements today are dominated by middle class and conservative types; they will downgrade the contributions of the Jewish Left. So, somebody has to defend that, somebody has to keep it [alive]. And then I'm very interested that new Jewish developments in the Soviet Union should also be known. Like, I've translated a few articles from the Soviet Yiddish press, that if I had not done it, nobody else would it. And I thought it was important for people to know these things and see these things. I think there's a role for the Jewish Left movement. As long as there's going to be a Jewish community, with Jewish political movements, of various kinds, there'll be a place for a Jewish left-wing movement. I hope it will be a movement that will continue the secular and socially progressive orientation.

DS: Some will say that it is conceivable that the left movement can continue to develop without necessarily any separate ethnic [component]. Not that it's desirable for it to end, but that without it, there would still be a viable movement. Would you say that it would be very difficult for you to conceive of a left movement without the Jewish—the ethnic—component?

SR: There will be, for a very considerable time, into the next century, maybe beyond—as long as there's going to be identifying or distinct ethnic groups in this country, there'll be a Jewish left-wing group.How long this can last, I don't know. Marxism has been woefully inadequate and wrong on the nationalities question.

DS: On that question, yeah.

SR: Woefully inadequate. I mean, a man like Karl Kautsky, the great [late nineteenth, early twentieth century] socialist theoretician, thought that the Jewish group in the United States would disappear before the 1950s. People would completely assimilate. And even Lenin agreed with it. Lenin agreed with him on that. And look at what's happening in the Soviet Union. Just the opposite has occurred. Where they had been thinking that they would tamp down and eliminate the nationalities factor, it now looms larger than it ever did before. Imagine in the Soviet Union today, hundreds of thousands of people are refugees from other republics, including Russians who had to flee from Azerbaijan or other places like that. So that the nationalities question has always been one of the weak points of the socialist movements. There will be ethnic left-wing movements for a long time to come, and the socialist movements have to learn how to work with them, and have to appreciate that they have a role to play. When the great millennium comes, and all people will merge, be one common mankind [sic], when that'll happen, there won't be any need for these movements. But until then, there'll be a need for these movements.

DS: So, you will continue to feel very committed to articulating a progressive position from the Jewish community.

SR: Right, that's right, that's right. And I want that this movement should also articulate a progressive position *to* the Jewish community and a Jewish progressive position to the broader community. So, we have a two-fold role: to be a—I don't want to say be a light unto the Gentiles [laughs]—but to let the non-Jewish movement know that there are Jewish group interests. Just as they respect that there are Hispanic group interests, or black group interests or Asian-American group interests, there are also Jewish group interests. We have a problem with anti-Semitism in the United States. Who's going to fight these things? Who's going to offer the counter-propaganda to anti-Semitism? Who's going to engage in defending the rights of Jewish people? And then, too, there are many Jews [who] don't understand, [who] have no knowledge of what Jewish people or Jewish culture is about. I see Jewish people from the Soviet Union who know nothing about the Jewish history of the Soviet Union, nothing. I mean, they don't know how to answer the anti-Semites. The anti-Semites say the Jews did this, and did that—they know nothing of Jewish history to know that they're wrong. They may feel in their gut [that] they're wrong, that the anti-Semitic arguments [are wrong], but they don't know how to answer it, because they have no knowledge of Jewish history.

DS: So, your contribution, principally, would be, in a sense, as a caretaker of that history that's been lost to them.

SR: That's right. Alright, you want to say caretaker, okay, but we [also] have to be popularizers of it, that's right. See, Jewish kids in the Soviet Union today should not only know that there were many Jewish revolutionaries in Jewish history—in Russian history—but that they were different kinds of revolutionaries, revolutionaries of different parties, and that there were Jews who made contributions to Russian culture, to every aspect of Russian culture, science, and like. And people don't know that. So, when they're assailed, that all the Jews are parasites in the Soviet Union, they don't know what to say, they don't know how to answer this. This can happen in the United States, too. In many ways, these questions become reborn. The need for them becomes reborn in unexpected ways, in unexpected ways. Like in the Soviet Union, they may have thought that assimilation from generation to generation will become so dominant that there won't be any differences among peoples, and so why bother studying differences among people. But you see that it didn't work out that way. And in other ways, these questions become restimulated. And it's there, it's there.

DS: Do you feel, here, as a person—you're now, let's see, 1922—

SR: I'm sixty eight.

DS: Sixty eight-years old.

SR: I'll [soon be] sixty-nine.

DS: Do you anticipate any diminution of your political activity or retirement from your paid employment in the near future?

SR: Maybe next year sometime, I'll quit for good.

DS: Your paid employment.

SR: My paid employment, yeah. I find the summertime is a hard time for me. So I may quit next year sometime. But I'll always be interested in politics. I have, if I retire completely—and even before I retire—I have a number of projects. For one thing, I'd like to write about the *Freiheit*. I was with the *Freiheit* in the last twenty years of its life. I knew the editor well. I've got a box of two hundred letters that he sent me over a twenty-year period. Some of the letters I want to give to a Jewish institution, because some of it is, you know, the history of our movement. I've got a lot of literature I would like to write about, people I would like to write about. Some of the Jewish communist history I would like to write about, because in 1966, [19]67, I was not in the middle of it, but I was close to the disputes in the communist movement on the Jewish question, you know, with Aptheker, with Hyman Lumer. I wrote contributions to the Communist Party press at the time about this. So, these are some of the things I would like to write about. And then, like I say, I want to do some things about the Soviet-Jewish literature, political developments that are taking place now. So, these are some of the things I have in mind to do. So, I won't be running around being a big political leader, but I'll be doing some of these things.

DS: So, certainly age is not necessarily going to be a hindrance in terms of your activity—

SR: I hope not [laughs].

DS: —but [may bring] a different level of activity.

SR: Yeah, yeah, yeah. Let me show you something that was in the paper a little while ago [gets up to search for a news clipping], a picture in the *Register*.

DS: The *New Haven Register*?

SR: Yeah, we had a demonstration against [right-wing demagogue Meyer] Kahane, when he spoke here.

DS: Oh, Meyer Kahane.

SR: We considered him a Jewish fascist. He was very right-wing.

DS: Very anti-Arab.

SR: Right. [Sid shows a picture of himself in the *Register* carrying a placard]

DS: So, you're still out on the picket lines when necessary.

SR: When we can, we are out there, that's right. Here, a lot of the Jewish community leadership here was very annoyed because [the headline says] "Jewish leaders denounce [Kahane]" [and] here *I* am. And I'm not the great Jewish leader in this town.

DS: So, they were irritated by the fact that it was your picture and not theirs.

SR: Well, they didn't picket, they issued little statements—I would say they were Casper Milquetoast statements, very mild. They were really not denunciations of the guy, which they should have done, because the guy actually said at the meeting that the Israeli government should let the Israeli army into the occupied territories, let 'em do what they want, and no questions asked. I mean, the guy is an advocate of murder. Instead of denouncing him for that, they give him a pat on the wrist.

DS: So, I think we can safely conclude, Sid, that if anything, age [has] given you a perspective, caused you to go through a lot of changes, but certainly has not diminished your—

SR: —yeah [laughs]—

DS: —commitment.

SR: I would say—you know, it's so embarrassing, like I'm the old codger who says certain things to the younger people. But, yeah, listen, you live through certain things. We went through very unusual history, people like us. I don't know how this is going to end, how it's gonna' turn. But I should imagine there'll be a left-wing movement. There's a need for a left-wing movement as long as there's a capitalist system. I feel that this is my movement, I'm associated with it and I feel my loyalty, my basic loyalty to it. And within this broader commitment I feel a special loyalty to the Jewish Left and would like to see it succeed [or] at least be a prominent influence in the Jewish community.

DS: So, it's safe to say that it will continue to be your, shall we call it, home—

SR: Oh yeah.

DS: —in the movement.

SR: Absolutely, absolutely, sure, oh sure, absolutely, yeah.

[After the interview was concluded, I asked Sid if he wanted to review the tape-recording or transcript of our conversation. He declined, feeling that he had nothing to add or reconsider.]

Summing Things Up

Chapter Eleven

Age of Wisdom, Age of Action: Narrative Theme and Variations

THEME AND VARIATIONS I: JOE

A review of the transcripts of my interviews with Joe Dimow reveals a depth of introspection unusual among activists that I have interviewed over the years. The apparent lack of self-reflection among many political activists might be attributed to the fact that they are constantly "in the moment," that is, fully engaged in tackling particular issues. Often this amounts to crisis intervention, since political events present continual challenges to the limited resources of the "movement" in which activists are involved, leaving little time for the relative luxury of introspection.

Another factor in the relative absence of self-reflection in personal narratives of activists is the public nature of the activities that have dominated their lives. Activists are accustomed to speaking in a "public voice" in defense of those issues of critical importance to their political lives. In any event, it is understandable that there will be a greater tendency to present and defend one's view as one would at a public forum rather than make a disingenuous attempt at "objectivity."Lack of self-criticism may reflect an effort at self-management or simply a genuine confidence in the certainty of one's views.

However, even among activists confident of their capacity to defend often-unpopular views in public forums, there may still be a certain amount of self-protective behavior in an interview situation, particularly when sensitive political issues are the topic of discussion.

Even when the interviewer lends an empathetic ear, it is not always possible or desirable to completely let down one's guard. An interview may have the appearance of a private conversation, but it does represent potential exposure to many other ears, not all of them sympathetic. On the other hand, it is also an opportunity to present one's views to a receptive audience—not only the audience-of-one of the interviewer, but also the potential audience of those who will eventually read the interview in the published book. This presents yet another source of dialectical tension within the interview process.

Given the pitfalls in attempting to elicit self-reflective discourse from a group of older activists, it is remarkable just how candid Joe's personal narratives were. As the transcripts show, during the course of three interviews he raised concerns about the very foundation of his beliefs and activities. I have asked myself whether or not this might be attributed, at least in some measure, to the reflectiveness of age. However, as an educator working for a state agency on aging for several years, I have found that the range in degree of self-reflection among older adults is just as wide as for other age groups, differing more in character (the depth of introspection informed by life experience) and frequency. This range was evident in the group of four activists that I interviewed.

From his opening remarks in the first interview, Joe demonstrated not only the depth and sharpness of his political vision, but also his capacity for self-scrutiny. Particularly noteworthy are his critical examination of the sources of his identity, his reflections upon the tension between his adaptation to changing personal and political circumstances and his desire to maintain a steady ideological bearing, and his willingness to reexamine his own views as our dialogue progressed.

The Politics of Retirement Versus the Retirement of Politics

In spite of the problematic nature of such key terms in this book as "work," "occupation," and "retirement" (not to mention socialism and Judaism), they may serve as useful categories provided that their use is carefully contextualized. The period following Joe's cessation of "work" (wage-earning employment) represents a real transition in terms of activities and is accompanied by a period of greater introspection. The fact that he has more free time *and* that he is aging may be coincidental, but Joe is aware of the fact that while retirement has allowed more time *for* reflection, old age is conventionally viewed as a time *of* introspection. Thus, "retirement," at least from wage-earning work, remains, with qualification, a meaningful category.

However, special acknowledgment must be made of the fact that Joe sees a vital distinction between wage-earning work and his true vocation—or "occupation" as he calls it—that of political activism. Since it is the latter rather than the former that has conditioned his core identity, it would be more appropriate to describe political activism as Joe's "career." "Retirement" is not a meaningful term in reference to Joe's political life; in fact, since his retirement from wage-earning work, the additional free time available to him has allowed him to become *more* politically active, though his overall activity level may have diminished somewhat with age. It is in this light that I will refer to the activity serving as Joe's primary source of identity as a "life career"—analogous to his use of the term "occupation" (Compare Myerhoff and Simic [1978] who describe aging as a late-life "career," presumably succeeding one's wage-earning [or unpaid housework career], and therefore linked with the distinction made here between work and retirement).

The literature on retirement has tended to exclude consideration of political activity as a distinct activity/career and source of identity for retired persons. Whether explicitly articulated or not, an apparent assumption of retirement studies is that (wage-earning) work was both the primary activity and primary source of identity for a worker prior to retirement. This is usually discussed in terms of social roles. Some studies refer to the "roleless role" of retirees; others point to role shifts and to retirement itself as a social role (Atchley 1976). However, activities of retired persons are categorized in ways that confound identification. The term "leisure" is used to cover virtually all activities conducted outside of (wage-earning) work. (An article on leisure in *The Gerontologist* [Kelly, Steinkamp and Kelly 1986] typically lists involvement in community organizations as a subcategory under this rubric.) Retirees are described as confronting the challenge of how to fill leisure time with meaningful activities (Brady 1988). Sometimes this includes social commitments such as volunteer work and community activism. These activities, as sources of personal identity and social role, are inadvertently "ghettoized"as they become subsumed under the "role" of retirement.

Ironically, with the growing acceptance of the "life-span" or "life-course" approach has come the acknowledgment that human personality is a product of a lifelong process in which both changes and continuities occur in such aspects of the self as identity and perceived social roles. This includes, one must assume, the persistence of aspects of identity and the specific activities/roles that have shaped and maintained that identity throughout one's life career (into old age). Those activities in particular that have not been directly associated with (wage-earning) work but that reflect important aspects of identity, such as political or cultural/religious activity, will be bound to criteria other than those conditioning work life (though boundaries may overlap if co-ethnics and political comrades work together in the same shop, or office). "Retirement" may represent a restructuring of time spent on those other activities but may not necessarily displace them as expressions of identity. In fact, the freeing of time in retirement may result in the expansion of commitment to such activity, potentially accompanied by an intensification of (political/ethnic/religious) self-identification.

Politics is rarely discussed as an integral aspect of identity among the aging. Keith (1977) notes the importance of prior political affiliation in the socialization of residents to an apartment for retired construction workers in a Paris suburb, but there is little or no reference to ongoing political activities engaged by residents in the surrounding community. In a discussion of forms of social practice in retirement, Guillemard (1982) acknowledges that, as one option, "Life in retirement may be concentrated on [the] political dimension. . . .It may acquire meaning from opposition versus acceptance of the place assigned by the social system to the aged person." But, once again, this political activity is "ghettoized"— restricted to issues affecting the elderly. Trela (1976) points to "status inconsistency" as an impetus for political action among the aging, but he avoids any consideration of the role of political activity among those older people for whom present involvement represents a continuity with past political actions and beliefs.

Political Activism as Life Career

While his work as a toolmaker dominated his time during most of his adult life prior to retirement, Joe has always viewed his role as a political activist as his primary "occupation" and source of identity. He made this clear at the beginning of our first conversation by his statement that he identifies himself not with his (wage-earning) work but with the political activities with which he has been involved (before and during retirement).

Joe also articulated in an unexpected way in the second interview his concern with placing political identity in a primary position. He understood that a major theme of our conversation was occupational identity, and since he saw political activism as his primary occupation, he felt uncomfortable about the amount of time spent discussing his work as a toolmaker in the first interview. It was as though he felt that the proportion of time spent discussing his (wage-earning) work life might de-emphasize his primary source of identification.

The focus of the second interview shifted entirely to aspects of Joe's life career and identity as a political activist. It also introduced another element—the role of "retrospective" political identity on present identity and its forms of expression. Joe and I, in reviewing the first interview, discussed the degree of candor with which he had talked about his political identity and activities. He had been open about his left-wing political background and orientation, but circumspect in our initial conversation about the specific nature of his involvement.

His hesitation on the question of "candidness" about his political background is not the result of his unwillingness to disclose his past—he has actually done this on several occasions in radio interviews as well as in newspaper articles. Rather, it is the fact that he continues to be associated with the Party in the minds of many people he meets—including those with whom he works in political organizations. The association is not always negative, as Joe recalls in the episode where members of an orthodox synagogue recognize him and remark, without rancor, "Oh, I know your family, you were from the Bolshevik Jews."

While Joe feels uncomfortable about being typecast by his continued association with a political party that he left thirty-four years before, it is clear from our conversations that it continues to be an important reference point—perhaps the most important—in his reflections on his sense of identity and purpose.

Ethnic Identity and Politics

Joe was raised in a family of poor, working-class, secular Jewish radicals—a configuration common to many Eastern European Jewish immigrants (his parents were from the "Old Country") and their children who, exposed to trade union and political movements, saw a means of confronting ethnic, occupational, and political oppression. Conflicts of identity occurred on several levels. Many Jewish political activists rejected Judaism as a religion of conservatism and conciliation, yet a significant number felt strong cultural and historical ties that they were not willing to abandon. Ethnicity also represented a dilemma vis-à-vis the "internationalism" of the left movement—the call to place loyalty to the international working class over potentially divisive ethnic loyalties. Yet the specter of anti-Semitism continued to place the "Jewish question" on the agenda of political activists; it especially hit home for Jewish radicals.

This dialectic of ethnicity and political identity has been a key issue in Joe's life. He confronted the issue while still in the Party, but he was never involved in any Party-affiliated Jewish organizations. The *Jewish Currents* was his first sustained "Jewish" involvement, political or otherwise, since childhood.

A Sense of Belonging

When asked, in our third conversation, to consider what areas he would address in an interview with those with similar backgrounds to his, Joe suggested that he would "try to probe more into the feelings of how they missed . . . the CP life." In our second conversation he had talked about missing "the theoretical discussions that took place . . . the sense of an ultimate goal beyond what we were working on." He had hinted at the sense of belonging that was as important as the ideology shared by his comrades, but he placed further emphasis on it as a way of explaining its lingering imprint on him after so many years.

Joe's association of the Party with "family" is particularly telling. The search for the missing sense of family characterized all the other political activity with which he was subsequently involved. He came closest to it with *Jewish Currents*, staffed, not surprisingly, by many former Party members. In describing his sense of feeling at home again in *Jewish Currents*, he calls to mind such things as the shared political "shorthand" that, like an occupational language, intensified the feeling of belonging and identity he had known in the Party.

As a whole, the feelings Joe describes in relationship to his "retirement" from the Communist Party are not unlike those expressed by older workers who have been displaced by plant layoffs or the closing down of a factory or other business where they have worked for many years, and who shared experiences—good and bad—with their co-workers, as well as special knowledge (often reflected in occupational language). I recently interviewed two older women who had known each other from their high-school days but became friends while working together in a department store. When asked what it felt like when the store closed down (one of them had worked there for over twenty years, the other for close to thirty), they said it was like losing a family, because of the close associations and friendships developed over the years with co-workers. Ironically, Joe never derived the same sense of "family" from his workplace.

To extend the analogy of "family" and "home," if retirement is seen as a "divorce" or separation from a place and a set of social relations that have exerted a dominant influence on self-concept, then Joe's departure from the Communist Party corresponded more to the textbook definition of "retirement" than his ceasing to work full time as a toolmaker. His situation may be compared in some ways to those who have chosen careers such as professional sports or the armed services, where early retirement is the norm. One speaks, in fact, of the "retirement" (with many of its associations, including pensions) of athletes or career soldiers in their thirties or forties. Joe left the Party when he was thirty-six. Yet, from our conversations, it appears that there has never been any other occupational experience with such intensity, family feeling, and centrality to his identity as that political affiliation. Again, analogous accounts may be found among many former athletes and soldiers, whose subsequent occupations never quite matched the peak experience of their early careers (and often whose subsequent activities—work-related or not—were, like many retirees, never as "familial," intense, or all-consuming [both in terms of time and consciousness]).

Retirement and Self-Concept

While retirement from the workplace did not involve, for Joe, a separation from roles, relationships, or activities crucial to his self-identity (it simply cannot be compared to his leaving the Party), it has played a role, albeit indirectly, in his evolving self-concept and sense of place. Its influence is felt in the availability of more time to engage in his primary occupation—political activism, the widening of his scope of involvement in "mainstream" Jewish activities (which his work schedule often did not permit), and the coincidence of retirement from (wage-earning) work with old age (Joe ceased working full time at age sixty-two).

Since leaving the Party in 1956, Joe has been involved in a variety of groups and activities inside and outside of the left-wing movement, including community organizations, peace groups, and even local electoral campaigns. However, he has, over the years, found himself in somewhat of a dilemma. In "non-left" groups he felt the lack of a more incisive political grounding; while in the "left" organizations he joined, he was haunted by the specter of his former Party membership.

However, when he became involved in left organizations other than the Party, he became embroiled in disputes between members and ex-members, which detracted from the unity necessary to carry out important tasks. Since he has retired, he has refrained from taking part in organizations where his presence might be divisive.

Whether or not Joe's reluctance to engage in factionalism is specifically associated with retirement and/or age is something about which he is uncertain. However, related to his avoidance of divisive activity is a widening of his involvement in certain "mainstream" activities that he would not have considered prior to retirement. Although he was involved in neighborhood organizations and other forms of local community activism prior to his retirement as a toolmaker, he had very little contact with "mainstream" organizations, including those in the organized Jewish community.

Acceptance within that mainstream has been conditional, for no matter how much he may be "welcomed" into mainstream Jewish activities, he is still viewed as a political outsider. While the boundaries of his Jewish identity may have expanded, it has tended to be a one-way process. This dilemma stems largely from the fact that, aside from his work with *Jewish Currents*, the other Jewish group with which he is involved, New Jewish Agenda, is also seen by the mainstream Jewish community as an "outsider" group.

This has been a persistent problem for Joe since he has retired—a contradiction between his expanded interests and involvement in Jewish community affairs (made possible because of the time made available by retirement) and his desire not to be typecast as a "Jewish left-winger," but simply identified as a leftist who happens to be Jewish. Ironically, Agenda itself is no haven from the sense of alienation he feels from those of his fellow Jews that do not understand or share his political outlook. This prevents him from finding the sense of "family" he has with *Jewish Currents*.

Joe's closeness to *Jewish Currents* comes not only from a dual ethnic/political solidarity, but also from membership in a cohort of older, Jewish, left activists who have shared not only a similar outlook, but also a set of shared experiences, going back in some instances (as noted earlier) to their youth.

Joe clearly feels that he has much to offer to a younger generation of activists, in terms of his background as a veteran left-wing political organizer, who throughout his long career has encountered many of the same kinds of situations that are being faced today. By typecasting him, these younger activists lose the benefits of Joe's sense of historical depth that age and experience have provided him.

Core Identity and the "True" Political Self

Joe has always accepted as accurate the Marxist critique of capitalism and its ills, and he continues to hold an abiding faith in socialism as a path toward the amelioration of capitalism's worst excesses. Yet much has changed over the years in his interpretation of what that means. The degree to which his core identity—his "true" political self—has qualitatively changed remains an open question. Clues are provided in our series of conversations, but it is possible to interpret them in ways that yield contradictory results.

Joe himself is uncertain about the influence, if any, that retirement and age have had on the evolution of his personal and political identity, though he recognizes markers of age identification in his interactions with his cohorts. Among these are factors related to historical experience. There is a profound disillusionment in a younger generation whose lack of historical experience has contributed to their confounding the actions of contemporary conservative and racist Jews—especially those in the American Jewish establishment and Israeli government—with Judaism itself. It is also an indication of the fact the contributions of these older, secular, Jewish-identified activists to the left movement have been eclipsed by the younger activists' rejection of a stereotypical Jewish identity that has nothing to do with that of Joe and his ethnic/political cohorts.

Ironically, Joe's sense of ethnicity has, if anything, become more expansive, partly an accommodation to his greater tolerance for the diversity of expressions of identity by those members of the Jewish community with whom he had little contact until he retired from toolmaking. In adjusting to the exigencies of working within an ideologically more conservative Jewish community as his primary sphere of activism, Joe has found himself compromising in the area of political tactics. A perennial argument within the Left is that concerning the point at which tactical compromises become compromises of principle. Certain of Joe's views on the Middle East (such as his opposition to using economic sanctions against Israel) may make some leftists uncomfortable; some might even question his allegiance to fundamental principles of Marxism.

Joe's tactical compromises in regard to his political activity within the Jewish community might lead one to believe that, if he has not abandoned ideology for transcendent personal values, then he has at the least allowed his ethnic identification to compromise the primacy of his political identity. Joe, however, is adamant about the transcendence of his political beliefs. His concluding statement in our third interview was, after all, an acknowledgment of the possibility that the social base for an expression of his politics through ethnic channels might erode. That scenario is acceptable to him, but the absence of political engagement altogether is not.

Summary: Selfhood, Politics, and Retirement as Narrative Themes

A number of themes emerge in the self-narratives of Joe; with each successive interview another dimension is added to the complex structure of his identity:

1. While aspects of his identity other than the political may play a dominant role as reflected in his activity during retirement, his political identity continues to be perceived as the dominant aspect of his selfhood and the ultimate arbiter of his actions.

2. While his political identity has always been primary, Joe's ethnic identity as a Jew has assumed a great importance for significant periods of his life. Significantly, the expression of his ethnicity has largely taken the form of involvement in Jewish political organizations.

3. A sense of belonging is just as important in identity formation in the political realm as it is in one's personal family/home life. Joe describes the sense of family/home that he has felt as a political activist, in which validation of self by members of that "family" is seen as important in sustaining a sense of political self-identity. Added to that are the "cohort effects" of membership in one group in particular to which he belongs, consisting primarily of older activists who have shared experiences, as well as shared political beliefs and ethnicity.

4. That retirement does play a role in Joe's evolving self-concept is revealed in at least three ways in his narratives: (a) the availability of more time has meant an intensity of political activity that raises new issues of personal and political identity; (b) the widening of his scope of involvement with members of the "mainstream" Jewish community has raised issues of his cultural identity vis-à-vis his political role; (c) he views the coincidence of old age and retirement as having some influence in his growing tendency toward introspection.

5. Although his political beliefs have undergone a radical transformation, he perceives a continuity in his core political identity.

6. There emerges in the course of Joe's conversations with me a sense of ambiguity about the self-identified aspects of his identity, life course, and sense of belonging and purpose. This is revealed in statements about regret over the lack of a college education, about

the sense of accomplishment he derived from his work as a
toolmaker, and his musings about the utility of his past and present
political involvements. There is little indication of despair; rather,
it seems to indicate a continued searching for a better relationship
between his beliefs and desires and the activities that articulate or
fulfill them.

Joe apparently shares this sense of ambiguity with middle-aged
and older autobiographers. Handel notes that the authors of
autobiography tend to compare their present selves not only with
"retrospective" selves but also with a "desired self." He points to a
sense of indeterminacy in autobiographical accounts of the self,
descriptions that present the self as in a perpetual state of emergence,
insinuating that there is always a gap between the present self and
the full realization of one's "true" self (Handel 1987). This notion
precludes the sense of closure that is the putative goal of self-
reflection in life review among the elderly, as argued by Butler (1963)
and others.

While Handel doesn't identify it as such, what he is describing is a
dialectical process of interaction among aspects of the evolving self
that is open-ended, unfolding, and therefore subject to ambiguity in
the assessment of its development. That this ambivalence does not
necessarily eclipse a strong sense of one's core identity is shown in
Joe's self-narrative, through his description of continued involvement
in political activity as a meaningful expression of his identity. In
dialectical fashion, there is both continuity and indeterminacy in
his life and self-assessment. Joe is acutely aware of the need to place
limits on indeterminacy in his own search for meaning. Immediately
following his statement that "we need a purpose in life," he cautions,
"I don't think you can examine it too deeply, 'cause if you go too
deeply there is no purpose anyway, there is no ultimate purpose in
anything. Life is to be lived, that's all."

An existential dilemma is resolved—or at least mediated—with
an existential solution: In activity there is meaning, even if tactics
shifts, even if ultimate goals aren't always clear, and even if tasks
are sometimes left unfinished. If meaning lies in doing, not
necessarily completing, including the life work of identity formation,
then "closure" is either an illusive goal or the ultimate form of denial.
As Joe put it early into our third conversation, "I'm pretty sure that
nobody is fully satisfied with their identification. People go around

with a smile on their face, but that doesn't mean that they're satisfied, that they are properly identified to themselves or to others." As seems apparent from Joe's observations, tolerance of ambiguity may well be a more realistic and perhaps more realizable goal. Certainly, such "tolerance," personally and politically, plays an important role, along with a sense of purpose, in the continued development and viability of self-concept.

THEME AND VARIATIONS II: LIL

What struck me as I reviewed the transcript of my interview with Lil Dimow was the way in which her narrative reveals a process of self-definition that stands in contrast to the "evolution" of Joe Dimow's discourse over three interviews. Joe began with certainty and ended with ambiguity. Lil began with self-doubt and concluded on a more affirmative note. There is great continuity in their shared lives and political outlook—an abiding commitment to the ideals of socialism and to each other—yet their contrasting narratives reveal differences in style, personality, and gender, reflected in different choices made that have had important consequences for their late-life transitions.

Lil's initial response to my opening inquiry was to exclaim that she was still searching for her core identity and was basically dissatisfied with her life. Whereas Joe gradually moved into an introspective mode, Lil was instantly self-critical, self-probing. At the conclusion of the interview, after she had reviewed what she considered to be the life activities that most closely reflected her personal and political identity, she was very clear about the crucial aspects of that identity: the "Yiddishist"; the socialist (actually, "Yiddishist" often implied "socialist"); the teacher of arts and crafts.

Part of the difficulty Lil experienced in offering her "first impression" of what I was looking for in my query may have been the fact that the activities she considers to be the prime manifestations of her identity are not necessarily the overt markers one might expect in a discussion of political belief and its forms of expression. Lil remarked at the beginning of our discussion that she had never felt complete satisfaction with the course of her life until she embarked upon a late life career as an arts-and-crafts teacher, a profession she practiced in public schools, housing projects, through social agencies, and in adult education programs for close to eighteen years, until her "retirement" (from paid employment) in 1986, at age seventy.

In the process of describing her experiences as an art teacher, it became clear that she saw this work as an expression, however indirect, of an interwoven family and political background. But her narrative also revealed the part played by serendipity (the chance encounter with a social worker) in bringing her into an unusual, yet somehow very fitting, occupation for someone with her life profile.

The fact was that Lil taught arts-and-crafts with inner-city children, choosing deliberately to work with those whose artistic development had been neglected for societal reasons. She even took on "difficult," emotionally troubled students, challenging them with creative activities as a positive pathway for their self-expression. Her encounter with the social worker may have been a stroke of good fortune, but it was no coincidence that Lil and Joe had lived for many years in a predominantly black neighborhood in New Haven, where they were active in local grassroots community groups, including a tenants organization that they helped create and for which they provided leadership. Lil was able to take advantage of a special rapport with her inner-city students that came partly from shared experience and partly from a perspective that she had developed from childhood.

An appreciation of the arts was something that Lil's own family felt was worth cultivating, in spite of economic hardship, a sentiment that no doubt contributed to her willingness to bring art to others who have faced hard times. More than that, cultural and political interests were, in Lil's family, parts of an integral whole, in which art and ideology were often inseparable.

While an appreciation for the arts and for Jewish culture were integrated into her overall political outlook, it was specifically her induction into the Communist Party, at a relatively early age, that provided her not only with political savvy, but with interpersonal skills that helped her immeasurably in her late career as an art teacher.

Lil, who loved school as a child and who spent much time in the public library, found herself unable to fulfill her desire to continue studying in pursuit of an advanced degree. She still looks back at this missed opportunity with some regret. Yet she realizes that it was a circumstance born partly of political choice and partly of economic necessity. She has, in late life, partly fulfilled her desire for formal education by enrolling in classes at local colleges and by attending Elderhostel (an educational program for older adults in which participants reside, usually on a university campus, for one week, taking in lectures, workshops and social activities).

Yet, in a real sense, her life in the Communist Party was an educational experience that not only provided a sense of purpose and direction, but that left her with practical skills that have come to her aid time and again, long after she and the organization parted ways. Ironically, Lil's "education" in the Party gave her life skills unmatched in any institution of formal learning, for it took place under unique conditions in which, struggling for common goals and facing common adversaries, she was able to develop a sense that her knowledge had a palpable relationship to the world she and her comrades struggled to change. Moreover, those with whom she shared a life of theory and practice developed relationships of a closeness and intensity that could be found in few strictly academic or intellectual circles.

Lil responded positively, as Joe had, when I asked her if she had ever felt that those ongoing and intense experiences shared with her comrades in the Party made it feel like being in a family. It was only during the late 1940s and early 1950s when the Party was hounded by the federal government (many Party members went underground during this period, a move about which there was divided opinion) that Lil felt that relationships with some of her comrades (those who, partly out of fear, avoided contact with her) became strained.

However, the difficulty of being under siege was not the only source of tension for Lil during the period of her involvement with the Communist Party. She learned, when she had her first child, that the Party's official position on "the woman question" was often at variance with actual practice. She speaks with not a little bitterness about her own treatment. She spares no bitterness in her description of the hypocrisy of the Party's lip service on the equality of women, given its shabby treatment of her following childbirth, yet she is willing to attribute this to cultural backwardness of Party members, not to a bankruptcy of their overall political outlook.

Ironically, it was indeed the exposure of political bankruptcy that ultimately did drive her out of the Party, when the sexism of some members would not. She experienced, as did Joe and many other comrades, a rude awakening during the course of Khrushchev's revelations of the crimes of Stalin, as well as disappointment in the

failure of the Communist Party in the United States to acknowledge
a profound contradiction in the socialist project. Yet Lil resisted the
impulse to reject a political theory because of historical failures in
its practice. Neither history nor age have diminished her socialist
outlook, in spite of the flaws in "existing socialism."

Further, in spite of her disillusionment with a party that she
suspects deliberately withheld knowledge that the socialist path in
Eastern Europe had become crooked, she feels no rancor toward the
organization that, whatever its faults, instilled in her a strength of
character and commitment.

When Joe left the Party, he experienced a profound sense of loss.
The level and intensity of his commitment were such that, in spite
of his subsequent involvement in various political and community
organizations over the years, he felt that none of it had been an
adequate substitute for the sense of satisfaction that came from the
unique integration of personal and political selves that Party life
represented. Lil, on the other hand, did not experience the break as
sharply. A partial explanation may be found in the socially distancing
effects she experienced while still a Party member, in particular, her
being relegated to the role of nonperson by some Party members
when she took on the responsibility of childrearing. In addition, she
was not as bound to the Party as was Joe, who occupied leadership
positions for many years. Moreover, Lil's late-life career as arts-and-
crafts teacher provided, directly and indirectly, personal ties and
channels of political expression analogous to those she had in the
Party.

Neither Lil nor Joe severed their relationships with everyone they
knew in the Party. "Some severed relationships with *us*. But some
we are still friendly with. We like them, feel warm towards them,
always have." Still, continued ties with some Party members was
little compensation for Joe for the sense of loss of a primary outlet
for the expression of his core identity. Lil, on the other hand, found
through her teaching another community that gave her a sense of
belonging. The rewards of teaching came not only from the joy of
reaching people through a creative medium, but from bringing to
her work a fresh perspective and level of commitment that came
from years of experience as a political organizer. In fact, while her
introduction to a new late-life career came through that chance
encounter with a social worker, it was a contact made in the course
of her political involvement as a local community activist.

A vital facet of Lil's identity, inseparable from her political outlook, is her abiding love of and commitment to "Yiddishkeit," a doctrine forged by Yiddish-speaking socialists that embraced a political vision with secular aspects of Jewish culture. Exposed to Yiddish language, song and literature in her home and to the Labor Lyceum in her neighborhood, where classes were held on matters cultural and political, she feels that her socialism has always had a "Yiddish" component.

THEME AND VARIATIONS III: JAKE

The life course of Joe and Lil Dimow's longtime friend and political comrade Jake Goldring represents yet another variation, one that parallels their experience and outlook in many ways and yet reveals the development of his own unique form and path of ideational expression. With Jake, I was once more confronted with a question of definition or, more to the point, the problematic equation of identity with activity. A dialectical model of self concept posits a core or dominant aspect of the self, reflected in thought and action. The problem arises in naming aspects of identity that are both distinct and significant parts of the self, yet interrelated to each other, and ultimately subordinate to the dominant or core self. The assumption that I brought to each interview (given my careful selection of subjects) was that the political aspect of the self has been the most important, the dominant, one for these activists throughout the course of their lives. In the first interview with Jake, my familiar leading question, "In your lifetime, what would you consider to be the one identity that you would like to be associated with?"—led him to equate "political identity" with political "occupation," to the extent that the period during which he considered his political identity to be dominant was the period of his membership and active participation in the Communist Party in Connecticut. And while he was not a full time (paid) organizer during this entire period, it was his membership and activity as a Party member that provided the ideational focal point for other aspects of his life and identity.

In this way, Jake sees the period of his membership in the Party as the time when his principal occupation and, therefore, source of identity was literally the "work" that dominated his activities in other areas.

A similar perspective emerged when I asked Jake about his principal wage-earning trade. He spoke of great pride in his skill as a carpenter and the fact that he derived a great deal of satisfaction in the process of work and the tangible products of his hands. Although his wage-earning career in construction ended, he never fully retired from construction work.

In our exchanges, Jake apparently equated his dominant identity with the specific nature of the activity that dominated his time. It wasn't until the end of the first interview, after we had reviewed the relationship among the various aspects of his life activities, that the common thread that emerged, if not always the most apparent, was the political.

To say that the political aspect of Jake's identity has been dominant is not to suggest, however, as Jake initially interpreted my query, that political activity has always been overt or has taken up the majority of his time. More telling is the way in which the political has informed all of Jake's interests and activities, both directly and indirectly, throughout his life course. Like both Lil and Joe, Jake was born into a family of Jewish socialists. But he sees influences both from within and outside of the family in his early political development.

In talking with Lil and Joe, one gets the impression that entry into the ranks of the Party was, for each of them, a natural outcome of their family upbringing. Jake experienced his initiation differently. He was not inducted into the Young Pioneers at an early age. In fact, his parents, unlike those of Lil or Joe, did not join that faction of the Workmen's Circle that broke away and joined forces with the Communist Party, so his family would not have provided such a direct route to Party membership. Moreover, Jake made a point, at the beginning of the second interview, of elaborating on the deliberate process of reflection about social conditions in the United States that led him to join the Party.

The integration of family and polity that Joe and Lil felt in the Party was analogous to the integration of family, politics, and Jewish culture that were intertwined in the homes in which they were raised. Jake was, indeed, exposed to Jewish tradition as a child, but he never experienced the same level of integration. Moreover, his Jewish education was apparently not linked with his parents' political life. Perhaps as a consequence of this, while Jake's ethnicity has never completely vanished as a component of his politics, it has never been a very demonstrative an aspect of his identity. Jake partly attributes his lack of ethnic engagement to circumstance: the absence of a significant left-wing Jewish community in Bridgeport. He links this with the cultural and political demographics of his adopted town, which historically lacked the requisite institutions.

Joe had suggested that, as involved as he was in Jewish, left politics, if the social base eroded, he would continue to be active without any specific (Jewish) ethnic forms for the expression of his political outlook. The implication of both Joe's and Jake's observations, coming from different vantage points, is that the expression of an overtly *Jewish*, left politics would, for them, be wholly contingent upon a sufficient community base to support such expression. Jake made this explicit toward the end of our first conversation, when he indicated that if there were a left-wing Jewish community in Bridgeport, he would have joined it.

Such a statement is telling, given his prior disclaimer in regard to his attachment to Jewish culture. It is in fact, an object lesson in the dialectics of self-determination versus circumstance in the formation of self-concept. What is remarkable is the willingness of both Joe and Jake to acknowledge the role still played in late life by circumstance in shaping the character and forms of expression of their self-identity.

In fact, the circumstance, noted by Jake, of the disproportionate number of Jews in Hartford and New Haven's Party chapters (this was also true of several other cities; the bulk of the Los Angeles and New York chapters were also Jewish) represents a convergence of politics and ethnicity of particular historical significance (see, for example, Liebman 1979). For one thing, it presents the possibility of an ethnic affinity among political cohorts not dependent on any particularly overt forms of ethnic expression, political or otherwise. Alternatively, it allows for the possibility that specifically ethnic forms of political expression might depend, as they have for Joe and Jake, as much on the presence (or absence) of a "critical mass" of ethnic/political cohorts as on a deeply felt motivation to maintain ethnicity as a component of self-identity. (This extrapolation from Joe's and Jake's remarks also presents an alternative view to those positing a tendency toward intensification of ethnic and/or religious identification among the aging [especially without mitigating historical conditions].)

I did not inquire of Jake whether the ethnic composition of the Bridgeport Communist Party played any part in the character of his relationships with local Party members. However, he did make the point (which he specifically identified in the second interview as requiring elaboration) that he felt on a number of occasions to be a "minority of one," often casting the sole dissenting vote on policy matters at local Party meetings.

Here, as on other, larger issues, such as the Stalin/Hitler Nonaggression Pact, Jake found himself among a small group of dissenters who yet refused to relinquish their embrace of the overall Party outlook and program. Hoping, in the wake of Khrushchev's denunciation of Stalin, to steer the Party out of the political mire, Jake, in fact, persisted (as did Sid) for several more years, while Joe, Lil, and many others left.

Nevertheless, to this day Jake resists the temptation to lash out against the Party itself. Like Joe, while he felt unhappy at the time about leaving the CP, he nevertheless recalls the positive impact it had on his life. Still, Jake, like Joe, felt a definite sense of loss, a feeling that something was missing in the terms of his "post-Party" political life. While it was not a substitute for his political involvement per se, Jake's return to the construction trade offered some solace; at least it provided rewards of another kind, while he searched for political alternatives.

While Jake eventually became active in a number of emergent, broad-based political groups, participating in the peace movement, becoming chairperson of the local SANE/Freeze group, and working for the national coalition Jobs for Peace, none of these has provided the sense of completeness that he experienced as a member of the Communist Party.

Though his work in the construction trade took the place of the Party as his principal "occupation" for many years, political concerns were never completely separate, in Jake's mind, from his work as a carpenter and later as a contractor and building inspector. In fact, the intersection of political and professional concerns has punctuated Jake's life as a carpenter and as an activist. When discussing his political involvements in the last twenty-five years, he noted that he was also active in the housing movement, recalling that his involvement in that issue goes back to the heyday of his Party organizing, when he fought for affordable housing. When Jake finally "retired" from this career, housing continued to be an important issue for him, from both professional and political perspectives. He does, in fact, still take on the occasional consulting job, especially if it involves a beneficial community impact.

Given the continuity of belief and activity through an active professional and political life, and the vigor with which he continues to draw from the lessons of carpentry and socialism, the issue of aging seems remote. But Jake reminded me toward the end of the second interview that the dissolution of that political world for which he still longs may be attributed not only to political and cultural demography, but also the demography of aging, the attrition of the "Old Left" with its shared outlook and culture. For Jake, the loss of a few political/age cohorts is more acute in the considerably smaller left community of Bridgeport than in cities like New Haven, with relatively larger cohort groups. In fact, the attrition of the Old Left in Bridgeport is so acute that the notion of "community" there is strained, at best. Jake and his wife commute to New Haven these days for most of their political as well as cultural activity, or they seek outlets farther afield.

The Party did champion not only political change, but the preservation and development of culture as well. Communists popularized the folklore of ethnic, regional, and occupational groups and favored public support for the arts. Ironically, though, being a full-time organizer for the Party often left little time for cultural pursuits.

Jake devoted time, in our second conversation, to outlining the role by the Party, or certainly specific members, in the development of his aesthetic sensibilities, especially the painter Mike Russo with whom Jake continues to be close friends long after their lives in the Party. In his discussion of his cultural interests, Jake makes it eminently clear that his self-concept in late life is solidly linked with that identity forged in his years with the Communist Party. Whatever the nature of his falling out over matters of political policy and principle, Jake still identifies his core self not only with the overall political vision the Party represented, but also with the community of comrades with whom he identified as sharing a common culture. In fact, he uses the term "heritage" to describe those influences whose impact remains undiminished in late life. Jake echoes the words of Joe when he suggests that, whatever the deficits might have been, he has "no regrets for the fact that my interests in certain directions are partly attributable to the Party."

THEME AND VARIATIONS IV: SID

Where Jake Goldring has felt removed from the ethnic component of his political identity, Sid Resnick has been totally immersed. Like Lil, Joe, and Jake, Sid is also a child of the old Jewish Left. In Sid's case, the political lineage was strictly maternal. What is remarkable about his narrative, in contrast to the more reflective discourse of the previous three narrators, is the depth, precision, and certainty with which he has carved out virtually every aspect of his ideational development, doing so in a single interview dense with detailed observations and delivered at a fast clip. (It is interesting to note that while the total length of my recorded conversations with Jake exceeded that of my interview with Sid, the transcript of my single conversation with Sid was almost as long as both of my interviews with Jake.)

There is a definite correlation between Sid's sense of certainly about the particularity of his self-identity and the relative lack of introspection evinced in his remarks. I might even be tempted to delete the term "emergent" when describing his self-concept, for it became apparent in the course of our conversation that he, most of all, has kept intact the agenda of his ethnic/political upbringing. Sid has carried with him, through several personal/political transitions, a self-identity forged in his youth, whose ideational configuration in late life has remained virtually intact.

This is not to say that Sid has experienced no change in specific aspects of his political outlook. His departure from the Party came about partly because of his growing realization of flaws in positions he had taken for granted for many years. Yet his core ethnic/political identity has been less challenged than with the others. In fact, in Sid's narrative the culture and world view of the Yiddish-speaking Old Left, with which he was raised, was apparently never far removed, if not always manifest in his political activities.

Sid recalls the rivalry between two principal factions of the Jewish Left, one that reflected both political lines of demarcation (as between the socialist paper *Forward* and the communist *Freiheit*) and differences in the conception of the role of culture in the left political movement. This is not just a detached historical observation for Sid, though, for not only did he grow up in this milieu, but he later became a contributor to the *Freiheit* himself. Much of what he describes constituted the world of his youth. This Yiddish, left subculture remained the solid core of Sid's self-concept, in spite of the fact that the majority of his years in the Party were spent in activities removed from this circle per se.

It is significant, however, that two of Sid's three reasons for quitting the Party involved the "Jewish question." Each represented a dilemma that confounded ethnicity with politics. In the one instance Sid took the Party to task for its failure to criticize the leaders of Poland, a nominally socialist state, for acts of anti-Semitism. In the other instance, Sid objected to the CPUSA's apparent echoing of the Soviet position on Israel. The former position is consistent with Sid's left politics and was shared by many progressives outside the Party. (In Europe, thousands of progressives, including Jean Paul Sartre and Simone de Beauvior signed a petition of protest.) Sid's position on this latter issue presents a problem of greater complexity, for the Left as a whole was virtually unanimous in its condemnation of Israel's military incursion into Arab lands.

Part of the explanation for this apparent anomaly in Sid's political logic may be the desire for consistency in his ethnic loyalties. The volatile and highly subjective issues of Israel and Zionism within the Jewish community have caused many Jews in the Left to temper their views so as not to be perceived as anti-Jewish. The Party's reluctance to criticize its *political* cohorts in another nation is in some ways analogous to the reluctance of Jews to criticize a nation that claims to represent their *ethnic* cohorts, even at the cost of political consistency. This was certainly true of those Jewish-identified activists in the Left who, facing a dwindling constituency of ethnic/ political cohorts, became more urgent in their effort to reach a larger segment of the Jewish community.

It is not surprising, therefore, that Sid's views mirror those of members of the group in which the specific form of his ethnic politics is heavily invested, namely the Old Jewish Left community whose newspaper he read as a child. Paradoxically, despite the lack of overt ethnic forms of expression in his political activities with the Party, the "ethnic question" became a primary one for Sid in his growing disillusionment with its positions. He eventually joined his ethno-political cohorts in their separation from the organization to which many of his elders had been wedded since the days of the Bolshevik Revolution. Having joined the Party because of its internationalism, he left because of its failure to correctly address the "national question."

Even though Sid was fluent in Yiddish, he was, ironically, born too late to fit in with those of his elders in the Old Yiddish Left who published the *Freiheit*. He encountered just enough of a generational difference in outlook and temperament to prevent him from feeling fully integrated with them. His solution was to join forces with the *Jewish Currents* but make regular contributions to the *Freiheit*.

Sid's recollection of his contributions to the *Freiheit* reveals another interesting paradox. He purposely sought to help make this small, ethnic publication, with a dwindling readership, more "internationalist" in scope, precisely by selecting the writings of *Jewish* communists throughout the world. It is yet another instance of a constant balancing act brought about by the dialectical tension between ethnicity and polity, a dilemma that has challenged all ethnic political activists.

In some ways, given the demonstrative ethnic component of Sid's core identity, it might be argued that the specifically Jewish Left was more of a "home" to him than the Party per se. Yet, as certain as he is of the particular configuration of his ethnic/political identity, he acknowledges the conflicting demands placed upon his political allegiance by ethnicity on the one hand and "internationalism" on the other.

It seems that much of Sid's political life has been spent reaching out to an older generation of left-wing Jews, the generation of his mother, the generation, in fact, that is itself but one step removed from the seedbed of the Jewish communist movement. This was made apparent in the historical overview Sid presented when I asked him whether he ever questioned Marxism as a guiding philosophy in light of the failure of many Marxists to deal adequately with the relationship between ethnicity and politics.

Sid took me on a historical journey from the founding of the Jewish socialist movement in the late 1880s by Morris Winchevsky to the Jewish section of the Communist Party in the United States that faced of hostility by those Party members opposed to autonomous ethnic formations. Ironically, the Jewish section of the Communist Party had its own publication, *Jewish Affairs*, but its editor allowed for no deviation from Party positions, effectively barring consideration of those troubling questions posed by Sid.

Yet, once again in our conversation, the paradox emerged. For all of his battles against the "assimilationist" stance of the Party, for its tendency, in his view, to dismiss the "Jewish question" in favor of larger concerns, it is precisely the broad political scope of the Party and the movement it represented that Sid feels was its greatest contribution.

The fact that Sid was disappointed in the Party's position on the Jewish question did not mitigate his pride in being a veteran of a movement that, at least in principle, united peoples of many cultures under one political banner while respecting cultural differences. Tenacious as he has been in defending his ethnicity, he has been equally adamant in defending his political outlook, though it has undergone a transformation in the years since he left the Party.

I mentioned to Sid that the changing character of his political views seemed to challenge the common assumption that, as people grow older, they become more rigid in their thinking. Sid's response to my remark is significant on a number of levels. First, he brushed aside the notion that older persons are either more or less prone to inflexibility in their thinking. Second, he suggested that there may be other factors than age that bear upon the question of rigidity, such as the reluctance to depart from group consensus. Third, he made the observation that there may well be a discrepancy between one's public positions, which may appear inflexible, and one's private "qualms" about such rigid views. In the final analysis, Sid suggested, at least implicitly, that over the years, one's "investment" in a particular political view (at least as publicly declared) becomes so heavy that it becomes more and more difficult to back down, let alone back out. (Sid himself persisted as a Party member longer than most of his ethno-political cohorts.) Thus, age may be seen as coinciding with length of commitment to a set of beliefs, as well as the intensity of social ties of long standing with one's comrades, to produce conditions under which one may be reluctant to change (regardless of one's actual chronological age).

Sid was reluctant for many years to challenge accepted Party wisdom, apparently not so much out of fear, but out of an initial lack of confidence in his own political knowledge. A remark he made in response to my inquiry as to whether he had felt a sense of family or home in the Communist Party is telling. Apparently that sense of communality existed for Sid primarily during the period when he was less sure of himself, less questioning of the views or motives of fellow Party members, that is, more in need of the "family" provided by CP membership. Sid did, of course, eventually offer a "minority platform" of dissenting opinions. And he left the Party rather than suppress his personal views in order to support official Party positions with which he disagreed in principle.

When I pressed him about the sense of loss, if any, that he felt in the wake of his departure from the Party, Sid did admit to a certain sadness at his rejection by many with whom he had struggled together for so long, those who were unforgiving for his "desertion" of the Party and, in their minds, the politics it represented. But he clearly indicated that any feeling of loss he might have felt was mitigated by a growing sense of alienation from those who continue along the path he left behind. Further, he felt compensated by his subsequent political involvements.Unlike Joe Dimow, he doesn't seem to feel that they are inadequate substitutes.

Sid also was buoyed by the fact that he was joined by those political, and age, cohorts, like Joe, Lil, and Jake, who have followed a similar path away from the Party. In addition, he saw some new, young faces in some of the organizations with which he became involved. The membership of New Jewish Agenda, for example, is composed of professionals largely in their twenties to forties, and Sid and Joe have found themselves in the role of elder statespersons to a younger generation. However, Sid has also confronted the generational question from a different perspective, that of the problem of passing on a political/cultural legacy inherited from the generation that *preceded him*, in the face of an erosion of its sociohistorical base. Sid shares with Joe a concern about the problem of attrition in the Yiddish communist movement and how he and his comrades—both his age contemporaries with *Jewish Currents* and his "elders" at the *Freiheit*— have dealt with the dilemma of an older generation up against relentless demographic odds. He also shares with Joe both the sense of irony in two directions that a "generation gap" exists(up to the *Freiheit*, down to the New Jewish Agenda) the realization that they, too, are also aging.

But in spite of attrition, Sid clings to the idea of the continued presence and viability of a Jewish socialist movement. He notes wryly that the failure of the Left to deal adequately with the issue of ethnicity will provide yet another reason for the persistence of ethnic politics in general and Jewish politics in particular.

We eventually got around to discussing the issue of occupational identity and "retirement," one made complicated not only by the varied nature of his work life (paid and nonpaid), but also by the fact that, at age sixty nine, he is not fully retired. His work as a

journalist and translator has occupied much of his adult life, yet it
has brought little or no financial remuneration. His principal wage-
earning skill was that of a typesetter, potentially a great asset for a
political activist. Ironically, he was only able to contribute his printer's
skills to the Party on the side. Still, he provided a political motivation
for his career choice, attributing it to the inspiration of a revolutionary
hero (Dimitrov) who had been a printer.

Sid balanced his work as a printer with his activity in the Party.
While devoted to the Party throughout his years of membership, he
resisted becoming a paid organizer. "In a way, I didn't cotton to the
idea of being a full-timer for the Party. Maybe when I was younger,
I had such ambitions, but after I got married I didn't want it, because
it was too uncertain, it was too time-consuming, so I didn't want
to."

Eventually, he was laid off as a printer. Trained in the old method
of metal, or "hot," type, he was made redundant with the advent of
computer typesetting. He then got a job updating loose-leaf volumes
in the Yale Law Library, one that he held for several years. He is
beginning to tire of this job a bit and looks forward to quitting paid
employment in the near future. Age may be a factor in his desire to
finally "retire" from wage-earning, but it has certainly not diminished
his desire to keep working, especially when it involves politics and
journalism.

Sid brought our conversation to an end with the remark that he
had become, in late life, "the old codger who says certain things to
the younger people." While it was an ironic comment, it was also
his tongue-in-cheek way of observing that, when "you live through
certain things," you are enabled (at least potentially) the perspective
that age may offer.

Unlike Joe, Sid has assured himself a certain continuity by declaring
that he envisions no end to the Jewish Left, to whom he declares "a
special loyalty," so long as the problems presented to the Left by its
nemesis, capitalism, persist (for Sid, capitalism and anti-Semitism
are inseparable). He concluded by concurring vigorously with my
affirmation of his abiding commitment to the politics of the Left; but
there was never any doubt in Sid's mind about that.

Chapter Twelve

Conclusion

In commenting about Joe Dimow's narratives, I observed that life stories are shaped by a dialectical tension between different aspects of identity in the process of development, including that between past and present selves. While reviewing Joe's discourse, and those of his life-partner and comrades, it has become clear that another dialectical relationship presents itself, one that is of particular relevance to the narratives of political activists. It consists of a tension between one's core identity as self-declared or revealed in the course of a dialogue and the profile one might draw from the description of those life activities that one chooses to recall when queried about this core identity. Sometimes the relationship is apparent, sometimes it requires illumination. It is, in a real sense, analogous to the relationship between theory (the political idea) and practice (its implementation).

In fact, perhaps one of the most difficult challenges that a political activist must face is the wide gulf between the grand vision of one's overall perspective and the practical reality of strategies and tactics employed in its fulfillment. There are often times when the direct outcomes of political work seem remote and out of reach, especially when the ultimate objective of one's efforts is the radical transformation of society.

Lil spoke of the tremendous satisfaction she got out of her work as an arts-and-crafts instructor. Part of that satisfaction derived from the fact that she came to see it as a transposed form of political expression. But she also was gratified by the fact that she could see tangible results from her work with her students.

Jake revealed a similar attitude in recalling the renewal of his career as carpenter after leaving the Party. While acknowledging that the work of his hands was no direct substitute for political work, it at least had the virtue of yielding a tangible, finished product. And the occasional political involvements associated with his skilled trade did provide some sense of a "tangible" connection.

Sid had a certain advantage with his writing skills, since he could at least point to the tangible results of his work in the newspapers and journals in which articles he had written or translated appeared over the years, during an active political life inside and out of the Party. But given his evident enthusiasm for the world of political and cultural ideas, reflected in the relish with which he told of his many ideological skirmishes, I suspect that he has found, perhaps even more than the others, palpable rewards in the polemics that have punctuated his political career. His tenacity in remaining in the Party as a gadfly long after his comrades had broken rank may have partly signaled a certain spirit of intellectual combat reflected in the sharpness of wit that he had honed with such great pride in years of political sparring.

Sid seems to have made tangible his labors in the world of ideas, allowing for an apparently successful and satisfying merging of his core identity with his political work. Lil and Jake, however, share in varying degrees the ambivalence expressed by Joe about the possibility of finding a palpable connection between one's core self and one's political activities, given the present and historical nature of the political climate. Though one might not infer from his narrative as strong a sense of the merging of theory and practice as from Sid's discourse, Joe does ultimately posit a theory of the "tangible" as activity itself. "To find things that are worth doing, and [to] try to do them, even if it's not totally successful" were his concluding remarks in our third conversation. In doing so, he has allowed for at least a qualified sense of satisfaction in the act of political engagement itself, even if the results are not immediately evident.

This willingness to seek reward in activity itself is not necessarily a product of age; it is often a necessary compensation for political activists who have long fought for lofty goals whose realization is acknowledged as beyond their immediate reach. Generativity, then, becomes an issue for many activists long before its textbook appearance as charted by life-stage theorists. For socialists and other visionaries whose goals loom beyond their life course, a "global" perspective (temporally as well as politically) is virtually mandatory. Under such conditions, the direct expression of one's core identity (that is, living as a socialist in a socialist society) may never be realized during one's lifetime. Still, it is possible, as Sid's experience with the staffs of both the *Freiheit* and *Jewish Currents* demonstrates, for activists to become so wrapped in up daily activities that they fail to adequately consider the steps necessary to pass on their political legacy to a younger generation that will, hopefully, come ever closer to the elusive goal. The irony for Sid's aging compatriots is the fact that while they have often written about the importance of their political legacy, they apparently have not taken concrete measures to ensure its continuity.

The issue of generativity is made more complicated by the fact that the chronological aging of these activists has coincided with the waning of the specific political and cultural milieu of the movement to which they belonged, referred to by many contemporary activists as the "Old Left" (a term applied to participants in the socialist and communist movements of the 1920s to 1950s). Adding to this dilemma is the even greater attrition seen in such ethno-political "subcultures" as the old Jewish Left. That the longevity of their movement is limited by changing historical conditions is acknowledged by Joe, Lil, Jake, and Sid, but it is met with varying reactions by each.

With Joe, I sensed a certain acceptance of the inevitable erosion of the cultural component of his political expression. He could accept the loss of overt outlets for his ethnic identification, since he does not view it as essential to the maintenance of his core identity (desirable, but not necessary). Lil clearly sees "Yiddishkeit" as a vital aspect of her core political identity. While it may not have been always linked with her political activity, she clearly indicated its importance to her core self. I did not press Lil on the issue of whether her sense of ethnic identification during her years as a member of the Communist Party was as intense as she clearly demonstrated in her presentation to the largely younger members of New Jewish Agenda. She did not indicate that she engaged in any overtly Jewish forms of political expression during her years as a Party member. Yet it was apparent in her discourse that ethnic identification—specifically ethno-political identification—had been an integral part of her upbringing and was certainly important to her in late life.

Jake felt no particular sense of, and apparently little need for, an overt ethnic component to his core political identity. It is, however, interesting to note his demographic explanation for this—the fact that there was no organized Jewish Left movement in the city in which he eventually settled. He implies that had he lived in New Haven, he might well have chosen, as have Lil, Joe, and Sid, a specifically Jewish outlet for at least part of his overtly political activity. One gets the impression from Joe's remarks on the subject that he might also have been less demonstrable in the overt expression of the ethnic component of his political identity had he shared Jake's demographic fate. (The role of strictly personal forms of ethnic expression remains to be explored.)

Sid apparently has made a greater investment in his ethno-political identity, deliberately choosing exclusively Jewish forms for the primary expression of his core identity. At one point in his discourse, he acknowledges the waning of the "Old Left" but denies that the Jewish left-wing movement will suffer a similar fate in the foreseeable future. "As long as there's going to be . . . distinct ethnic groups in this country, there'll be a Jewish left-wing group." Historians may argue about the viability of this position, but for Sid, it is a firmly held conviction, one that (with the coterminus existence of the Left in general and its capitalist antithesis) ensures the perpetuation of the specific conditions (ethnic and political) that have nurtured his ideational core. Thus, he feels assured, in late life, that conditions for the continued marriage of fundamental political belief and its forms of expression will outlast him.

Perhaps the most important lesson to be learned from the narratives of Joe, Lil, Jake, and Sid is that self-identity is not strictly speaking a *product* of individual development, personal choice, or environment (social and physical). Rather, it is an emergent aspect of the dialectical relationship between the individual and social self, set within ever-changing historical conditions. Within such parameters, the overt manifestation of self-identity may depend as much on (historically) available forms for its expression as upon a self-determined molding of personal identity.

My initial reading of Joe's route to successful integration of core identity with life activity was that he displayed a high "tolerance of ambiguity." Transposed into political terms, what is revealed in his narratives and those of his life-partner and friends is the degree to which, in spite of such readily acknowledged contingencies, these activists have demonstrated a willingness to accept contradiction, to embrace it as a lived-in experience. Such a capacity to accept personal, social, and historical paradox may stem from their political perspective. The philosophical core of the Marxist outlook is dialectical materialism—the theory that phenomena are defined by a process of continual emergence through the interrelationship of contradictory aspects of their being. Perhaps this gives revolutionaries too much credit for successful education of their cadre in the ideological underpinnings of the Left. (Many socialists have, in fact, complained of the lack of sufficient ideological understanding among their political compatriots.)

Nevertheless, Joe, Lil, Jake, and Sid have managed to maintain a vision that incorporates the unevenness of life into their ideational equation. Differing in the nature and degree of the overt forms of expression of their core identities, they are similar in their understanding of the interrelationship of the various aspects of their lives; they are united in their embrace of a political perspective that has enabled them to incorporate disparate parts of their identity into an integrated, ideological whole. They have also offered an alternative view of the notion of "life satisfaction." While not always happy with specific life conditions, they have been sustained and nourished by a social movement that has offered an abiding sense of purpose. Regardless of its illusive goal, the vision held by members of that movement has provided lifelong meaning in the process of struggling for a common cause.

Bibliography

Bibliography

Andrews, Molly. *Lifetimes of Commitment: Aging, Politics, Psychology.* Cambridge: Cambridge University Press, 1991.

Atchley, Robert C. *The Sociology of Retirement.* New York: John Wiley and Sons, 1976.

Bair, Deirdre. *Simone de Beauvoir: A Biography.* New York: Summit Books, 1990.

Bakhtin, M. M. *The Dialogic Imagination: Four Essays by M. M. Bakhtin* [ed. by Michael Holquist]. Austin: University of Texas Press, 1981.

Bertaux, Daniel. *Biography and Society: The Life History Approach in the Social Sciences.* Beverly Hills, Calif.: Sage, 1981.

Blank, Thomas. "Macro-dialectics and Micro-dialectics of Aging and Politics." Np., 1990. Typescript.

Blythe, Ronald. *The View in Winter: Reflections on Old Age.* Middlesex: Penguin, 1979.

Bornat, Johanna, Chris Phillipson, and Sue Ward. *A Manifesto for Old Age.* London: Pluto Press, 1985.

Brady, Michael. *Retirement: The Challenge of Change.* Portland, Maine: University of Southern Maine, 1988.

Breytspraak, Linda M. *The Development of the Self in Later Life.* Boston: Little, Brown, 1983.

Breytspraak, Linda M., and Linda K. George. "Self-Concept and Self-Esteem." In David J. Mangen and Warren A. Peterson, eds., *Clinical and Social Psychology,* (vol. I of series *Research Instruments in Social Gerontology.*) Minneapolis: University of Minnesota Press, 1982.

Burgos, Martine. "Life Stories, Narrativity, and the Search for Self." *Life Stories/ Recits de vie* 5 (1989), 29-37.

Butler, Robert. "The Life Review: An Interpretation of Reminiscence in the Aged." *Psychiatry* 26 (1963); 65-76.

Chappell, Neena L., and Harold L. Orbach. "Socialization in Old Age: A Meadian Perspective." In Victor W. Marshall, ed., *Later Life: The Social Psychology of Aging.* Beverly Hills, Calif.: Sage,1986, 75-106.

Cohler, Bertram J. "Personal Narrative and Life Course." In Paul B. Baltes, and Orville G. Brim, eds., *Life Span Development and Behavior.* Vol. 4. New York: Academic Press, 1982, 205-241.

Coleman, Peter. "The Past in the Present: A Study of Elderly People's Attitudes to Reminiscence." *Oral History* 14 (1986), 50-59.

Coles, Robert. *The Old Ones of New Mexico.* Albuquerque: University of New Mexico Press, 1973.

de Beauvoir, Simone. *The Coming of Age.* New York: G. P. Putnam's Sons, 1972.

_____*The Second Sex.* New York: Alfred A. Knopf, 1957.

De Grazia, Sebastian. *Of Time, Work and Leisure.* New York: Twentieth Century Fund, 1962.

Dennis, Peggy. *The Autobiography of an American Communist: A Personal View of a Political Life, 1925-1975.* Westport, Conn.: Lawrence Hill & Co., 1977.

Denzin, Norman. *Interpretive Biography.* Newbury Park, Calif.: Sage, 1989.

Disman, Milada. "Explorations in Ethnic Identity, Oldness and Continuity." In Donald E. Gelfand and Charles M. Barresi, eds., *Ethnic Dimensions of Aging.* New York: Springer, 1987, 6 4-74.

Ekerdt, David J. "The Busy Ethic: Moral Continuity Between Work and Retirement."*The Gerontologist* 26 (1986) ; 239-44.

Eldridge, Mary, ed. "Older, Wiser, Stronger: Southern Elders." *Southern Exposure* 8:2-3 (1985), special issue.

Erikson, Erik H. *Life History and the Historical Moment.* New York: W. W. Norton, 1975.

Estes, Carroll L. "Political Gerontology: The Politics of Aging." *Society* 15:5 (1978); 43, 49.

Fox, Richard G. "The Welfare State and the Political Mobilization of the Elderly." In Sara B. Kiesler, James N. Morgan, and Valerie Kincade Oppenheimer, eds., *Aging: Social Change.* New York: Academic Press, 1981, 159-82.

Fry, Christine, Jennie Keith and contributors. *New Methods for Old Age Research.* South Hadley, Mass.: Bergin & Garvey, 1986.

Gelfand, Donald E., and Charles M. Barresi, eds. *Ethnic Dimensions of Aging.* New York: Springer, 1987.

Georgoudi, Marianthi. "Modern Dialectics in Social Psychology: A Reappraisal *European Journal of Social Gerontology* 13 (1983); 77-93.

Gergen, Kenneth J., and Mary M. Gergen. "Narratives of the Self." In Theodore R. Sarbin and Karl E. Scheibe, eds., *Studies in Social Identity.* New York: Praeger, 1983.

Gergen, Mary M., and Kenneth J. Gergen. "The Social Construction of Narrative Accounts." In Kenneth J. Gergen and Mary M. Gergen, eds., *Historical Social Psychology.* Hillsdale, NJ: Lawrence Erlbaum, 1984.

Goffman, Erving. *The Presentation of Self in Everyday Life.* New York: Anchor Books, 1959.

Goffman, Erving. *Relations in Public.* New York: Harper & Row, 1971.

Gordon, Milton. *Assimilation in American Life.* New York: Oxford University Press, 1964.

Gornick, Vivian. *The Romance of American Communism*. New York: Basic Books, 1977.

Graebner, William. *A History of Retirement: The Meaning and Function of an American Institution, 1885-1978*. New Haven and London: Yale University Press, 1980.

Guillemard, Anne-Marie. "Old Age, Retirement, and the Social Class Structure: Towards an Analysis of the Structural Dynamics of the Latter Stage of Life. In Tamara K. Hareven and Kathleen J. Adams, eds., *Aging and Life Course Transitions: An Interdisciplinary Perspective*. New York: Guilford Press, 1982.

Halamandaris, Val J. "Tribute to Maggie Kuhn: Compassionate Revolutionary." *Caring* 8:2 (1986), 34-36+.

Handel, Amos. Personal Theories About the Life-Span Development of One's Self in Autobiographical Self-Presentations of Adults. *Human Development*, Volume 30 (1987), 83-98.

Hareven, Tamara K. *Family Time and Industrial Time: The Relationship Between the Family and Work in a New England Industrial Town*. Cambridge: Cambridge University Press, 1982.

Harris, Alice Kessler. "Introduction." In Ronald J. Grele, *Envelopes of Sound: The Art of Oral History*. New York: Praeger, 1991, 6-7.

Hareven, Tamara K. and Kathleen J. Adams. *Aging and Life Course Transitions: An Interdisciplinary Perspective*. New York: The Guilford Press, 1982.

Haywood, Harry. *Black Bolshevik: Autobiography of an Afro-American Communist*. Chicago: Liberator Press, 1978.

Healey, Dorothy, and Maurice Isserman. *Dorothy Healey Remembers: A Life in the American Communist Party*. New York: Oxford University Press, 1990.

Hessel, D., ed. *Maggie Kuhn on Aging: A Dialogue*. Philadelphia: Westminster Press, 1977.

Howell, Sandra C. "The Meaning of Place in Old Age." In Graham D. Rowles and Russell J. Ohta, eds., *Aging and Milieu: Environmental Perspectives on Growing Old*. New York: Academic Press, 1983, 97-107.

Jackson, Jacquelyne Johnson. "Race, National Origin, Ethnicity, and Aging." In Robert H. Binstock and Ethel Shanas, *Handbook of Aging and the Social Sciences*. 2d ed. New York: Van Nostrand Reinhold, 1985.

Kann, Kenneth. *Joe Rapoport: The Life of a Jewish Radical*. Philadelphia: Temple University Press, 1981.

Kaufman, Sharon R. *The Ageless Self: Sources of Meaning in Late Life*. Madison: University of Wisconsin Press, 1986.

Kaufman, Sharon. "Cultural Components of Identity in Old Age: A Case Study." *Ethos* 9 (1981); 51-87.

Keith, Jennie. *Old People, New Lives*. Chicago: University of Chicago Press, 1977.

Kelly, John R., Marjorie W. Steinkamp, and Janice R. Kelly. "Later Life Leisure: How They Play in Peoria." *The Gerontologist* 26 (1986); 531-37.

Kleemeier, Robert W. *Aging and Leisure: A Research Perspective Into the Meaningful Use of Time*. New York: Oxford University Press, 1961.

Kleyman, Paul. *Senior Power: Growing Old Rebelliously*. San Francisco: Glide Publishing, 1974.

Kuhn, Maggie. "Advocacy in This New Age." *Aging* 297/298 (1979); 2-5.

Langness, L. L., Gelya Frank. *Lives: An Anthropological Approach to Biography.* Novato, Calif.: Chandler & Sharp, Publishers.

Lewis, C. N. "Reminiscing and Self-Concept in Old Age." *Journal of Gerontology* 26 (1971); 240-43.

Lieberman, Morton A., and Sheldon S. Tobin. *The Experience of Old Age: Stress, Coping and Survival.* New York: Basic Books, 1983.

Liebman, Arthur. *Jews and the Left.* New York: John Wiley, 1979.

Lindeman, Les. "Taking the Long Road to Peace." *50 Plus* 27:10 (1987); 50-55.

Lyman, F. "Maggie Kuhn [interview]." *Progressive* 52 (January 1988); 29-31.

MacKinnon, Janice, and Stephen R. MacKinnon. *Agnes Smedley: The Life and Times of an American Radical.* Berkeley, Calif.: U. of California Press, 1988.

Markides, Kyriakos S., Jersey Liang, and James S. Jackson. "Race, Ethnicity, and Aging: Conceptual and Methodological Issues." In Robert H. Binstock and Gordon F. Streib, eds., *Handbook of Aging and the Social Sciences.* 3d ed. New York: Academic Press, 1990.

_____and Charles H. Mindel. *Aging & Ethnicity.* Newbury Park, Calif.: Sage, 1987.

Marshall, Victor, and Joseph A. Tindale. "Notes for a Radical Gerontology." *International Journl of Aging and Human Development* 9 (1978-1979); 163-75.

Mead, George Herbert. *Mind, Self and Society.* Chicago: U. of Chicago Press, 1934.

Metropoulos, N. D. "The Retirement Years: Disengagement or Reengagement?" *Lifelong Learning* 4:4 (1980), 12-15.

Miller, William D. *Dorothy Day: A Biography.* New York: Harper & Row, 1982.

Misztal, Bronislaw. "Autobiographies, Diaries, Life Histories and Oral Histories of Workers as a Source of Socio-Historical Knowledge." *International Journal of Oral History* 2 (1981), 181-194.

Moody, Harry. *Abundance of Life.* New York: Columbia University Press, 1988.

Murphy, James F. *Concepts of Leisure: Philosophical Implications.* Englewood Cliffs, N.J.: Prentice-Hall, 1974.

Myerhoff, Barbara. *Number Our Days.* New York: E. P. Dutton, 1978.

_____and Andrei Simic. *Life's Career—Aging: Cultural Variations on Growing Old.* Beverly Hills, Calif.: Sage, 1978.

Nelson, Steve, James R. Barrett, and Rob Ruck. *Steve Nelson, American Radical.* Pittsburgh: University of Pittsburgh Press, 1981.

Neugarten, Bernice L., and Gunhild O. Hagestad. "Age and the Life Course." In R. H. Binstock and E. Shanas, eds., *Handbook of Aging and the Social Sciences.* New York: Van Nostrand Reinhold, 1976, 35-55.

Olson, Laura Katz. *The Political Economy of Aging: The State, Private Power, and Social Welfare.* New York: Columbia University Press, 1982.

Painter, Nell Irvin. *The Narrative of Hosea Hudson: His Life as a Negro Communist in the South.* Cambridge, Mass.: Harvard University Press, 1979.

Personal Narratives Group. *Interpreting Women's Lives: Feminist Theory and Personal Narratives.* Bloomington: Indiana University Press, 1989.

Phillipson, Chris. *Capitalism and the Construction of Old Age.* London: Macmillan, 1982.

Phillipson, Chris. "The State, Economy & Retirement." Anne-Maire Guillemard ed., *Old Age and the Welfare State.* Calif.: Sage, 1983, 127- 139.

Plummer, Ken. *Documents of Life: An Introduction to the Problems and Literature of a Humanistic Method*. London: George Allen and Unwin, 1983.

Polkinghorne, Donald E. *Narrative Knowing and the Human Sciences*. Albany: State University of New York Press, 1988.

Portelli, Alessandro. "Uchronic Dreams: Working Class Memory and Possible Worlds." *Oral History* 16 (1988); 46-56.

Pratt, Henry J. *The Gray Lobby*. Chicago: University of Chicago Press, 1976.

Richmond, Al. *A Long View From the Left: Memoirs of an American Revolutionary*. Boston: Houghton Mifflin, 1973.

Riegel, Klaus. "Toward a Dialectical Theory of Development ." *Human Development* 18 (1975), 50-64.

Rosengarten, Theodore. *All God's Dangers: The Life of Nate Shaw*. New York: Alfred A. Knopf, 1974.

Rosengarten, Theodore. "Stepping Over Cockleburs: Conversations with Ned Cobb." In Marc Pachter, ed., *Telling Lives: The Biographer's Art*. Philadelphia: University of Pennsylvania Press, 1985 (1979), 104-131.

Rosenmayr, Leopold. "Biography and Identity." In Tamara K. Hareven and Kathleen J. Adams, eds., *Aging and Life Course Transitions: An Inter-disciplinary Perspective*. New York: Guilford Press, 1982.

Rosow, Irving. *Socialization to Old Age*. Berkeley: Univ. of California Press, 1974.

Ryff, Carol D. "The Subjective Construction of Self and Society: An Agenda for Life-Span Research." In Victor Marshall, ed., *Later Life: The Social Psychology of Aging*. Beverly Hills, Calif.: Sage, 1986, 33-74.

Santino, Jack. *Miles of Smiles, Years of Struggles: Stories of Black Pullman Porters*. Champaign, Ill.: University of Illinois Press, 1989.

Sauer, William J., and Rex Warland. "Morale and Life Satisfaction." In David J. Mangen and Warren A. Peterson, eds., *Clinical and Social Psychology*, (vol. I of series *Research Instruments in Social Gerontology*.) Minneapolis: University of Minnesota Press, 1982.

Seve, Lucien. *Man in Marxist Theory and the Psychology of Personality*. Atlantic Highlands, N.J.: Humanities Press, 1978.

Shotter, John H., Kenneth J. Gergen, eds. *Texts of Identity*. London: Sage, 1989.

Shuldiner, David. *Of Moses and Marx: Folk Ideology Within the Jewish Labor Movement in the United States*. Dissertation, University of California, Los Angeles, 1984.

_____ "Work, Class, Ethnicity, Gender and Age: Sources of Identity and Expression in Occupational Folklore." Paper presented to the American Folklore Society, Philadelphia, 1989.

Smith, Robert J. "Propositions to a Marxist Theory of Personality." *Human Development* 28 (1985); 10-24.

Strong, Tracy B., and Helene Keyssar. *Right in Her Soul: The Life of Anna Louise Strong*. New York: Random House, 1983.

Titon, Jeff. "The Life Story." *Journal of American Folklore* 93 (1980); 276-92.

Tolman, Charles. "The Metaphysics of Relations in Klaus Riegel's 'Dialectics' of Human Development." *Human Development* 24 (1981); 33-51.

Trela, James E. "Status Inconsistency and Political Action in Old Age." In Jaber F. Gubrium, ed., *Time, Roles, and Self in Old Age*. New York: Human Sciences Press, 1976.

Watson, Lawrence C., and Maria-Barbara Watson-Franke. *Interpreting Life Histories: An Anthropological Inquiry.* New Brunswick, N.J.: Rutgers University Press, 1985.
Weisbord, Vera Buch. *A Radical Life.* Bloomington: Indiana University Press, 1977.
Wexler, Philip. *Critical Social Psychology.* London: Routledge & Kegan Paul, 1983.
White, Robert W., ed. *The Study of Lives: Essays in Honor of Henry A. Murray.* New York: Atherton Press, 1963.

Index

About the Author

DAVID P. SHULDINER holds dual appointments as Visiting Professor with the School of Family Studies at the University of Connecticut and as Humanities Program Coordinator with the State of Connecticut, Department of Social Services, Elderly Services Division. Trained in anthropology and gerontology, he has conducted research among the aging since 1980 when he began interviewing veterans of the Jewish Labor Movement who were active in the United States in the first half of the 20th century.

ISBN 0-275-95045-X

90000>

EAN

9 780275 950453

HARDCOVER BAR CODE